THE CATHOLIC ALL YEAR
PRAYER COMPANION

KENDRA TIERNEY

The Catholic All Year
Prayer Companion

The Liturgical Year in Practice

IGNATIUS PRESS   SAN FRANCISCO

Texts contained in this work derived whole or in part from liturgical texts copyrighted by the International Commission on English in the Liturgy (ICEL) have been published here with the confirmation of the Committee on Divine Worship, United States Conference of Catholic Bishops. No other texts in this work have been formally reviewed or approved by the United States Conference of Catholic Bishops.

All Vatican documents are © Libreria Editrice Vaticana and used with permission.

This book is dedicated to all priests, but above all to the priests dearest to me: the priest who baptized me; the priests who absolved me from my sins; the priests at whose Masses I assisted and who gave me Jesus' Body and Blood in Holy Communion; the priests who taught and instructed me; and all the priests to whom I am indebted in any other way, most especially Father Philip Sullivan, O.C.D., a shepherd who would lay down his life for his sheep.

CONTENTS

PREFACE

Over two years have passed since I wrote the preface to my previous book *The Catholic All Year Compendium*.[1] It's interesting to go back and read all the goings-on I faced while writing that book. I've been working on compiling this book since shortly after that one was published. The crazy has been different, but still very crazy. During the writing of this book, our family has faced treatment decisions for the husband's stage IV metastatic melanoma, welcomed baby number ten (our lovely Barbara Josephine), endured two-year-old George's five-week hospitalization when he contracted bacterial meningitis, and celebrated my great-grandmother's hundredth birthday, followed by her peaceful passing one month later. Now, here I sit, sheltered at home in week twelve of a COVID-19 lockdown, having just given my oldest son a pretty passable at-home haircut so he can get his socially distanced senior high school portrait taken. The years 2019 and 2020 will not soon be forgotten in the Tierney house, or in the world.

As an "expert" in liturgical living at home, I've been called upon many times over the past months to share ideas for celebrating Holy Week, Easter, and now Pentecost with those who are physically separated from Mass and the sacraments. I've never been more grateful for the liturgical living traditions that have given our days order and light and a feeling of normalcy in trying times. I'm grateful to have been able to share them with so many others. I've also never understood so strongly the profound importance of our physical churches, our beloved priests, and our parish communities, when it comes to our faith life—and how very essential are the sacraments. I hope this book finds you with time for prayer at home, access to the sacraments, and health of body and soul.

[1] San Francisco: Ignatius Press, 2018.

INTRODUCTION

The family that prays together, stays together.

—Venerable Patrick Peyton,
"the Rosary Priest"

We've all heard the above quotation. Probably, we believe it. But is it inspiring ... or is it intimidating? Maybe it's both?

There are so many different prayers and devotions available to us as Catholics. It would be literally impossible to get to all of them every day. But that's the great thing about the liturgical calendar. It's a framework for our prayer life. It tells us when to try what.

We are probably familiar with the liturgical seasons of Advent, Christmas, Lent, Easter, and Ordinary Time. Each of them has its own character and its own associated prayers and pious practices. Each month of the year has a devotion traditionally associated with it. Feast days throughout the year honor saints and historic events in the lives of Jesus, the Holy Family, and the early Church. These are associated with particular prayers and pious practices. Particular saints have particular patronages and are often associated with particular devotions.

Liturgical living allows us to sample from the rich bounty of Catholic prayers and practices. The ones we like best can be incorporated more often. Others maybe we won't try again for a whole year. Liturgical living–based prayer is an especially great way to introduce different spiritual practices to children. Repeated exposure to various devotions over the years in the domestic church can help us all grow in faith together.

Here in *The Catholic All Year Prayer Companion*, you'll find the Bible passages, prayers, songs, and devotions that our family uses. These are the prayers and practices that I recommend in my earlier book *The Catholic All Year Compendium*. I ran out of room there to include the actual words of these things, so when a particular feast day came around, I would consult one of the various prayer books we have, or, more often, start looking on my phone for the prayer I wanted in a translation I liked.

That's not an ideal method when dinner is already on the table. And, like the Church, I prefer paper over screens when it comes to religious use.[1] So I put all the texts together here, in one (big ol') handy volume. That way, all of us can have easy access to them and dinner won't get cold. For history, tradition, and backstories surrounding these devotions and the feast days to which they are attached, please consult the *Compendium*.

A few prayers and hymns are included in both Latin and English, as we aim to facilitate at least a rudimentary familiarity with Latin in our home. I think it's a good practice for all Catholics.

Some prayers, especially blessings and novenas that are conducive to group use, are available in a printable format at CatholicAllYear.com. I've noted those in the text. Also available at my website are liturgical year wall calendars, planners, and other resources specifically designed to support *The Catholic All Year Compendium* and *The Catholic All Year Prayer Companion*.

Something to keep in mind as you use this book: The Catholic Church is very big. It encompasses the whole world. It embraces people from every race and culture. It is for all people in all circumstances. My family and I are American. We attend Masses in the Ordinary Form of the Latin Rite, so that is the foundation of our knowledge and experience. We've also incorporated prayers and devotions from other rites and eras into our family traditions. It's my hope that in these pages you will find prayers and devotions that you can add or adapt to your own family's practice of the faith, whatever your background might be.

Indulgences

You will see indulgences attached to various prayers and practices in this book. (Please see appendix B of *The Catholic All Year Compendium* or the *Manual of Indulgences* for a thorough explanation of indulgences.) Indulgences can be plenary (full) or partial, and so remove

---

[1] United States Conference of Catholic Bishops, "The Sacred Liturgy in the Digital Age", *Newsletter of the Committee on Divine Worship*, March–April 2011.

either all or part of the temporal punishment due to sins. Indulgences can be gained for oneself, or applied to the Holy Souls in purgatory, but cannot be gained for another living person. They can be gained so long as the following usual conditions are met:[2]

- One must be a baptized Catholic, not excommunicated, and not in a state of mortal sin at the time of the actions taken for the indulgence.
- One must have the intention of gaining the indulgence, and perform the required actions in the required amount of time and in a devout manner.
- One can gain many partial indulgences but only one plenary indulgence per day, except that one can gain a second plenary indulgence at the point of death.
- If the indulgence requires visiting a church or oratory, devoutly recite the Our Father and the Creed[3] during the visit.
- To gain a plenary indulgence, one must be free from all attachment to sin, even venial sin. This does not mean we don't often commit the same sins. However, we must not excuse or love the sin. We must struggle against it, even if we fail and must confess and begin again.
- One must perform the required actions, receive Holy Communion, make a sacramental confession, and pray for the intentions of the Holy Father. The usual prayers offered for the intentions of the Holy Father are one Our Father and one Hail Mary.
- It is preferred to receive Communion and pray for the intentions of the Holy Father on the same day that one performs the actions, but within about twenty days before or after is acceptable. Reception of Communion and prayer for the Holy Father's intentions must be completed for each indulgence sought.
- Confession should be made within about twenty days before or after the actions for the indulgence. One confession can apply to many indulgences.

[2] The list below is adapted from Cardinal William Wakefield Baum, Apostolic Penitentiary, "The Gift of the Indulgence", January 29, 2000, http://www.vatican.va/roman_curia/tribunals/apost_penit/documents/rc_trib_appen_pro_20000129_indulgence_en.html.
[3] Any of the three approved Creeds is acceptable: Apostles, Nicene, or, if you've got some time to spare, Athanasian.

- If all the conditions are not met, the indulgence becomes partial rather than plenary. A partial indulgence is still very good and worthwhile!

Things that we are obliged to do, like attend Mass, are understood to confer graces and are not enhanced with indulgences.

Feast Days

Feast days are designated as solemnity, feast, memorial, optional memorial, or historical. (See chapter 1 of *The Catholic All Year Compendium* for more on the ordering of feast days.) These categories apply to how the Mass is celebrated, and they give us an indication of how important the Church considers that day either in the universal Church or in a particular country. We can use the categories at home to prioritize the observance of the more important feasts, along with those of the saints to whom our family has a particular connection or devotion. Solemnities are the highest priority, then feasts, then memorials, then optional memorials. Feasts designated as historical no longer appear on the universal calendar, but a couple are included here because they have noteworthy associated traditions. A designation of holy day of obligation means that Catholics are required to attend Mass on that day as on a Sunday.

Easter is what we call a "movable feast", meaning that it doesn't fall on the same date each year.[4] Many other days, from Ash Wednesday to Trinity Sunday, are ordered around Easter and are also movable.

In this book, you'll find a chapter for each month, as well as four chapters for the movable feast days of Lent, Holy Week, Eastertide, and the weeks following Pentecost. (See appendix B for lists of the dates of movable feasts in upcoming years.) Before the content of the actual liturgical year, you'll find a chapter on how we incorporate prayer into our family life, and one on the differences between types of included prayers. Prayers that don't quite sort into the liturgical calendar, but that we like for daily use or for special undertakings, are included in appendix A.

---

[4] Easter is celebrated on the first Sunday after the first full moon occurring on or after the vernal equinox.

I

Liturgical Living in Practice

A Kick in the Pants

In our home, liturgical living serves as both a framework and a kick in the pants. It's so easy to put off family prayer. It's so easy to think things will "calm down" at some point with work or family life and we'll focus on prayer then. But, of course, nothing really ever calms down. It just becomes crazy in a different way. Liturgical living gives our prayer life the urgency it needs actually to happen. It helps us move beyond the aspiration to, generally, um, "pray more" by giving us this particular prayer to say on this particular day. That's the motivation my family needs.

The facets of liturgical living in the home, as we practice it, include instruction, veneration, nourishment, and—occasionally—singing, crafts, and activities. My book *The Catholic All Year Compendium*[1] focuses on the instruction piece of the puzzle with histories, stories, legends, and suggested practices for over a hundred feast days and every season of the liturgical year. The goal of this volume is to tackle the veneration aspect. This *Prayer Companion* functions as just that, a companion to the *Compendium*. Either volume can be used without the other. But if you're wondering what particular terms in this book mean or why certain prayers and blessings are associated with particular feast days, the *Compendium* will have more answers. If you like the suggestions found in the *Compendium* but wish for an easy way to find the prayers and readings, this *Prayer Companion* is it. Someday, I hope to tackle the nourishment angle with a book focused on cooking

---

[1] Kendra Tierney, *The Catholic All Year Compendium: Liturgical Living for Real Life* (San Francisco: Ignatius Press, 2018).

and hospitality, and perhaps more of the fun with other volumes of hymns, crafts, and activities.

In this book, you'll find ways of praying associated with different feast days and seasons throughout the year. It seems like rather a lot when you're holding it all in your hands at once, but these pages shouldn't be seen as a mandate or a burden. They're a resource and an opportunity!

What Is Prayer?

Before we get too far, let's talk about prayer itself. According to the *Catechism of the Catholic Church*, "prayer is the raising of one's mind and heart to God or the requesting of good things from God."[2] It can be directed to any of the three Persons of God (the Father, the Son, the Holy Spirit). We can ask a saint to intercede with God for our desires. Prayer can be focused on a particular devotion like Jesus' Sacred Heart or his Divine Mercy. Prayer can be expressed mentally or vocally.

Mental prayer is characterized by the use of one's own words, thoughts, and feelings to communicate with God. Saint Teresa of Avila explained, "Mental prayer is nothing else, in my opinion, but being on terms of friendship with God."[3] A friend is often in our thoughts. We can raise our minds to God during times of anxiety or gratitude, and in all the moments of joy, sorrow, effort, and humdrum of daily life. We can spend dedicated time in meditative or contemplative prayer, focused on particular aspects of Jesus' life or the perfections of God.

Vocal prayer is the type of prayer with which this book is predominantly concerned. This type of prayer typically uses some approved form of words that are read, sung, or recited. Vocal prayer counts as such even if it's said in your head rather than out loud. It can be individual or communal. We can use vocal prayer to praise God, petition

---

[2] John Damascene, *De fide orth.* 3.24, PG 94:1089C, quoted in *Catechism of the Catholic Church*, 2nd ed., updated 2016 (Vatican City: Libreria Editrice Vaticana / Washington, D.C.: United States Catholic Conference, 1997), 2559 (hereafter cited as CCC).

[3] Teresa of Avila, *The Life of St. Teresa of Avila*, trans. David Lewis (London: Burns & Oates, 1962), 51.

him for a need for ourselves, or intercede with God for the needs of another. Some examples of vocal prayer include the Rosary, blessings, hymns, novenas, litanies, and the Mass itself. Vocal prayer can be used as its own end or as preparation for a time of mental prayer.

I like to think of the relationship between us, God, and prayer in terms of a concert. God is the audience and we are the performers. Mental prayer is like a spontaneous composition. Maybe it's childlike and simple like the little songs my toddler sings for me about what I just served him for lunch. Maybe it's complex improvisational jazz or an extemporaneous operetta. The songs of a toddler are charming to the ears of a parent. With time and practice a musician's spontaneous composition can ascend to the heights of musical achievement. Vocal prayers, on the other hand, are the greatest hits list. No matter our virtuosity, singing God a selection of his old-time favorites is sure to please, and the more people we have "singing" together, the better it's going to sound.

What Prayer Looks Like in Our House

We have a space set apart in our home for meditative mental prayer, and we also encourage all members of the family to cultivate a running conversation with God throughout the day, during and between tasks. Additionally, we spend time in vocal prayer, together and individually. The prayers included in this book are ones we have used together over the years. Some, like the Christmas Novena on the nine days before Christmas, and the Stations of the Cross on Fridays during Lent, are flagship family devotions. These happen every year, during their liturgical season. We move things around and make sacrifices to make these devotions happen amid busy schedules. They are part of our family culture, and my kids have fond memories of returning to them each year. Some, like the family Rosary, are part of our prayer life all year, and something we strive to get to each day—even if we reach only a couple times a week.

Some years, we have to pare back our family prayer life because of challenging seasons and circumstances, but the framework of the liturgical year is there waiting for us, so we can pick up where we left off at any time. This book is intended to be a resource you could use every single day of the year, if you choose. But if that's not where your family is at the moment, or how your year is going, it will be there for when the time and the season are right.

On an Ideal Day

As I write this, my ten children range in age from seven months to seventeen years. We've been praying together as a family since my oldest kids were little. On an ideal day, we weave prayer throughout, with a Morning Offering, mealtime prayers, an Angelus at noon, a family Rosary on a long car ride or after dinner, and an examination of conscience and Act of Contrition before bed. We attend Sunday Mass together each week, and usually two weekday Masses as well.

As a family, we also incorporate different prayerful practices based on the liturgical calendar over the course of the year. We'll do a Seven Sorrows of Our Lady scripture activity on the feast of Our Lady of Sorrows and a blessed bonfire on the eve of the Nativity of Saint John the Baptist, as schedules allow, and with whomever is available. Some devotions, especially novenas, I'll often do on my own in quiet prayer time without the kids. While doing things like these together as a whole family is my preference, we try not to let the ideal keep us from getting to things at all.

Our whole-family saint day observances are largely dinner-table based. Family dinners are a very important and prioritized part of our family culture. Since we'll be sitting down together around the table most every evening, it's easy to include an extra prayer following our regular Blessing before Meals or a Bible reading.

My husband works long hours out of the house, but with the prep work done ahead of time he can easily lead our family in prayer around the table with resources that I just hand to him. Participation by all members of the family, from the youngest to the oldest, is good and important, and participation by the head of the household is especially important. I don't want to give my children the impression that prayer and the practice of our faith is "kids' stuff". We make it a point to avoid encouraging participation of little kids to the exclusion of adults and teenagers. I want my little kids to see an active life of faith leadership as something to which they can aspire as they grow older.

I find it's helpful in most cases to reserve the role of prayer leader for someone who is a leader in the family. In our home that's most often going to be Dad. If he's not available, Mom or the oldest child is tasked with leading. Other kids can do readings or lead songs, and all can do the responses.

Blessings are the liturgical living practice for which the participation of the head of the household is most important. More on that in the next chapter.

The Apostolate of Family Dinner

At our house, we all wait to eat until everyone is served and seated, even the littlest kids. We say the Blessing before Meals together, led by Dad, and often a short extra prayer for the monthly devotion or liturgical season. Then people can start eating. If it's a feast day that we usually celebrate, the husband or I will read the Collect prayer for the feast while the rest of the family is eating, and we all take turns reading any extra prayers for a saint's day or the appropriate story in the Bible for a feast day recalling a historic event. If there's a hymn or a litany attached to the feast, we wait until after dinner, so we're not trying to sing or shout responses with mouths full. Special blessings for the occasion are led by Dad whenever possible and might happen before or after eating, depending on what or who is being blessed.

The goal—after offering to God his due praise—is to set the stage for a conversation about the feast day over the dinner table. All the aspects of liturgical living in the home—the saint stories, historic and legendary; the traditional feast day foods and decorations and activities; the prayers and the scriptures—lead us to a deeper engagement with the truths of our faith.

What gives the martyrs the strength to confess their belief even when it will mean torture and death? What does it mean to say that God is three in one? Why do we call Mary the Tower of David? All these conversations around our dinner table have been sparked by prayers in this book.[4]

If around the dinner table isn't the best place for your family to have deep conversation, feel free to employ these devotions in other situations. I also use the prayers in this book to pray on my own, for family morning prayer, in our classroom, and in the car. I am a huge fan of in-the-car prayers. We're all buckled in and stuck there. We might as well use the time for something edifying. Of course, unless you've got the prayers memorized, it will require that someone other than the driver be of reading age and able to lead the devotions.

And that leads me to what is probably my most frequently asked question over a dozen years of blogging, posting on social media, and doing speaking engagements: What do I do if my spouse/toddler/kid/teenager doesn't want to participate in family prayer?

Good question!

Encouraging a Reluctant Spouse

A reluctant spouse is a challenge for the faith life of a family but not necessarily an insurmountable one. My own childhood experience was of a Catholic mother and a not-particularly-anything father. My mom taught my sister and me our prayers, presented us for our sacraments, and took us to Mass on Sundays. We said a prayer together as a family before meals, but otherwise, while he wasn't hostile to the Catholic faith, my father wasn't doing anything to promote it either.

My mother's approach with him was one of prayer, good example, and quiet steadfastness. She prayed for my dad's conversion, unceasingly. She befriended Catholic families that became an influence on his worldview. She set the example of Mass attendance—with

---

[4] Usually our family dinners are device free, but we sometimes have to make an exception to this rule to discover something like the following: "A tower in its simplest idea is a fabric for defence against enemies. David, King of Israel, built for this purpose a notable tower; and as he is a figure or type of our Lord, so is his tower a figure denoting our Lord's Virgin Mother", according to my friend Fr. Juan Velez in his article "Mary, Tower of David" on his blog *Cardinal John Henry Newman*, https://www.cardinaljohnhenrynewman.com /mary-tower-of-david-cardinal-newman/.

two sometimes unenthusiastic little girls in tow—even when it was inconvenient. She didn't argue or threaten or cajole—she just did her thing with us and let him do his thing on his own. He was always welcome to join us at Mass, and did so at Christmas and Easter. And then, when I was in college, seemingly out of the blue, but actually out of the grace of twenty-five years of my mom's prayers, my dad signed himself up for RCIA (Rite of Christian Initiation of Adults) and came into full communion with the Church. Now I can hardly remember that he wasn't always Catholic, and my kids have always known a grandad who is an active participant in all our liturgical living traditions.

That's just one example of a reluctant spouse, of course, and with that pesky free will and all, even the most devoted prayer is no guarantee of results. But I think my mom's approach was a good one, with a reasonable likelihood of success, whether a reluctant spouse is not Catholic, or not Christian, or not anything at all. Involving the reluctant spouse in as many of the faith practices of the family as possible, according to his comfort level, and allowing him to be a witness to the fun and informative aspects of liturgical living in the home is a good place to start.

All must be undertaken with the understanding that you may not see the fruits of your prayers for the conversion of your spouse in this life but that living a life of personal holiness is always going to be the best advertisement for our faith and our best hope of salvation for ourselves and those we love. That example you set with your spouse will also be an advertisement to your children. They will grow up seeing that the faith isn't a constant cause of argument or strife but is rather a source of peace and strength in you.

So for a wife hoping to inspire a husband or a husband hoping to inspire a wife to live a more fully Catholic life, a somewhat hands-off approach might have the best chance of success. But how about our kids? Shall we let *them* do their own thing when it comes to religion? After all, the medium of ceramic figurines suggests that small children are naturally inclined to closed-eye, folded-hand, symmetrical, kneeling prayer. So pious. So quiet.

This has not, however, been *my* personal experience with my small children.

Encouraging Reluctant Kids

It's easy for us parents to think our kids should naturally want to pray, and if they don't, we don't want to spoil it for them by "making" them. But, of course, we are all fallen creatures, even our children, and so none of us naturally desires what's good for us. Sure, it's troubling if kids say they don't want to go to Mass or pray a family Rosary. But don't they also prefer not to wear their seatbelts, not to do their schoolwork, and not to brush their teeth? Viewed in that light, it's not really a piety issue—it's a parenting issue.

It's our job as parents to encourage and even insist upon behaviors that are in the best interests of our children. In our house, we present saying our prayers as a family activity that members of the family must participate in. If they don't, they get a couple of reminders, and then they incur the same sorts of consequences they would for breaking other family rules.

What we begin doing out of obedience, we can learn to do out of love.

My husband and I also don't, in general, indulge pointless grumbling from the kids about things they have to do. Complaining is not going to change our family rules, and it tends to spiral into more unhappiness in the complainer and those around him. We find it best to practice more constructive speech.

Raising children with prayer and the sacraments and liturgical living in a faithful Catholic home is, unfortunately, not a guarantee that they'll never err or stray as they get older. But it means that if they do, they'll have graces and good habits (and their mother's prayers) tugging them back toward faith and family.

Ages and Expectations

Family prayers are going to look different in different families. Some parents value formality and reverence; some parents value casualness and intimacy. I think both approaches can work. In our home, we try to strike a middle chord of comfortable respectfulness. Our expectations for a child's behavior vary depending on the age and development level of the child.

Babies can do whatever they want during prayer time. Pretty much all planned activities in our house happen at the pleasure of the currently reigning baby, so our babies get considerable latitude to eat, sleep, roll around on the floor, be carried about, or whatever.

Around one and a half or two, our kids start to be able to understand and comply with instructions, so at about this age we start requiring a basic level of nondisruption from them during prayer time. Quietly playing with a stuffed toy is probably fine; knocking over block towers is not. Moving from the lap of one sibling to another is okay; running around isn't. We expect that they'll stay in the same area of the house as the rest of us and not hinder us in our devotions. If they join in for a few words here or there of a prayer, there is great rejoicing. If it's just not working, we'll pause to put the little offender down for a nap.

Probably by school age, and certainly by the age of reason,[5] we expect that our kids will actively participate in what we're doing as a family. For the purposes of this book, we are focusing on religious activities, but we also have the expectation that our kids participate with a minimum of grumbling in, say, driving four hours to go see the poppies or watching a black-and-white movie. The activity doesn't have to be the child's favorite, but he still needs to participate politely. After all, group activities of all sorts create memories and shared experiences and help strengthen our family culture.

As far as prayers go specifically, our goal for kids above the age of reason is that they (1) promptly and pleasantly report when called; (2) stay in one spot; (3) not distract one another; and (4) speak up loudly enough for everyone to hear. Of course, we often fall short of our goal. When that happens there are verbal reminders, and if those don't work, explanations of—and then realizations of—consequences for behavior.

We try to have age-appropriate expectations and generally understood consequences for failing to live up to expectations, and to

---

[5] A minor before the completion of the seventh year is called an infant and is considered not responsible for himself (*non sui compos*). With the completion of the seventh year, however, a minor is presumed to have the use of reason. *Code of Canon Law* (Vatican City: Libreria Editrice Vaticana, 1983), can. 97 §2, https://www.vatican.va/archive/cod-iuris-canonici /eng/documents/cic_lib1-cann96-123_en.html. All references to canon law in this book are to the 1983 code.

apply them calmly and consistently. We try not to take kid behavior personally or to put undue weight on something a child does just because it's associated in that moment with a religious activity. It's probably just kid stuff. We're still going to work on it, but we don't have to worry more than we would otherwise.

If prayer and devotion time in your home is chaos and you can't get a handle on it, there might be larger disciplinary issues that need to be sorted for this time to be fruitful. If you're banging your head on the wall, the problem isn't that "Catholic devotions are just not for us." They can be! This will require some additional effort but might also make other aspects of family life more manageable.

They Are Animals

If we are, as Saint Paul suggests, to "pray constantly" (1 Thess 5:17), it will mean that we pray while walking, lying down, tying shoes, wiping noses, and doing the dishes. That kind of prayer of mindfulness of God and pious invocations in the midst of daily life is good and necessary. But more dedicated prayer is probably going to benefit from a more dedicated body position.

In C. S. Lewis' *Screwtape Letters*, the senior demon writes: "At the very least, they [people] can be persuaded that the bodily position makes no difference to their prayers; for they constantly forget, what you must always remember, that they are animals and that whatever their bodies do affects their souls."[6]

In the knowledge that our kids are animals (and so are we), we pay attention to bodily position during prayers. Even our little kids are expected to stand and kneel with the congregation during Mass. After Mass we kneel and pray in thanksgiving. We bow to the altar and genuflect before the Blessed Sacrament. At home we kneel for our morning prayers before our school day begins and for bedtime prayers at night. We stand for the noon Angelus. For dinner-table prayers and the family Rosary, we are most often seated around the table or on the couch, but we try to maintain a reverent posture: no melting into the floor or the furniture.

---

[6] C. S. Lewis, *The Screwtape Letters, with Screwtape Proposes a Toast* (London: HarperCollins, 2002), 16.

The *General Instruction of the Roman Missal* (*GIRM*) instructs the faithful: "A bow of the head is made when the three Divine Persons are named together and at the names of Jesus, of the Blessed Virgin Mary, and of the saint in whose honor Mass is being celebrated."[7] These instructions are associated specifically with the Mass, but the practice of bowing the head when these names are mentioned is one that can be used in the home as well, so our bodies can help to convince our souls of important truths.

Encouraging Reluctant Teens

Our oldest kids are now teenagers. They attend a brick-and-mortar Catholic school and have the busy schedules to show for it. Sometimes they can't be home for family dinners or weekend activities because of sports and social commitments, and that's okay. But when they're home, they hang out with the rest of the family and do what we're doing.

I know that this isn't a given in all families. If you're in a challenging time with your teenagers, you'll have to decide whether you might still be able to get through to them with the reluctant-kid method or whether it's time to move to the Saint Monica method, which is basically the same as the reluctant-spouse method but with more crying.[8]

In our home, keeping the teenagers involved, even in goofy or religious family activities, has been relatively painless because it's been an expectation that we've had with them since they were little. We work hard to model respectful behavior between the adults in our family, and to speak respectfully to our kids, and to apologize when we don't. We require our kids to speak respectfully to us and to each other, and there are coaching sessions and consistently employed consequences as needed when they fall short of expectations.

---

[7] United States Conference of Catholic Bishops, *General Instruction of the Roman Missal* (Washington, D.C.: United States Conference of Catholic Bishops, 2010), no. 275a, http://www.vatican.va/roman_curia/congregations/ccdds/documents/rc_con_ccdds_doc_2003 0317_ordinamento-messale_en.html.

[8] Joking aside, St. Monica *is* a powerful intercessor for mothers and children. See p. 302 for a lovely prayer for this situation (Prayer for the Conversion of Loved Ones).

If ever we find ourselves having over- or undershot our parenting goals in a particular area of older kid or teen behavior, we call a family meeting. We talk about what needs to change and why, and we discuss strategies for how we can meet our goals for our family going forward. It's not a democracy. But it's a good strategy for winning our teens' support by incorporating their ideas whenever possible.

I think it helps that we avoid TV and movies in which kids and parents are disrespectful toward one another. I also think it helps that as long as we've had teenagers, we've also had babies and toddlers and little kids. Our older kids have stayed excited about our liturgical living traditions because they get to share them with enthusiastic little kids.

Sometime between seven and ten years old, our kids transition from "Team Little Kid" to "Team Grown-ups and Big Kids". Members of Team Grown-ups and Big Kids get to stay up late and fill Christmas stockings. They hide the silver coins on Spy Wednesday. They get to go to the Easter Vigil and then to the drive-through for fast-busting burgers and milkshakes afterward. They memorize comically morbid epic poems for our Memento Mori Poetry Recital on Halloween. They do the baking and grilling for particular feast days. They build our liturgical bonfires. We keep them involved by letting them invite friends to join us for feast day dinners, prayers and all.

The draw of helping to create the same fun experiences for their younger siblings that they had when they were the little kids can't last forever, of course. At some point we are going to run out of babies around here, and we'll probably have many years to wait before grandchildren show up to start the cycle of wonder over again.

Perhaps there will come a day when we have only teenagers in the house, and no one much feels like making candle crowns for the feast of Saint Lucy or processing around the yard on the feast of the Assumption. I don't know, I feel that *I* would have been up for that stuff as a teenager, especially if I had invited some friends over to make on-fire hats with me. But I allow for the possibility that we will graduate from some of the activities that I discuss in *The Catholic All Year Compendium*. That's why I also want us to have *this* book, which will continue to be a useful resource for my family no matter our ages or the season.[9]

If we've achieved what we've set out to achieve, we'll have a family culture in which prayer and family time are valued by everyone in our home. These habits we've cultivated with our little ones and reinforced with our teenagers will grow deeper and more meaningful as we all get older. That's my hope for my family and for yours!

[9] I also have the liturgically correct cocktail recipe book by Michael P. Foley, *Drinking with the Saints: The Sinner's Guide to a Holy Happy Hour* (Washington, D.C.: Regnery History, 2015), which I'm looking forward to sharing with adult children!

2

A Prayer Primer

You'll see many different types of prayers as you page through the liturgical year. Let's take a few moments to look at a few of the different types and how they can be used in our families.

Who Can Bless and Why

A blessing, in the liturgical sense, is "a rite, consisting of a ceremony and prayers performed in the name and with the authority of the Church by a duly qualified minister, by which persons or things are sanctified as dedicated to Divine service, or by which certain marks of Divine favour are invoked upon them".[1]

Blessings can be divided into two classes, traditionally called *invocative* and *constitutive*. The distinction is whether the blessing is simply *invoking* God's help or protection or whether the blessing is meant to change the *constitution*, or fundamental nature, of a person or thing. Invocative blessings include those given to children and to food and can be called for by a layperson. Constitutive blessings permanently dedicate persons or things to God's service by imparting to them some sacred character. These become spiritually new and different things, so they cannot be returned to regular use. The blessings given to churches and anything that will be used on the altar fall into this category and must be performed by an ordained minister.

There is also an intermediate sort of blessing, by which things are dedicated to specifically religious use without at the same time

---

[1] Patrick Morrisroe, "Blessing", in *The Catholic Encyclopedia*, vol. 2 (New York: Robert Appleton, 1907), 4, New Advent, http://www.newadvent.org/cathen/02599b.htm.

becoming irrevocably sacred, such as blessed chalk, candles, and homes. These blessings are ideally performed by a bishop, priest, or deacon but can also be said by a layperson.

Blessings are not sacraments. They do not in and of themselves give sanctifying grace. Rather, they are what we call *sacramentals*. Sacramentals help prepare us better to better receive the graces available to us in the sacraments. If the sacraments are paint, sacramentals are a base coat. The term *sacramental* applies to the blessing performed on an object or a person, and also to objects that have been so blessed by a priest, like holy water, palms, or rosaries. These items can help the faithful to sanctify their homes and the actions of their daily lives.

To perform a blessing, a person must have both the faculties and the authority to do so. All rightful authority begins with God, and Jesus Christ himself is the founder and head of the Catholic Church. Our Lord passed authority to his apostles.[2] They were the first bishops. Catholic bishops of today can trace their authority through a line of apostolic succession back to the first apostles. Foremost among the bishops is the Bishop of Rome, whom we call the pope. He is assisted by archbishops, patriarchs, prelates, and ordinaries who have authority over the people of particular physical areas, rites, or communities.[3]

Bishops are assisted by priests and deacons. A parish is led by a pastor, who exercises authority over the members of that parish. Below the pastor in the chain of ecclesiastical authority are heads of families and households, who exercise authority over those for whom they are responsible.

A subordinate cannot bless a superior or exercise ordinary powers in his presence. A priest, for instance, who is the principal celebrant of a Mass at which a bishop is present, is not to give the final blessing.[4]

Faculties, in the context of blessings, mean permission from the Catholic Church to perform a certain religious action. The *Catechism*

---

[2] See Mt 10:1; 16:19; Lk 9:1; 10:16; 22:29; Jn 16:14–15.

[3] There also exist honorary distinctions that can be conferred by the pope. Examples of these are the honorary title of monsignor for diocesan priests, and cardinal for bishops. Priests and bishops so honored are considered members of the papal household but do not wield additional hierarchical authority, although individual cardinals often hold important positions in the Vatican and as a group have the honor of electing the pope.

[4] Catholic Church and International Commission on English in the Liturgy, *Ceremonial of Bishops* (Collegeville, Minn.: Liturgical Press, 1989), no. 18.

of the Catholic Church states, "Every baptized person is called to be a 'blessing,' and to bless. Hence lay people may preside at certain blessings; the more a blessing concerns ecclesial and sacramental life, the more is its administration reserved to the ordained ministry (bishops, priests, or deacons)."[5]

To sum up: not every person can give every blessing. For laypeople, our faculties and authority to bless are largely confined to our food, homes, possessions, animals, and people for whom we are responsible. Parents are especially encouraged to bless their children.[6] With one exception, all the blessings in this book are appropriate for use by nonordained persons.[7]

For some prayers, the fullness of the blessing is dependent on who performs it. A layperson can ask God's blessing upon his possessions, but a layperson's blessing cannot create a sacramental. Therefore, it is preferable for a priest or deacon to bless things like candles and chalk and branches or herbs that will be used over time for religious purposes in the home, so that those items take on the character of sacramentals. Some of the blessings included here have additional instructions for when they are used by a priest or deacon either at church or in your home.[8] However, when that isn't possible, it is permissible—and always better than nothing—for a member of the family to perform these blessings at home.

Blessings are rightly performed by a person with ecclesiastical authority over the home. Commonly that is the father of the family.

---

[5] CCC 1669.

[6] An ordained minister or the child's own parents, grandparents, or godparents are in fact the only people with the authority to confer a blessing on a child. This is among the reasons that it is not appropriate for a lay extraordinary minister of Holy Communion to give blessings to children in the Communion line. See also CCC 1669; can. 1169. The practice was officially discouraged in a letter (Protocol No. 930/08/L), dated November 22, 2008, signed by Fr. Anthony Ward, S.M., undersecretary of the Congregation for Divine Worship.

[7] The blessing part of the Blessing of a Bonfire on the Eve of the Nativity of St. John the Baptist is reserved to a priest, but the rest of the prayers are appropriate for use by the laity.

[8] Pro tip: Invite a priest or deacon over for dinner! It's a wonderful way to strengthen the ties of our parish communities and can help our children to consider a vocation to the priesthood or religious life as a familiar option. While you've got him at your house, ask him to bless some stuff! Also effective is bringing to church the items you would like blessed, plus a copy of the prayers for blessing them, in case Father would like to use them. Some priests are happy to do such blessings after Mass; others prefer that you call ahead and make an appointment.

For single people, or roommates, or families without a father in the home, it would be whoever is the person most responsible for the home. It's not going to be little Timmy, even if he really, really wants to. Just as a priest cannot bless a bishop, a child doesn't have the authority to bless his parents (until he is an adult and responsible for their care) or the family meal if his parents are present.

Some family situations are more complex than others. If the father of the family doesn't wish to participate in liturgical living practices, or isn't available for some or all of them, then that authority must be exercised by another responsible adult.

It's important to note that the outward sign-of-the-cross hand gesture of blessing is reserved to ordained persons. A layperson performing a blessing over an object makes the usual sign of the cross on his own body while asking God's blessing on the thing. A parent asking God's blessing on a child may trace the sign of the cross on the child's forehead as a reminder of having done so at his baptism.[9]

Litanies

Litanies are a series of petitions announced by a leader to which people make fixed responses. Litanies probably originated with the fourth-century tradition of public recitation of the Kyrie, encouraged by the Council of Vaison in 529. That developed into the custom of large public processions of prayer through the streets led by a priest or deacon, often on feast days or in response to a public crisis. The popularity of the practice led to hundreds of different litanies being composed and promulgated, not all of which were appropriately expressive of the fullness of the Truth. To prevent abuse, Pope Clement VIII in 1601 forbade the publication of any litany except the Litany of All Saints (in which only the saints of the universal calendar could be invoked) and the Litany of Loreto. Later, litanies of the Holy Name of Jesus, the Sacred Heart, the Precious Blood, and Saint Joseph were also approved for publication and public recitation.

---

[9] Bishops' Committee on the Liturgy, *Catholic Household Blessings and Prayers* (Washington, D.C.: United States Conference of Catholic Bishops, 2007), 239.

Partial indulgences are offered for the public recitation of these approved litanies.[10] Public recitation is considered to be in a church, family, religious community, or group of the faithful. Other, unapproved litanies may be used in private prayer by one person only. With one exception, all the litanies in this book are approved by the magisterium for public use.[11] I highly recommend their use in families. Litanies are a really fun, participatory way for kids to pray. Sometimes we do them around the table, sometimes in procession around the house or yard. Sometimes I'll print out copies of the prayer so everyone can read the responses aloud. If not, the leader just announces what the next response will be.

Novenas

The word *novena* comes from the Latin *novem*, meaning "nine", so *any* prayer recited for nine days—or nine months—in a row is a novena. Novenas are often undertaken for a specific prayer request, and if they are offered to invoke the intercession of a particular saint, they are usually begun such that the ninth and final day's prayers are said on the day *before* that saint's feast day. The *Manual of Indulgences* specifically recommends undertaking novenas before Christmas, Pentecost, and the feast of the Immaculate Conception and offers a partial indulgence if they are said publicly.[12] No particular formula is required. A novena for each of those three feast days is included in this book. Also included is a novena for Divine Mercy Sunday, the feast of Saint Thérèse of Lisieux, and the feast of Saints Anne and Joachim (this last novena is often prayed by those seeking a spouse or struggling with infertility).

Any of the prayers included here could also be used for a private novena. All you have to do is say the prayer for nine days in a row. Easier said than done, I know. The fear of not being able to complete a novena successfully is enough to scare a lot of folks away from even

---

[10] Apostolic Penitentiary, *Manual of Indulgences: Norms and Grants* (Washington, D.C.: United States Conference of Catholic Bishops, 2006), grant 22.

[11] The Litany of Humility on p. 360 is included for private use.

[12] *Manual of Indulgences*, grant 22.2.

attempting one. But it's important to remember that a novena isn't a magic spell. The idea isn't that we say the prayers just right and then God or the saints are somehow required to submit to our demands. That's not how prayer works. If the goal of prayer is always to reconcile our will to God's, then the goal of a novena is to pray in a more dedicated way and so have more opportunity to reconcile our will to God's.

If we miss a day of a novena, it's up to us to figure out how to handle it. We can start the whole novena over, or skip a day, or do two days' prayers at once. But, of course, the best thing to do is not miss a day to begin with. What works best for me is to put an alarm on my phone for a time when I'm usually able to stop and do the novena prayers—and then a backup alarm in case I get pulled away to do something else. This trick works well for the noon Angelus, too, especially if you have a church bell option for the alarm sound.

And Rosaries, Oh My!

Outside of Mass and the sacraments, the Marian Rosary is probably the most defining devotion of the Catholic Church. It comes highly recommended and incentivized. A plenary indulgence is available *every day* for a family Rosary, which is pretty mind-boggling.[13] The Rosary is both instructive and meditative. While reciting the Our Father and the Hail Mary prayers, we reflect upon events in the lives of Jesus and his Mother Mary. The Rosary fosters obedience and unity. Our Lady herself, in multiple apparitions, has requested that the faithful all over the world pray the Rosary, and our bishops have reiterated that request.[14] The Rosary can be a beautiful and pious experience for a family, or it can be a real soup sandwich, but either

[13] *Manual of Indulgences*, grant 17.1.1–2. To gain the plenary indulgence, one must recite the Rosary in a church or oratory, or in a family, religious community, or group. In addition to fulfilling the usual conditions, one must recite the five decades without interruption, announce the mysteries, and combine meditation upon the mysteries with the vocal prayer, or else the indulgence becomes partial. See the introduction of this book for the usual conditions for indulgences.

[14] Public Affairs Office, United States Conference of Catholic Bishops, "Bishops Urge Catholics to Pray for Life, Marriage, Religious Liberty" (December 6, 2012), no. 2, https://www.usccb.org/news/2012/bishops-urge-catholics-pray-life-marriage-religious-liberty.

way it's worth doing. An imperfect Rosary is better than no Rosary. If we are unable to fulfill the conditions of a plenary indulgence, the indulgence becomes partial, which is still very good!

Saint Josemaría Escrivá said, "The holy Rosary is a powerful weapon. Use it with confidence and you will be amazed at the results."[15] And I'm thinking, Saint Josemaría, please stop giving my children ideas about weapons. Their confidence is not lacking, I promise. We've had the most success with family Rosaries in the car or at home in the evening after dinner—but before dessert, so we still have something with which to motivate the behavior of the "powerful weapon" wielders.

Other prayers said using a standard five-decade rosary include the Divine Mercy Chaplet, based on the messages of Jesus to Saint Faustina Kowalska, and the Chaplet of Reparation, said as an act of reparation for our sins and the sins of priests. The Chaplet of Reparation is based on the messages of Jesus to a Benedictine monk and is popular as a response to the sexual abuse crisis in the Church.

These and other prayers can be said using a typical fifty-nine-bead rosary, a single-decade rosary bracelet or ring, or your fingers!

Devotions and Consecrations

All prayer is intended to honor God and help us grow closer to him. Different devotions honor God in different ways, whether through the saints, Our Lady, the Persons of the Trinity, or different aspects of Jesus' life and character. Different devotions appeal to people of different temperaments or in different circumstances. None of us should feel obligated to pursue any one particular devotion, no matter how fruitful it's been for someone else. I have found it useful to explore different devotions. If it seems that one will be especially useful in my attempt to grow in personal holiness, I can make it part of my usual prayer routine. If it doesn't resonate as much, maybe I'll try again next year, or maybe I'll just leave it off. That's okay. We aren't required to enjoy every flavor of ice cream equally.

---

[15] Josemaría Escrivá de Balaguer, *The Way*, no. 558, Fundación Studium, https://www.escrivaworks.org/book/the_way.htm.

When we've found our very favorite "flavors", we can consider making things official. An act of consecration to a particular devotion is a decision to give oneself entirely to God though that devotion. The act of consecration itself is a prayer recited by a family or an individual, or ideally by a deacon, priest, or bishop on behalf of an individual, a family, a country, or even the whole world. Usually one prepares for an act of consecration with a period of thirty-three days of prayer culminating in the consecration prayer.[16]

Latin Lover

A few prayers and hymns are included here in both English and Latin. In case you're wondering why, here's a quick rundown of the language of prayer.

Aramaic was the native language of the apostles, who also knew Hebrew. Since Greek was a dominant language in the Roman Empire at the time of Jesus, the apostles wrote the books of the New Testament in Greek, which was also used in early Christian worship. Greek fell into disuse in the West in the fourth century and began to be replaced by a form of Latin. In A.D. 420 Saint Jerome's Latin Vulgate translation of the Bible facilitated the birth of what developed into ecclesiastical Church Latin. In the sixteenth century the Council of Trent chose to maintain the use of Latin in the liturgy even though it had long ceased to be a living language. In the twentieth century the Second Vatican Council allowed for the use of the vernacular tongue in the Mass but maintained Latin as the official language of the Catholic Church. The official liturgical books of the Roman Rite, as well as letters and encyclicals of the popes, are all still written in Latin.

The fact that Latin prayers are the same all over the world helps unite us as a universal Church. Since Latin words and phrases are no longer in secular use, they don't change over time and so unite us with the faithful of the past. Pope Saint John Paul II wrote, "The Roman Church has special obligations towards Latin, the splendid language of ancient Rome, and she must manifest them whenever

---

[16] See especially Michael E. Gaitley, *33 Days to Morning Glory: A Do-It-Yourself Retreat in Preparation for Marian Consecration* (Stockbridge, Mass.: Marian Press, 2014).

the occasion presents itself."[17] Pope Benedict XVI said, "Nor should we forget that the faithful can be taught to recite the more common prayers in Latin."[18]

He's right! We can! I've had no formal training in Latin but have been able to muddle along. The nice thing about it being a dead language is that almost nobody is going to give you a hard time if you pronounce something wrong. There are online recordings of Latin hymns and prayers if you'd like to hear how people who know what they're doing sing and say them.

Let's Do This!

We try to work all these different types of prayer into our days in a way that doesn't add to our stress and busyness. We keep track of upcoming feast days using a liturgical year wall calendar.[19] We add a short prayer to the end of our Blessing before Meals for the month to help us stay mindful of the recommended devotion for that month, and we add special litanies, prayers, and songs to our evening prayers as often as we are able, always depending on the circumstances of the day, week, and year. If we miss the prayers for a feast day that we usually observe, we make them up on another day or skip them for that year and try again next year.

See appendix C for space to record the dates of what we call the "three special days" (birthday, baptism day, and name day or patron saint day) for the members of your family, plus other favorite family prayers you would like to add to those available here.

Please remember, you do not have to do everything in this book! You can do all the prayers or just a few here and there. You can find

[17] John Paul II, apostolic letter *Dominicae Cenae* (February 24, 1980), no. 10, https://w2
.vatican.va/content/john-paul-ii/en/letters/1980/documents/hf_jp-ii_let_19800224
_dominicae-cenae.html.

[18] Benedict XVI, apostolic exhortation *Sacramentum Caritatis* (February 22, 2007), no. 62,
http://www.vatican.va/content/benedict-xvi/en/apost_exhortations/documents/hf_ben
-xvi_exh_20070222_sacramentum-caritatis.html.

[19] Liturgical year wall calendars are often available for free from your parish before Advent
begins. I also offer them in PDF and printed versions at CatholicAllYear.com. The Catholic
All Year calendars feature all the feast days discussed in the *Compendium* and reminders for
novenas and indulgenced prayers recommended here in the *Prayer Companion*.

other prayers and jot them in the margins or print them out and stuff them between the pages. You can use this book with your family, or in a classroom, or on your own. *You* can grow in faith, devotion, and understanding through the prayerful traditions of the Church associated with the liturgical calendar. It's all right here!

3

The Liturgical Year Begins: December

Immaculate Conception Novena[1]

Traditionally recited daily from November 29 to December 8 in preparation for the feast of the Immaculate Conception on December 9.

Immaculate Virgin! Mary, conceived without sin!

Remember, you were miraculously preserved from even the shadow of sin, because you were destined to become not only the Mother of God, but also the mother, the refuge, and the advocate of man; penetrated therefore, with the most lively confidence in your never-failing intercession, we most humbly implore you to look with favor upon the intentions of this novena, and to obtain for us the graces and the favors we request.

You know, O Mary, how often our hearts are the sanctuaries of God, who abhors iniquity. Obtain for us, then, that angelic purity which was your favorite virtue, that purity of heart which will attach us to God alone, and that purity of intention which will consecrate every thought, word, and action to his greater glory. Obtain also for us a constant spirit of prayer and self-denial, that we may recover by penance that innocence which we have lost by sin, and at length attain safely to that blessed abode of the saints, where nothing defiled can enter.

Leader: O Mary, conceived without sin,

All: Pray for us who have recourse to you.

Leader: You are all fair, O Mary.

All: You are all fair, O Mary.

Leader: And the original stain is not in you.

[1] Francis Xavier Lasance, *With God: A Book of Prayers and Reflections* (New York: Benziger Brothers, 1911), 691.

All: And the original stain is not in you.

Leader: You are the glory of Jerusalem.

All: You are the joy of Israel.

Leader: You are the honor of our people.

All: You are the advocate of sinners.

Leader: O Mary, Virgin, most prudent,

All: O Mary, Mother, most tender,

Leader: Pray for us.

All: Intercede for us with Jesus our Lord.

Leader: In your conception, Holy Virgin, you were immaculate.

All: Pray for us to the Father whose Son you brought forth.

Leader: O Lady, aid my prayer,

All: And let my cry come unto you.

Leader: Let us pray. Holy Mary, Queen of Heaven, Mother of our Lord Jesus Christ, and mistress of the world, who forsakes no one, and despises no one, look upon me, O Lady, with an eye of pity, and entreat for me of your beloved Son the forgiveness of all my sins; that, as I now celebrate, with devout affection, your holy and immaculate conception, so, hereafter I may receive the prize of eternal blessedness, by the grace of him whom you, in virginity, brought forth, Jesus Christ our Lord: who, with the Father and the Holy Ghost, lives and reigns, in perfect Trinity, God, world without end.

All: Amen.

November 30: Saint Andrew, Apostle (Feast)

The season of Advent, and the new liturgical year, begins on the Sunday closest to the feast of Saint Andrew. See the prayers and devotions for the rest of the month of November beginning on p. 335.

COLLECT PRAYER

We humbly implore your majesty, O Lord, that, just as the blessed Apostle Andrew was for your Church a preacher and pastor, so he may be for us a constant intercessor before you. Through our Lord Jesus Christ, your Son, who lives and reigns with you in the unity of the Holy Spirit, one God, for ever and ever. Amen.

A reading from the Holy Gospel according to Saint John. (Jn 1:35–42)

The next day again John was standing with two of his disciples; and he looked at Jesus as he walked, and said, "Behold, the Lamb of God!" The two disciples heard him say this, and they followed Jesus. Jesus turned, and saw them following, and said to them, "What do you seek?" And they said to him, "Rabbi" (which means Teacher), "where are you staying?" He said to them, "Come and see." They came and saw where he was staying; and they stayed with him that day, for it was about the tenth hour. One of the two who heard John speak, and followed him, was Andrew, Simon Peter's brother. He first found his brother Simon, and said to him, "We have found the Messiah" (which means Christ). He brought him to Jesus. Jesus looked at him, and said, "So you are Simon the son of John? You shall be called Cephas" (which means Peter).

The Gospel of the Lord.

All: Praise to you, Lord Jesus Christ.

Christmas Anticipation Prayer

The Christmas Anticipation Prayer (p. 41) is traditionally recited fifteen times a day until Christmas, often for a particular intention, beginning on the feast of Saint Andrew. This is a meditative prayer that helps increase our awareness of the season of Advent and prepares us spiritually for the coming of Jesus. It's sometimes called the Saint Andrew Christmas Novena, even though it's not actually a novena.

Prayer for Fishermen and All Those Who Travel by Sea

O God, who brought our fathers through the Red Sea and carried them safely through the deep as they sang praises of your name, we humbly beseech you to guard your servants aboard ship, and having repelled all adversities, bring them to the desired port after a calm voyage. Through our Lord, Jesus Christ, your Son, who lives and reigns with you in the unity of the Holy Spirit, world without end. Amen.

DECEMBER

The month of the Immaculate Conception

Prayer after Blessing before Meals I: Christmas Anticipation Prayer

Hail and blessed be the hour and moment in which the Son of God was born of the most pure Virgin Mary, at midnight, in Bethlehem, in the piercing cold. In that hour vouchsafe, I beseech you, O my God, to hear my prayer and grant my desires, through the merits of our Savior Jesus Christ and of his blessed Mother. Amen.

or

Prayer after Blessing before Meals II: Miraculous Medal Prayer

O Mary, conceived without sin, pray for us who have recourse to you. Amen.

Marian Antiphon I: Alma Redemptoris Mater

One of the four seasonal liturgical Marian antiphons sung, chanted, or recited at the end of the office of Compline, or Night Prayer (the other three being Ave Regina Caelorum, p. 146; Regina Caeli, p. 223; and Salve Regina, p. 250), this antiphon is used during both Advent and Christmastide (through Candlemas). The text is credited to Hermann the Lame, an eleventh-century monk. The English translation is by Father Adrian Fortescue, 1913.

Alma Redemptoris Mater, quae pervia caeli porta manes et stella maris, succurre cadenti, surgere qui curat, populo: tu quae genuisti, natura mirante, tuum sanctum genitorem, Virgo prius, ac posterius, Gabrielis ab ore sumens illud ave, peccatorum miserere.

Holy Mother of our Redeemer, gate leading to heaven and star of the sea, help the falling people who seek to rise, you who, all nature wondering, gave birth to your holy Creator. Virgin always, hearing the greeting from Gabriel's lips, take pity on sinners.

ADVENT SONG SUGGESTIONS: O Come, O Come, Emmanuel; Come, Thou Long Expected Jesus; Creator of the Stars of Night; O Come, Divine Messiah; Let All Mortal Flesh Keep Silence; People Look East; Of the Father's Love Begotten

First Sunday of Advent (Stir-Up Sunday)

COLLECT PRAYER

Grant your faithful, we pray, almighty God, the resolve to run forth to meet your Christ with righteous deeds at his coming, so that, gathered at his right hand, they may be worthy to possess the heavenly Kingdom. Through our Lord Jesus Christ, your Son, who lives and reigns with you in the unity of the Holy Spirit, one God, for ever and ever. Amen.

Prayer to One's Patron Saint[2]

Each person in our family has a "forever" patron saint (a saint with whom he shares a name or is otherwise dedicated to), but each year we also like to choose a new saint (or let a new saint choose us!) for the new liturgical year. We pray this prayer and randomly choose a saint from a book of saints or from the Saint's Name Generator (saintsnamegenerator.com).

O Heavenly Patron, in whose name I glory, pray ever to God for me: strengthen me in my faith; establish me in virtue; guard me in the conflict; that I may vanquish the foe malign and attain to glory everlasting. Amen.

---

[2] Joseph Patrick Christopher, Charles E. Spence, and John F. Rowan, *The Raccolta; or, A Manual of Indulgences, Prayers, and Devotions Enriched with Indulgences* (New York: Benziger Brothers, 1957), no. 581. Prayers from the *Raccolta* are used with permission.

Advent Wreath Blessing[3]

The Book of Blessings *states: "The use of the Advent Wreath is a traditional practice which has found its place in the Church as well as in the home. The blessing of an Advent Wreath takes place on the First Sunday of Advent or on the evening before the First Sunday of Advent. . . . When the blessing of the Advent Wreath is celebrated in the home, it is appropriate that it be blessed by a parent or another member of the family."*[4]

All make the sign of the cross.

Leader: Our help is in the name of the Lord.
All: Who made heaven and earth.

A reading from the book of the prophet Isaiah.
(Is 9:1–2, 5–6, NAB)

> The people who walked in darkness
> have seen a great light;
> Upon those who dwelt in the land of gloom
> a light has shone.
> You have brought them abundant joy
> and great rejoicing,
> As they rejoice before you as at the harvest,
> as men make merry when dividing spoils.
> For a child is born to us, a son is given us;
> upon his shoulder dominion rests.
> They name him Wonder-Counselor, God-Hero,
> Father-Forever, Prince of Peace.
> His dominion is vast
> and forever peaceful,
> From David's throne, and over his kingdom,
> which he confirms and sustains
> By judgment and justice, both now and forever.

[3] International Commission on English in the Liturgy, *Book of Blessings*, approved for use in the dioceses of the United States of America, © 1988 United States Conference of Catholic Bishops, Washington, D.C. (Collegeville, Minn.: Liturgical Press, 1989). Used with permission. All rights reserved. Nos. 1509, 1514, 1537, 1538, 1540. For the history of the Advent wreath and instructions on how to make a simple home version, see *The Catholic All Year Compendium.*

[4] Ibid., nos. 1509, 1514.

The Word of the Lord.

All: Thanks be to God.

With hands joined, the leader says:

Leader: Lord our God,
we praise you for your Son, Jesus Christ:
he is Emmanuel, the hope of the peoples,
he is the wisdom that teaches and guides us,
he is the Savior of every nation.

Lord God,
let your blessing come upon us
as we light the candles of this wreath.
May the wreath and its light
be a sign of Christ's promise to bring us salvation.
May he come quickly and not delay.
We ask this through Christ our Lord.

All: Amen.

All make the sign of the cross.

After the blessing, the wreath (and everyone in the splash zone) can get sprinkled with holy water, if you have some handy. Many parishes have a holy water dispenser in the church; just bring your own container. If you're not sure how to get some, ask your priest or someone in the parish office.

Advent Wreath Prayers

These prayers can be said before family meals.

First Week

Leader: O Lord, stir up your might, we beg you, and come, that by your protection we may deserve to be rescued from the threatening dangers of our sins and saved by your deliverance. Through Christ our Lord.

All: Amen.

Light the first purple candle. Let it burn during the meal. This is repeated each day of the week.

Second Week

Leader: O Lord, stir up our hearts that we may prepare for your only-begotten Son, that through his coming we may be made worthy to serve you with pure minds. Through Christ our Lord.

All: Amen.

Light the first and second purple candles. Let them burn during the meal. This is repeated each day of the week.

Third Week

Leader: O Lord, we beg you, incline your ear to our prayers and enlighten the darkness of our minds by the grace of your visitation. Through Christ our Lord.

All: Amen.

Light the first and second purple candles and the pink candle. Let them burn during the meal. This is repeated each day of the week.

Fourth Week

Leader: O Lord, stir up your power, we pray you, and come; and with great might help us, that with the help of your grace, your merciful forgiveness may hasten what our sins impede. Through Christ our Lord.

All: Amen.

Light all four candles. Let them burn during the meal. This is repeated each day of the week.

December 6: Saint Nicholas, Bishop (Optional Memorial)

COLLECT PRAYER

We humbly implore your mercy, Lord: protect us in all dangers through the prayers of the Bishop Saint Nicholas, that the way of salvation may lie open before us. Through our Lord Jesus Christ, your

Son, who lives and reigns with you in the unity of the Holy Spirit, one God, for ever and ever. Amen.

Prayer for Children[5]

Saint Nicholas is the patron saint of children.

O God, we pray that through the intercession of Saint Nicholas you will guide and protect our children. Keep them safe from all harm and help them grow to become loving disciples of Jesus in your sight. Give them strength always to mature into deeper faith in you, and to keep alive joy in your creation. Through Jesus Christ our Lord. Amen.

Nicene Creed[6]

This prayer was developed and adopted at the Council of Nicaea in 325 as a definitive statement of the doctrinal beliefs of the Church, in opposition to the heretical beliefs being promoted by Arius. Saint Nicholas is understood to have been in attendance at the council, debated Arius, lost his temper, and slapped the heretic right across the face!

I believe in one God,
the Father almighty,
maker of heaven and earth,
of all things visible and invisible.

I believe in one Lord Jesus Christ,
the Only Begotten Son of God,
born of the Father before all ages.
God from God, Light from Light,

[5] Composed by Fr. David R. Engbarth, St. Nicholas Church, Aurora, Ill.

[6] International Commission on English in the Liturgy Corporation, *The Roman Missal*, 3rd ed., approved by the United States Conference of Catholic Bishops and confirmed by the Apostolic See (New Jersey: Catholic Book Publishing Corp., 2011), Order of Mass, no. 18. All rights reserved. Used with permission.

true God from true God,
begotten, not made, consubstantial with the Father;
through him all things were made.
For us men and for our salvation
he came down from heaven,

At the words that follow, up to and including and became man, *all bow.*

and by the Holy Spirit was incarnate of the Virgin Mary, and
   became man.
For our sake he was crucified under Pontius Pilate,
he suffered death and was buried,
and rose again on the third day
in accordance with the Scriptures.
He ascended into heaven
and is seated at the right hand of the Father.
He will come again in glory
to judge the living and the dead
and his kingdom will have no end.

I believe in the Holy Spirit, the Lord, the giver of life,
who proceeds from the Father and the Son,
who with the Father and the Son is adored and glorified,
who has spoken through the prophets.

I believe in one, holy, catholic and apostolic Church.
I confess one Baptism for the forgiveness of sins
and I look forward to the resurrection of the dead
and the life of the world to come. Amen.

December 7: Saint Ambrose, Bishop and Doctor of the Church (Memorial)

COLLECT PRAYER

O God, who made the Bishop Saint Ambrose a teacher of the Catholic faith and a model of apostolic courage, raise up in your Church men after your own heart to govern her with courage and wisdom.

Through our Lord Jesus Christ, your Son, who lives and reigns with you in the unity of the Holy Spirit, one God, for ever and ever. Amen.

Penitential Prayer of Saint Ambrose

O Lord, who has mercy upon all, take away from me my sins, and mercifully kindle in me the fire of your Holy Spirit. Take away from me the heart of stone, and give me a heart of flesh, a heart to love and adore you, a heart to delight in you, to follow and enjoy you, for Christ's sake. Amen.

See also Te Deum, p. 107.

December 8: THE IMMACULATE CONCEPTION OF THE BLESSED VIRGIN MARY
(Solemnity, Holy Day of Obligation [U.S.])

COLLECT PRAYER

O God, who by the Immaculate Conception of the Blessed Virgin prepared a worthy dwelling for your Son, grant, we pray, that, as you preserved her from every stain by virtue of the Death of your Son, which you foresaw, so, through her intercession, we, too, may be cleansed and admitted to your presence. Through our Lord Jesus Christ, your Son, who lives and reigns with you in the unity of the Holy Spirit, one God, for ever and ever. Amen.

Prayer to the Immaculate Conception[7]

Blessed be the holy and Immaculate Conception of the Blessed Virgin Mary, Mother of God. You are all fair, O Mary; the original stain is not in you. You are the glory of Jerusalem. You, the joy of Israel;

---

[7] *Raccolta*, nos. 356, 359.

you, the great honor of our people; you, the advocate of sinners. O Mary, O Mary, virgin most prudent, mother most merciful, pray for us. Intercede for us with our Lord Jesus Christ. Amen.

Prayer for the Consecration of the United States to Its Patroness, the Immaculate Conception[8]

In 1789 John Carroll of Baltimore, Maryland, was appointed the first bishop in the United States. In 1792 he consecrated the country to the Blessed Virgin Mary under the title of the Immaculate Conception with the following prayer.

Most Holy Trinity: Our Father in heaven, who chose Mary as the fairest of your daughters; Holy Spirit, who chose Mary as your spouse; God the Son, who chose Mary as your Mother; in union with Mary, we adore your majesty and acknowledge your supreme, eternal dominion and authority.

Most Holy Trinity, we place the United States of America into the hands of Mary Immaculate in order that she may present the country to you. Through her, we wish to thank you for the great resources of this land and for the freedom which has been its heritage.

Through the intercession of Mary, have mercy on the Catholic Church in America. Grant us peace. Have mercy on our president and on all the officers of our government.

Grant us a fruitful economy born of justice and labor. Protect the family life of the nation.

Guard the precious gift of many religious vocations.

Through the intercession of Mary our Mother, have mercy on the sick, the poor, the tempted, sinners, on all who are in need.

Mary, Immaculate Virgin, our Mother, patroness of our land, we praise you and honor you and give ourselves to you. Protect us from every harm. Pray for us, that acting always according to your will and the will of your divine Son, we may live and die pleasing to God. Amen.

---

[8] John Carroll, "Prayer of Consecration of America", http://childrenoftheeucharist.org /wp-content/uploads/2021/01/Archbishop-Carroll-First-Bishop-Consecrates-USA.pdf.

See also Litany of Loreto, p. 52.

SONG SUGGESTIONS: Lo, How a Rose E'er Blooming; Ave Maria

December 9: Saint Juan Diego Cuauhtlatoatzin (Optional Memorial)

COLLECT PRAYER

O God, who by means of Saint Juan Diego showed the love of the most holy Virgin Mary for your people, grant, through his intercession, that, by following the counsels our Mother gave at Guadalupe, we may be ever constant in fulfilling your will. Through our Lord Jesus Christ, your Son, who lives and reigns with you in the unity of the Holy Spirit, one God, for ever and ever. Amen.

Homily at the Canonization of Juan Diego Cuauhtlatoatzin[9]

By Pope Saint John Paul II, Mexico City, July 31, 2002 (excerpt).

Blessed Juan Diego, a good, Christian Indian, whom simple people have always considered a saint! We ask you to accompany the Church on her pilgrimage in Mexico, so that she may be more evangelizing and more missionary each day. Encourage the bishops, support the priests, inspire new and holy vocations, help all those who give their lives to the cause of Christ and the spread of his Kingdom.

Happy Juan Diego, true and faithful man! We entrust to you our lay brothers and sisters so that, feeling the call to holiness, they may imbue every area of social life with the spirit of the Gospel. Bless families, strengthen spouses in their marriage, sustain the efforts of parents to give their children a Christian upbringing. Look with favor upon the pain of those who are suffering in body or in spirit, on those

---

[9]John Paul II, Homily at the Canonization Mass of Blessed Juan Diego Cuauhtlatoatzin (Mexico City, July 31, 2002), no. 5, http://www.vatican.va/content/john-paul-ii/en/homilies /2002/documents/hf_jp-ii_hom_20020731_canonization-mexico.html.

afflicted by poverty, loneliness, marginalization or ignorance. May all people, civic leaders and ordinary citizens, always act in accordance with the demands of justice and with respect for the dignity of each person, so that in this way peace may be reinforced.

Beloved Juan Diego, "the talking eagle"! Show us the way that leads to the "Dark Virgin" of Tepeyac, that she may receive us in the depths of her heart, for she is the loving, compassionate Mother who guides us to the true God. Amen.

December 10: Our Lady of Loreto (Optional Memorial)[10]

COLLECT PRAYER

O God, who at the announcement of your angel willed that your Word would take flesh in the womb of the Blessed Virgin Mary, grant, we pray, to us who remember this great mystery in this holy place, the ability to celebrate both in faith and in holiness of life, the immensity of your mercy. Through our Lord Jesus Christ, your Son, who lives and reigns with you in the unity of the Holy Spirit, one God, forever and ever. Amen.

Prayer to Our Lady of Loreto

O Mary, Immaculate Virgin, for the sake of your blessed house, which the angels moved to the pleasant hills of Loreto, turn your benevolent eyes toward us. For the holy walls within which you were born and lived as a child, with prayers and the most sublime love; for the fortunate walls that listened to the greetings of the angel who called you "blessed among all women" and which remind us of the Incarnation of the Word in your purest bosom; for your blessed

---

[10] *The Catholic All Year Compendium* was released in October 2018 and contained a listing for the then-historical feast of Our Lady of Loreto. In October 2019 Pope Francis restored the feast of Our Lady of Loreto to the universal Roman calendar as an optional memorial. Just sayin'.

house, where you lived with Jesus and Joseph, and which became during the centuries the fervently longed-for destination of the saints, who considered themselves lucky to kiss your sacred walls, bestow upon us the graces which we humbly ask, and the fortune of coming to heaven after the exile, to repeat to you the greetings of the angel: Hail Mary. Amen.

Litany of Loreto (Litany of the Blessed Virgin Mary)[11]

The Litany of the Blessed Virgin Mary is a Marian prayer originally approved in 1587 by Pope Sixtus V. Also known as the Litany of Loreto, it has been in use at the Marian shrine at the Holy House in Loreto, Italy, since at least 1558. The litany is usually recited as a call and response in a group setting but can also be recited alone. A partial indulgence is attached to the prayer at any time. In our home, we recite the Litany of Loreto on all Marian feast days. There are four different concluding prayers, which can be used during particular liturgical seasons. In June 2020 Pope Francis added three new invocations to the litany: "mother of mercy", "mother of hope", and "solace of migrants".

Leader: Lord, have mercy.

All: Christ, have mercy.

Leader: Lord, have mercy; Christ, hear us.

All: Christ, graciously hear us.

Leader: God, the Father of heaven,

All: Have mercy on us.

Leader: God the Son, Redeemer of the world,

All: Have mercy on us.

Leader: God the Holy Spirit,

All: Have mercy on us.

---

[11] *Manual of Indulgences*, grant 22, and press release Letter of the Prefect of the Congregation for Divine Worship and the Discipline of the Sacraments to the Presidents of the Conferences of Bishops on the Invocations "Mater misericordiæ", "Mater spei", and "Solacium migrantium" to Be Inserted into the Litany of Loreto (June 20, 2020), https://press.vatican.va/content/salastampa/en/bollettino/pubblico/2020/06/20/200620c.html.

Leader: Holy Trinity, One God,

All: Have mercy on us.

The leader announces each title of Mary.

All reply: pray for us.

Holy Mary, *pray for us.*
Holy Mother of God, *pray for us.*
Holy Virgin of virgins, *pray for us.*
Mother of Christ, *pray for us.*
Mother of the Church, *pray for us.*
Mother of mercy, *pray for us.*
Mother of divine grace, *pray for us.*
Mother of hope, *pray for us.*
Mother most pure, *pray for us.*
Mother most chaste, *pray for us.*
Mother inviolate, *pray for us.*
Mother undefiled, *pray for us.*
Mother most amiable, *pray for us.*
Mother most admirable, *pray for us.*
Mother of good counsel, *pray for us.*
Mother of our Creator, *pray for us.*
Mother of our Savior, *pray for us.*
Virgin most prudent, *pray for us.*
Virgin most venerable, *pray for us.*
Virgin most renowned, *pray for us.*
Virgin most powerful, *pray for us.*
Virgin most merciful, *pray for us.*
Virgin most faithful, *pray for us.*
Mirror of justice, *pray for us.*
Seat of wisdom, *pray for us.*
Cause of our joy, *pray for us.*
Spiritual vessel, *pray for us.*

Vessel of honor, *pray for us.*
Singular vessel of devotion, *pray for us.*
Mystical rose, *pray for us.*
Tower of David, *pray for us.*
Tower of ivory, *pray for us.*
House of gold, *pray for us.*
Ark of the covenant, *pray for us.*
Gate of heaven, *pray for us.*
Morning star, *pray for us.*
Health of the sick, *pray for us.*
Refuge of sinners, *pray for us.*
Solace of migrants, *pray for us.*
Comfort of the afflicted, *pray for us.*
Help of Christians, *pray for us.*
Queen of Angels, *pray for us.*
Queen of Patriarchs, *pray for us.*
Queen of Prophets, *pray for us.*
Queen of Apostles, *pray for us.*
Queen of Martyrs, *pray for us.*
Queen of Confessors, *pray for us.*
Queen of Virgins, *pray for us.*
Queen of all Saints, *pray for us.*
Queen conceived without original sin, *pray for us.*
Queen assumed into heaven, *pray for us.*
Queen of the most holy Rosary, *pray for us.*
Queen of families, *pray for us.*
Queen of Peace, *pray for us.*

Leader: Lamb of God, you take away the sins of the world;

All: Have mercy on us.

Leader: Lamb of God, you take away the sins of the world;

All: Have mercy on us.

Leader: Lamb of God, you take away the sins of the world;

All: Have mercy on us.

Leader: Pray for us, O holy Mother of God,

All: That we may be made worthy of the promises of Christ.

General Concluding Prayer

Leader: Let us pray. Eternal God, let your people enjoy constant health in mind and body. Through the intercession of the Virgin Mary free us from the sorrows of this life and lead us to happiness in the life to come.

All: Amen.

During Advent

Leader: Let us pray. O God, you willed that, at the message of an angel, your Word should take flesh in the womb of the Blessed Virgin Mary; grant to your suppliant people, that we, who believe her to be truly the Mother of God, may be helped by her intercession with you. Through the same Christ our Lord.

All: Amen.

From Christmas to Candlemas (February 2)

Leader: Let us pray. O God, by the fruitful virginity of Blessed Mary, you bestowed upon the human race the rewards of eternal salvation; grant, we beg you, that we may feel the power of her intercession, through whom we have been made worthy to receive the Author of life, our Lord Jesus Christ your Son. Who lives and reigns with you forever and ever.

All: Amen.

During Eastertide

Leader: Let us pray. O God, who by the Resurrection of your Son, our Lord Jesus Christ, granted joy to the whole world; grant, we beg you, that through the intercession of the Virgin Mary, his Mother, we may attain the joys of eternal life. Through the same Christ our Lord.

All: Amen.

December 12: Our Lady of Guadalupe (Feast)

COLLECT PRAYER

O God, Father of mercies, who placed your people under the singular protection of your Son's most holy Mother, grant that all who invoke the Blessed Virgin of Guadalupe, may seek with ever more lively faith the progress of peoples in the ways of justice and of peace. Through our Lord Jesus Christ, your Son, who lives and reigns with you in the unity of the Holy Spirit, one God, for ever and ever. Amen.

Nican Mopohua

A description of the apparitions of Our Lady of Guadalupe written in the Nahuatl language, probably by Don Antonio Valeriano in the mid-sixteenth century. This excerpt describes the fourth apparition on Monday, December 11, 1531.[12]

The next day Juan Diego did not return, for his uncle, Juan Bernardino, was gravely ill. He called a doctor in the morning and at night his uncle, feeling that his hour had come, asked him to go early to Tlaltelolco to find a priest. Juan did as he was bid, leaving at dawn, by his usual road; but drawing near to the hill of Tepeyac, he stopped and thought. "If I go forward, I shall meet Our Lady, who will divert me to give the sign the prelate has asked for." So he turned to the west from the easterly road he was following, believing

---

[12] Antonio Valeriano, "Nican Mopohua: The Story of Our Lady of Guadalupe in Nahuatl", University of Dayton, Ohio, n.d., https://udayton.edu/imri/mary/n/nican-mopohua.php. The excerpt is adapted from English translations by David K. Jordan, https://pages.ucsd.edu /~dkjordan/nahuatl/nican/NicanMopohua.html, and Johann Roten, S.M.

it paramount to fetch the priest to his dying uncle. As he circled the hill, he saw Our Lady treading majestically down the slope: she drew right near him and said, "What is happening, my son? Where are you going?"

"My daughter," replied Juan Diego, "it will grieve you to know that one of your poor servants, my uncle, is very ill and dying of plague. I am going in a great hurry to call the priest to confess him and will come back here to take your message. Forgive me, lady and daughter mine, be patient with me, I am not deceiving you, I will come tomorrow in all haste."

"Be not troubled or afraid," replied the Virgin. "Do not let it disturb you. Do not fear this sickness or any other sickness or any sharp and hurtful thing. Am I not here, I, who am your Mother? Are you not under the shadow of my protection? Am I not the source of your joy? Are you not in the hollow of my mantle, in the crossing of my arms? Do you need something more? Let not the sickness of your uncle distress you anymore, for he will not die yet. You can rest assured that he is well even now."

When Juan heard these words, he felt comforted and happy.

"Go to the hilltop, my son," the Virgin went on. "There you will find flowers in plenty; pluck them, gather them into a bouquet, and come down at once to bring them here to me."

Juan Diego at once went off and, when he reached the top, he stood astonished before a choice variety of flowers blooming before their due season. They were fresh, covered with the night's dew, whose drops shone like precious pearls. Juan plucked the flowers and, descending at once, he offered the Virgin the heavenly blooms.

"My son," Our Lady said to him, "these flowers are the sign you shall take to the bishop. You shall tell him in my name to see my will in them. You shall be my emissary, full worthy of my whole trust. I charge you strictly to unfold thy cloak only before the bishop and show him the flowers. You shall tell him all you have seen and wondered at."

In haste and with joy Juan Diego took the road to Mexico, with the wonderful flowers he was carrying in his arms.

See also Litany of Loreto, p. 52.

December 13: Saint Lucy, Virgin and Martyr (Memorial)

COLLECT PRAYER

May the glorious intercession of the Virgin and Martyr Saint Lucy give us a new heart, we pray, O Lord, so that we may celebrate her heavenly birthday in this present age and so behold things eternal. Through our Lord Jesus Christ, your Son, who lives and reigns with you in the unity of the Holy Spirit, one God, for ever and ever. Amen.

Prayer to Saint Lucy of Syracuse

O God, our Creator and Redeemer, mercifully hear our prayers that as we venerate your servant, Saint Lucy, for the light of faith you bestowed upon her, you would increase and preserve this same light in our souls, that we may be able to avoid evil, to do good, and to abhor nothing so much as the blindness and the darkness of evil and of sin.

Relying on your goodness, O God, we humbly ask you, by the intercession of your servant, Saint Lucy, that you would give perfect vision to our eyes, that they may serve for your greater honor and glory, and for the salvation of our souls in this world, that we may come to the enjoyment of the unfailing light of the Lamb of God in paradise. Saint Lucy, virgin and martyr, hear our prayers and obtain our petitions. Amen.

SONG SUGGESTION: *This Little Light of Mine*

Ember Days Prayer

The winter Ember Days—voluntary days of fasting and abstinence—fall on the Wednesday, Friday, and Saturday after the feast of Saint Lucy.[13] *This*

[13] For more on Ember Days, vigils, and general fasting and abstinence requirements and recommendations, see appendix A of *The Catholic All Year Compendium*.

season's days are offered for the olive harvest in anticipation of the holy oils used for the sacrament of extreme unction, or anointing of the sick. Saturday is also offered as a day of prayer for priests and for vocations.

All: Bless the Lord, O my soul, and never forget all he has done for you.

Leader: Lord, you have been our refuge.

All: From generation to generation.

Leader: Let us pray. Grant, we beseech you, almighty God, that as year by year we devoutly keep these holy observances, we may be pleasing to you both in body and soul. Through Christ our Lord. Amen.

See Farmer's Prayer, p. 235; Blessing for the Products of Nature, p. 124; Prayer for Priests, p. 102; Prayer for Vocations, p. 357.

December 14: Saint John of the Cross, Priest and Doctor of the Church (Memorial)

COLLECT PRAYER

O God, who gave the Priest Saint John an outstanding dedication to perfect self-denial and love of the Cross, grant that, by imitating him closely at all times, we may come to contemplate eternally your glory. Through our Lord Jesus Christ, your Son, who lives and reigns with you in the unity of the Holy Spirit, one God, for ever and ever. Amen.

A Spiritual Canticle of the Soul and the Bridegroom Christ[14]

Composed by Saint John of the Cross during his imprisonment by the Carmelite order (excerpt).

[14]John of the Cross, "A Spiritual Canticle of the Soul and the Bridegroom Christ", trans. Rhina P. Espaillat, *First Things*, November 1, 2003, https://www.firstthings.com /article/2003/11/a-spiritual-canticle-of-the-soul-and-the-bridegroom-christ.

Where have you fled and vanished,
Beloved, since you left me here to moan?
Deer-like you leaped; then, banished
and wounded by my own,

I followed you with cries, but you had flown.
Shepherds, if you discover,
going about this knoll to tend your sheep,
the dwelling of that lover
whose memory I keep,
tell him I sicken unto death and weep.

To seek him, I shall scour
these trackless woods to where the rivers flow—
not stop to pick a flower,
not run from beasts—but go
past every fort and border that I know.

O forests darkly glooming,
seeded by my beloved's very hand!
O pasture richly blooming,
you flower-jeweled band!
I beg you, say if he has crossed your land.

Yes, with his thousand graces
streaming from him, he crossed these groves with speed,
and, glancing at these places—
with no more word or deed—
left them in his own beauty liveried.

The Christmas Novena[15]

The Christmas Novena, traditionally said from December 16 through December 24, has been a part of our family's preparation for Christmas for over a

[15] Originally composed by Fr. Charles Vachetta, pastor of the Church of the Immaculate in Turin, Italy, 1721. This version is adapted from Mary Lewis, *Living and Celebrating the Advent-Christmas Seasons* (Boston: St. Paul Books & Media, 1982), and Elsa Chaney and Jeanne Heiberg, *The Twelve Days of Christmas* (Collegeville, Minn.: Liturgical Press, 1955), and appears online at Catholic Culture, https://www.catholicculture.org/culture/liturgicalyear/prayers/view.cfm?id=939. A printable version of the novena is available at CatholicAllYear.com.

decade now. We have a lot of liturgical living traditions in our home, but if I had to choose just one, I would say that this novena has been the most meaningful of them all.

It includes beautiful prayers, Old and New Testament scripture readings, and an Advent hymn sing-along with the traditional O Antiphons. It takes about fifteen minutes to finish, depending on the length of the readings.

Opening Prayers

Recited on each of the nine days.

Leader 1: O Lord, open my lips.

All: And my mouth shall proclaim your praise.

Leader 1: O God, come to my assistance.

All: O Lord, make haste to help me. Glory to the Father, and to the Son, and to the Holy Spirit. As it was in the beginning, is now, and will be forever. Amen. Alleluia.

Leader 1: Our Lord and King is drawing near, O come, let us adore him.

All: Our Lord and King is drawing near, O come, let us adore him.

Leader 2: Rejoice, O you daughter of Zion and exult fully, O daughter of Jerusalem! Behold, the Lord and Master comes, and there shall be a brilliant light in that day, and the mountains shall drop down sweetness, and hills flow with milk and honey, for in that day the Great Prophet will come, and he himself will renew Jerusalem. (cf. Zeph 3:14–18)

All: Our Lord and King is drawing near, O come, let us adore him.

Leader 2: Behold, the God-man of the house of David will come to sit upon the royal throne, and you will see him and your heart will rejoice. (cf. Jer 23:5–8)

All: O come, let us adore him.

Leader 2: Behold, the Lord our Protector will come to save us, Israel's Holy One, wearing the crown of royalty on his noble brow, and he will exercise his rule from sea to shining sea, and from the waters of the river to the ends of the earth. (cf. Is 33:22)

All: O come, let us adore him.

Leader 2: Behold, the Lord and King will appear, and he will not deceive; but if he should delay, wait for him to come; he will surely come and will not tarry. (cf. Hab 2:3)

All: O come, let us adore him.

Leader 2: The Lord will come down like rain upon the fleece of Gideon; justice will thrive and an abundance of true peace; all the kings of the lands of the earth will adore him, and every nation will serve him. (cf. Judg 6:38; Ps 72:3–4; Is 2:3)

All: O come, let us adore him.

Leader 2: A Child will be born to us, and he will be called God the almighty; he will sit upon the royal throne of David his father, and he will hold sway, the sign of his power on his shoulder. (cf. Is 9:6–7)

All: O come, let us adore him.

Leader 2: Bethlehem, city of the Most High God, from you will come forth the King of Israel, and he will proceed forth from his eternity; and he will be greatly praised in the midst of the entire universe; and there will be peace in our land when he will have come. (cf. Mic 5:2–5)

All: Our Lord and King is drawing near, O come, let us adore him.

On the final day of the novena add:

Leader 2: Tomorrow the wickedness of the whole world will be destroyed, and over us will reign the Savior of the world.

All: Our Lord and King is drawing near, O come, let us adore him.

Leader 2: Near at last is Christ our King.

All: O come, let us adore him.

Let the Heavens Be Glad

Recited on each of the nine days. All take turns saying a response line.

All: Blow ye the trumpet in Zion, for the day of the Lord is nigh: behold, he will come to save us, alleluia, alleluia! (cf. Joel 2:1)

Responses
1. Let the heavens be glad and the earth rejoice. O all you mountains, praise the Lord.
2. Let the mountains break forth into gladness, and the hills with justice.
3. For the Lord shall come, and to the poor he shall show mercy.
4. Drop down dew, you heavens, from above and let the clouds rain the Just One.
5. Let the earth be opened and bud forth the Savior.
6. Be mindful of us, O Lord, and visit us in your salvation.
7. Show to us, O Lord, your mercy, and grant us your salvation.
8. Come, O Lord, in peace visit us, that with a perfect heart we may rejoice before you.
9. Come, O Lord, do not tarry; do away with the offenses of your people.
10. Come and show to us your countenance, O Lord. You sit upon the cherubim.

Leader 1: Glory to the Father, and to the Son, and to the Holy Spirit.

All: As it was in the beginning, is now, and will be forever. Amen.

All: Blow ye the trumpet in Zion, for the day of the Lord is nigh: behold, he will come to save us, alleluia, alleluia!

Scripture Reading

Each day has two readings from the Bible.

Day 1: December 16

A reading from the book of Genesis. (Gen 3:1–13)

Now the serpent was more subtle than any other wild creature that the LORD God had made. He said to the woman, "Did God say, 'You shall not eat of any tree of the garden'?" And the woman said to the serpent, "We may eat of the fruit of the trees of the garden; but God said, 'You shall not eat of the fruit of the tree which is in the midst of the garden, neither shall you touch it, lest you die.'" But the serpent said to the woman, "You will not die. For God knows that when you eat of it your eyes will be opened, and you will be like God, knowing good and evil." So when the woman saw that the tree was good for food, and that it was a delight to the eyes, and that the tree was to be desired to make one wise, she took of its fruit and ate; and she also gave some to her husband, and he ate. Then the eyes of both were opened, and they knew that they were naked; and they sewed fig leaves together and made themselves aprons.

And they heard the sound of the LORD God walking in the garden in the cool of the day, and the man and his wife hid themselves from the presence of the LORD God among the trees of the garden. But the LORD God called to the man, and said to him, "Where are you?" And he said, "I heard the sound of thee in the garden, and I was afraid, because I was naked; and I hid myself." He said, "Who told you that you were naked? Have you eaten of the tree of which I commanded you not to eat?" The man said, "The woman whom you gave to be with me, she gave me fruit of the tree, and I ate." Then the LORD God said to the woman, "What is this that you have done?" The woman said, "The serpent beguiled me, and I ate."

The Word of the Lord.

All: Thanks be to God.

A reading from the Letter of Saint Paul to the Romans.
(Rom 1:15–25)

I am eager to preach the gospel to you also who are in Rome.

I am not ashamed of the gospel: it is the power of God for salvation to every one who has faith, to the Jew first and also to the Greek. For in it the righteousness of God is revealed through faith for faith; as it is written, "He who through faith is righteous shall live."

For the wrath of God is revealed from heaven against all ungodliness and wickedness of men who by their wickedness suppress the truth. For what can be known about God is plain to them, because God has shown it to them. Ever since the creation of the world his invisible nature, namely, his eternal power and deity, has been clearly perceived in the things that have been made. So they are without excuse; for although they knew God they did not honor him as God or give thanks to him, but they became futile in their thinking and their senseless minds were darkened. Claiming to be wise, they became fools, and exchanged the glory of the immortal God for images resembling mortal man or birds or animals or reptiles.

Therefore God gave them up in the lusts of their hearts to impurity, to the dishonoring of their bodies among themselves, because they exchanged the truth about God for a lie and worshiped and served the creature rather than the Creator, who is blessed for ever! Amen.

The Word of the Lord.

All: Thanks be to God.

After the readings:

Leader 1: Drop down dew from above, O you heavens, and let the clouds rain the Just One.

Turn to pp. 77–81 for O Antiphon for the day, the Magnificat, and the closing prayers.

Day 2: December 17

A reading from the book of Genesis.   (Gen 3:14–20)

The LORD God said to the serpent,

"Because you have done this,
    cursed are you above all cattle,
    and above all wild animals;
upon your belly you shall go,
    and dust you shall eat
    all the days of your life.
I will put enmity between you and the woman,
    and between your seed and her seed;
he shall bruise your head,
    and you shall bruise his heel."

To the woman he said,

"I will greatly multiply your pain in childbearing;
    in pain you shall bring forth children,
yet your desire shall be for your husband,
    and he shall rule over you."

And to Adam he said,

"Because you have listened to the voice of your wife,
  and have eaten of the tree
of which I commanded you,
  'You shall not eat of it,'
cursed is the ground because of you;
  in toil you shall eat of it all the days of your life;
thorns and thistles it shall bring forth to you;
  and you shall eat the plants of the field.
In the sweat of your face
  you shall eat bread
till you return to the ground,
  for out of it you were taken;
you are dust,
  and to dust you shall return."

The man called his wife's name Eve, because she was the mother of all living.

The Word of the Lord.

All: Thanks be to God.

A reading from the Letter of Saint Paul to the Romans.
(Rom 5:12–21)

Therefore as sin came into the world through one man and death through sin, and so death spread to all men because all men sinned— sin indeed was in the world before the law was given, but sin is not counted where there is no law. Yet death reigned from Adam to Moses, even over those whose sins were not like the transgression of Adam, who was a type of the one who was to come.

But the free gift is not like the trespass. For if many died through one man's trespass, much more have the grace of God and the free gift in the grace of that one man Jesus Christ abounded for many. And the free gift is not like the effect of that one man's sin. For the judgment following one trespass brought condemnation, but the free gift following many trespasses brings justification. If, because of one man's trespass, death reigned through that one man, much more will those who receive the abundance of grace and the free gift of righteousness reign in life through the one man Jesus Christ.

Then as one man's trespass led to condemnation for all men, so one man's act of righteousness leads to acquittal and life for all men. For as by one man's disobedience many were made sinners, so by one man's obedience many will be made righteous. Law came in, to increase the trespass; but where sin increased, grace abounded all the more, so that, as sin reigned in death, grace also might reign through righteousness to eternal life through Jesus Christ our Lord.

The Word of the Lord.

All: Thanks be to God.

Leader 1: Drop down dew from above, O you heavens, and let the clouds rain the Just One.

Turn to pp. 77–81 for O Antiphon for the day, the Magnificat, and the closing prayers.

Day 3: December 18

A reading from the book of Genesis.   (Gen 17:15–22)

And God said to Abraham, "As for Sarai your wife, you shall not call her name Sarai, but Sarah shall be her name. I will bless her, and moreover I will give you a son by her; I will bless her, and she shall be a mother of nations; kings of peoples shall come from her." Then Abraham fell on his face and laughed, and said to himself, "Shall a child be born to a man who is a hundred years old? Shall Sarah, who is ninety years old, bear a child?" And Abraham said to God, "O that Ishmael might live in your sight!" God said, "No, but Sarah your wife shall bear you a son, and you shall call his name Isaac. I will establish my covenant with him as an everlasting covenant for his descendants after him. As for Ishmael, I have heard you; behold, I will bless him and make him fruitful and multiply him exceedingly; he shall be the father of twelve princes, and I will make him a great nation. But I will establish my covenant with Isaac, whom Sarah shall bear to you at this season next year."

When he had finished talking with him, God went up from Abraham.

The Word of the Lord.

All: Thanks be to God.

A reading from the Letter of Saint Paul to the Romans.
(Rom 4:13–23)

The promise to Abraham and his descendants, that they should inherit the world, did not come through the law but through the righteousness of faith. If it is the adherents of the law who are to be the heirs, faith is null and the promise is void. For the law brings wrath, but where there is no law there is no transgression.

That is why it depends on faith, in order that the promise may rest on grace and be guaranteed to all his descendants—not only to the adherents of the law but also to those who share the faith of Abraham, for he is the father of us all, as it is written, "I have made you the father of many nations"—in the presence of the God in whom he believed, who gives life to the dead and calls into existence the things that do not exist. In hope he believed against hope, that he should become the father of many nations; as he had been told, "So shall your descendants be." He did not weaken in faith when he considered his own body, which was as good as dead because he was about a hundred years old, or when he considered the barrenness of Sarah's womb. No distrust made him waver concerning the promise of God, but he grew strong in his faith as he gave glory to God, fully convinced that God was able to do what he had promised. That is why his faith was "reckoned to him as righteousness." But the words, "it was reckoned to him," were written not for his sake alone.

The Word of the Lord.

All: Thanks be to God.

Leader 1: Drop down dew from above, O you heavens, and let the clouds rain the Just One.

Turn to pp. 77–81 for O Antiphon for the day, the Magnificat, and the closing prayers.

Day 4: December 19

A reading from the book of Deuteronomy. (Deut 18:15–22)

[Moses summoned all Israel, and said to them,] "The LORD your God will raise up for you a prophet like me from among you, from your brethren—him you shall heed—just as you desired of the LORD your God at Horeb on the day of the assembly, when you said, 'Let me not hear again the voice of the LORD my God, or see this great fire any more, lest I die.' And the LORD said to me, 'They have rightly said all that they have spoken. I will raise up for them a prophet like you from among their brethren; and I will put my words in his mouth, and he shall speak to them all that I command him. And whoever will not give heed to my words which he shall speak in my name, I myself will require it of him. But the prophet who presumes to speak a word in my name which I have not commanded him to speak, or who speaks in the name of other gods, that same prophet shall die.' And if you say in your heart, 'How may we know the word which the LORD has not spoken?'—when a prophet speaks in the name of the LORD, if the word does not come to pass or come true, that is a word which the LORD has not spoken; the prophet has spoken it presumptuously, you need not be afraid of him."

The Word of the Lord.

All: Thanks be to God.

A reading from the Acts of the Apostles.   (Acts 3:18–26)

"But what God foretold by the mouth of all the prophets, that his Christ should suffer, he thus fulfilled. Repent therefore, and turn again, that your sins may be blotted out, that times of refreshing may come from the presence of the Lord, and that he may send the Christ appointed for you, Jesus, whom heaven must receive until the time for establishing all that God spoke by the mouth of his holy prophets from of old. Moses said, 'The Lord God will raise up for you a prophet from your brethren as he raised me up. You shall listen to him in whatever he tells you. And it shall be that every soul that does not listen to that prophet shall be destroyed from the people.' And all the prophets who have spoken, from Samuel and those who came afterwards, also proclaimed these days. You are the sons of the prophets and of the covenant which God gave to your fathers, saying to Abraham, 'And in your posterity shall all the families of the earth be blessed.' God, having raised up his servant, sent him to you first, to bless you in turning every one of you from your wickedness."

The Word of the Lord.

All: Thanks be to God.

Leader 1: Drop down dew from above, O you heavens, and let the clouds rain the Just One.

Turn to pp. 77–81 for O Antiphon for the day, the Magnificat, and the closing prayers.

Day 5: December 20

A reading from the book of the prophet Isaiah.   (Is 28:14–20)

Therefore hear the word of the LORD, you scoffers,
   who rule this people in Jerusalem!
Because you have said, "We have made a covenant with death,
   and with Sheol we have an agreement;
when the overwhelming scourge passes through
   it will not come to us;
for we have made lies our refuge,
   and in falsehood we have taken shelter";
therefore thus says the Lord GOD,
"Behold, I am laying in Zion for a foundation
   a stone, a tested stone,
a precious cornerstone, of a sure foundation:
   'He who believes will not be in haste.'
And I will make justice the line,
   and righteousness the plummet;
and hail will sweep away the refuge of lies,
   and waters will overwhelm the shelter."
Then your covenant with death will be annulled,
   and your agreement with Sheol will not stand;
when the overwhelming scourge passes through
   you will be beaten down by it.
As often as it passes through it will take you;
   for morning by morning it will pass through,
   by day and by night;
and it will be sheer terror to understand the message.
For the bed is too short to stretch oneself on it,
   and the covering too narrow to wrap oneself in it.

The Word of the Lord.

All: Thanks be to God.

A reading from the Letter of Saint Paul to the Romans.
(Rom 10:5–11)

Moses writes that the man who practices the righteousness which is based on the law shall live by it. But the righteousness based on faith says, Do not say in your heart, "Who will ascend into heaven?" (that is, to bring Christ down) or "Who will descend into the abyss?" (that is, to bring Christ up from the dead). But what does it say? The word is near you, on your lips and in your heart (that is, the word of faith which we preach); because, if you confess with your lips that Jesus is Lord and believe in your heart that God raised him from the dead, you will be saved. For man believes with his heart and so is justified, and he confesses with his lips and so is saved. The scripture says, "No one who believes in him will be put to shame."

The Word of the Lord.

All: Thanks be to God.

Leader 1: Drop down dew from above, O you heavens, and let the clouds rain the Just One.

Turn to pp. 77–81 for O Antiphon for the day, the Magnificat, and the closing prayers.

Day 6: December 21

A reading from the first book of Samuel.   (1 Sam 2:1–10)

Hannah also prayed and said,

> "My heart exults in the LORD;
>   my strength is exalted in the LORD.
> My mouth derides my enemies,
>   because I rejoice in thy salvation.
>
> "There is none holy like the LORD,
>   there is none besides thee;
>   there is no rock like our God.

Talk no more so very proudly,
    let not arrogance come from your mouth;
for the LORD is a God of knowledge,
    and by him actions are weighed.
The bows of the mighty are broken,
    but the feeble gird on strength.
Those who were full have hired themselves out for bread,
    but those who were hungry have ceased to hunger.
The barren has borne seven,
    but she who has many children is forlorn.
The LORD kills and brings to life;
    he brings down to Sheol and raises up.
The LORD makes poor and makes rich;
    he brings low, he also exalts.
He raises up the poor from the dust;
    he lifts the needy from the dung heap,
to make them sit with princes
    and inherit a seat of honor.
For the pillars of the earth are the LORD's,
    and on them he has set the world.

"He will guard the feet of his faithful ones;
    but the wicked shall be cut off in darkness;
    for not by might shall a man prevail.
The adversaries of the LORD shall be broken to pieces;
    against them he will thunder in heaven.
The LORD will judge the ends of the earth;
    he will give strength to his king,
    and exalt the power of his anointed."

The Word of the Lord.

All: Thanks be to God.

A reading from the Holy Gospel according to Saint Luke.
(Lk 1:26–38)

In the sixth month the angel Gabriel was sent from God to a city of Galilee named Nazareth, to a virgin betrothed to a man whose name was Joseph, of the house of David; and the virgin's name was Mary.

And he came to her and said, "Hail, full of grace, the Lord is with you!" But she was greatly troubled at the saying, and considered in her mind what sort of greeting this might be. And the angel said to her, "Do not be afraid, Mary, for you have found favor with God. And behold, you will conceive in your womb and bear a son, and you shall call his name Jesus.

> He will be great, and will be called the Son of the Most High;
> and the Lord God will give to him the throne of his father David,
> and he will reign over the house of Jacob for ever;
> and of his kingdom there will be no end."

And Mary said to the angel, "How can this be, since I have no husband?" And the angel said to her,

> "The Holy Spirit will come upon you,
> and the power of the Most High will overshadow you;
> therefore the child to be born will be called holy,
> the Son of God.

And behold, your kinswoman Elizabeth in her old age has also conceived a son; and this is the sixth month with her who was called barren. For with God nothing will be impossible." And Mary said, "Behold, I am the handmaid of the Lord; let it be to me according to your word." And the angel departed from her.

The Gospel of the Lord.

All: Praise to you, Lord Jesus Christ.

Leader 1: Drop down dew from above, O you heavens, and let the clouds rain the Just One.

Turn to pp. 77–81 for O Antiphon for the day, the Magnificat, and the closing prayers.

Day 7: December 22

A reading from the book of Deuteronomy. (Deut 7:6–21)

For you are a people holy to the LORD your God; the LORD your God has chosen you to be a people for his own possession, out of all the peoples that are on the face of the earth. It was not because you were more in number than any other people that the LORD set his love upon you and chose you, for you were the fewest of all peoples; but it is because the LORD loves you, and is keeping the oath which he swore to your fathers, that the LORD has brought you out with a mighty hand, and redeemed you from the house of bondage, from the hand of Pharaoh king of Egypt. Know therefore that the LORD your God is God, the faithful God who keeps covenant and merciful love with those who love him and keep his commandments, to a thousand generations, and repays to their face those who hate him, by destroying them; he will not be slack with him who hates him, he will repay him to his face. You shall therefore be careful to do the commandment, and the statutes, and the ordinances, which I command you this day.

And because you listen to these ordinances, and keep and do them, the LORD your God will keep with you the covenant and the merciful love which he swore to your fathers to keep; he will love you, bless you, and multiply you; he will also bless the fruit of your body and the fruit of your ground, your grain and your wine and your oil, the increase of your cattle and the young of your flock, in the land which he swore to your fathers to give you. You shall be blessed above all peoples; there shall not be male or female barren among you, or among your cattle. And the LORD will take away from you all sickness; and none of the evil diseases of Egypt, which you knew, will he inflict upon you, but he will lay them upon all who hate you. And you shall destroy all the peoples that the LORD your God will give over to you, your eye shall not pity them; neither shall you serve their gods, for that would be a snare to you.

If you say in your heart, "These nations are greater than I; how can I dispossess them?" you shall not be afraid of them, but you shall remember what the LORD your God did to Pharaoh and to all Egypt, the great trials which your eyes saw, the signs, the wonders, the mighty hand, and the outstretched arm, by which the LORD your God brought you out; so will the LORD your God do to all the peoples of whom you are afraid. Moreover the LORD your God will send hornets among them, until those who are left and hide themselves from you are destroyed. You shall not be in dread of them; for the LORD your God is in the midst of you, a great and terrible God.

The Word of the Lord.

All: Thanks be to God.

A reading from the Letter of Saint Paul to the Ephesians.
(Eph 2:11–22)

Therefore remember that at one time you Gentiles in the flesh, called
the uncircumcision by what is called the circumcision, which is made
in the flesh by hands—remember that you were at that time separated from Christ, alienated from the commonwealth of Israel, and
strangers to the covenants of promise, having no hope and without
God in the world. But now in Christ Jesus you who once were far off
have been brought near in the blood of Christ. For he is our peace,
who has made us both one, and has broken down the dividing wall
of hostility, by abolishing in his flesh the law of commandments and
ordinances, that he might create in himself one new man in place
of the two, so making peace, and might reconcile us both to God
in one body through the cross, thereby bringing the hostility to an
end. And he came and preached peace to you who were far off and
peace to those who were near; for through him we both have access
in one Spirit to the Father. So then you are no longer strangers and
sojourners, but you are fellow citizens with the saints and members
of the household of God, built upon the foundation of the apostles
and prophets, Christ Jesus himself being the cornerstone, in whom
the whole structure is joined together and grows into a holy temple
in the Lord; in whom you also are built into it for a dwelling place
of God in the Spirit.

The Word of the Lord.

All: Thanks be to God.

Leader 1: Drop down dew from above, O you heavens, and let the
clouds rain the Just One.

*Turn to pp. 77–81 for O Antiphon for the day, the Magnificat, and the
closing prayers.*

Day 8: December 23

A reading from the book of the prophet Isaiah. (Is 7:10–16)

Again the LORD spoke to Ahaz, "Ask a sign of the LORD your God;
let it be deep as Sheol or high as heaven." But Ahaz said, "I will not
ask, and I will not put the LORD to the test." And he said, "Hear

then, O house of David! Is it too little for you to weary men, that you weary my God also? Therefore the Lord himself will give you a sign. Behold, a virgin shall conceive and bear a son, and shall call his name Immanuel. He shall eat curds and honey when he knows how to refuse the evil and choose the good. For before the child knows how to refuse the evil and choose the good, the land before whose two kings you are in dread will be deserted."

The Word of the Lord.

All: Thanks be to God.

A reading from the Holy Gospel according to Saint Matthew. (Mt 1:18–25)

Now the birth of Jesus Christ took place in this way. When his Mother Mary had been betrothed to Joseph, before they came together she was found to be with child of the Holy Spirit; and her husband Joseph, being a just man and unwilling to put her to shame, resolved to send her away quietly. But as he considered this, behold, an angel of the Lord appeared to him in a dream, saying, "Joseph, son of David, do not fear to take Mary your wife, for that which is conceived in her is of the Holy Spirit; she will bear a son, and you shall call his name Jesus, for he will save his people from their sins." All this took place to fulfil what the Lord had spoken by the prophet:

"Behold, a virgin shall conceive and bear a son, and his name shall be called Emmanuel"

(which means, God with us). When Joseph woke from sleep, he did as the angel of the Lord commanded him; he took his wife, but knew her not until she had borne a son; and he called his name Jesus.

The Gospel of the Lord.

All: Praise to you, Lord Jesus Christ.

Leader 1: Drop down dew from above, O you heavens, and let the clouds rain the Just One.

Turn to pp. 77–81 for O Antiphon for the day, the Magnificat, and the closing prayers.

Day 9: December 24

A reading from the book of the prophet Micah.   (Mic 5:2–6)

But you, O Bethlehem Ephrathah,
   who are little to be among the clans of Judah,
from you shall come forth for me
   one who is to be ruler in Israel,
whose origin is from of old,
   from ancient days.
Therefore he shall give them up until the time
   when she who has labor pains has brought forth;
then the rest of his brethren shall return
   to the people of Israel.
And he shall stand and feed his flock in the strength of the
   LORD,
   in the majesty of the name of the LORD his God.
And they shall dwell secure, for now he shall be great
   to the ends of the earth.
And this shall be peace,
   when the Assyrian comes into our land
   and treads upon our soil,
that we will raise against him seven shepherds
   and eight princes of men;
they shall rule the land of Assyria with the sword,
   and the land of Nimrod with the drawn sword;
and they shall deliver us from the Assyrian
   when he comes into our land
   and treads within our border.

The Word of the Lord.

All: Thanks be to God.

A reading from the Holy Gospel according to Saint Luke.
(Lk 2:1–7)

In those days a decree went out from Caesar Augustus that all the world should be enrolled. This was the first enrollment, when Quirinius was governor of Syria. And all went to be enrolled, each to his

own city. And Joseph also went up from Galilee, from the city of
Nazareth, to Judea, to the city of David, which is called Bethlehem,
because he was of the house and lineage of David, to be enrolled
with Mary his betrothed, who was with child. And while they were
there, the time came for her to be delivered. And she gave birth to
her first-born son and wrapped him in swaddling cloths, and laid
him in a manger, because there was no place for them in the inn.

The Gospel of the Lord.

All: Praise to you, Lord Jesus Christ.

Leader 1: Drop down dew from above, O you heavens, and let the
clouds rain the Just One.

*Continue with the O Antiphon for the day, the Magnificat, and the closing
prayers.*

O Antiphons

*From December 17 to December 23, the O Antiphons beg God with mount-
ing impatience to come and save his people. The order of the antiphons climbs
climactically through our history of redemption: O Sapientia, at the beginning
of eternity; O Adonai, at the time of Moses, about 1250 B.C.; O Radix
Jesse, O Clavis David, O Oriens, and O Rex Gentium focused on Jesse
and his son King David around 1000 B.C.; and finally, O Emmanuel, on
the first Christmas Eve.*

*The Advent hymn "O Come, O Come, Emmanuel"[16] is a metrical
paraphrase of the O Antiphons. Traditionally an O Antiphon is sung or
chanted before and after the Magnificat during Evening Prayer in the final
days before Christmas. Sing the O Antiphon for the day, then turn to
p. 80 to recite, chant, or sing the Magnificat prayer, then sing the day's O
Antiphon again.*

---

[16] Music: T. Helmore (1811–1890), adapted from a first-mode Responsory in a fifteenth-
century French processional. Text: *Veni, Veni, Emmanuel*, a paraphrase of Latin twelfth- and
thirteenth-century Great O Antiphons in *Psalteriolum Cantionum Catholicarum* (1770). Trans-
lators: John Neale (1818–1866), et al.

December 16

All sing:

O Come, O come, Emmanuel,	Veni, veni, Emmanuel,
And ransom captive Israel,	Captivum solve Israel,
That mourns in lonely exile here	Qui gemit in exsilio,
Until the Son of God appear.	Privatus Dei Filio.
Rejoice! Rejoice! Emmanuel	Gaude! Gaude! Emmanuel,
Shall come to thee, O Israel!	Nascetur pro te Israel!

December 17: O Wisdom (O Sapientia)

All sing:

O come, thou Wisdom, from on high,	Veni, O Sapientia,
And order all things far and nigh;	Quae hic disponis omnia,
To us the path of knowledge show,	Veni, viam prudentiae
And teach us in her ways to go.	Ut doceas et gloriae.
Rejoice! Rejoice! Emmanuel	Gaude! Gaude! Emmanuel,
Shall come to thee, O Israel!	Nascetur pro te Israel!

December 18: O Lord (O Adonai)

All sing:

O come, o come, thou Lord of might,	Veni, veni, Adonai,
Who to thy tribes on Sinai's height	Qui populo in Sinai
In ancient times did give the law,	Legem dedisti vertice
In cloud, and majesty, and awe.	In maiestate gloriae.
Rejoice! Rejoice! Emmanuel	Gaude! Gaude! Emmanuel,
Shall come to thee, O Israel!	Nascetur pro te Israel!

December 19: O Root of Jesse (O Radix Jesse)

All sing:

O come, thou Rod of Jesse's stem,	Veni, O Iesse virgula,
From ev'ry foe deliver them	Ex hostis tuos ungula,
That trust thy mighty power to save,	De spectu tuos tartari
And give them vict'ry o'er the grave.	Educ et antro barathri.
Rejoice! Rejoice! Emmanuel	Gaude! Gaude! Emmanuel,
Shall come to thee, O Israel!	Nascetur pro te Israel!

December 20: O Key of David (O Clavis David)

All sing:

O come, thou Key of David, come,	Veni, Clavis Davidica,
And open wide our heav'nly home,	Regna reclude caelica,
Make safe the way that leads on high,	Fac iter tutum superum,
That we no more have cause to sigh.	Et claude vias inferum.
Rejoice! Rejoice! Emmanuel	Gaude! Gaude! Emmanuel,
Shall come to thee, O Israel!	Nascetur pro te Israel!

December 21: O Dayspring (O Oriens)

All sing:

O come, thou Dayspring from on high,	Veni, veni, O Oriens,
And cheer us by thy drawing nigh;	Solare nos adveniens,
Disperse the gloomy clouds of night	Noctis depelle nebulas,
And death's dark shadow put to flight.	Dirasque mortis tenebras.
Rejoice! Rejoice! Emmanuel	Gaude! Gaude! Emmanuel,
Shall come to thee, O Israel!	Nascetur pro te Israel!

December 22: O King of Nations (O Rex Gentium)

All sing:

O come, Desire of nations, bind	Veni, veni, Rex Gentium,
In one the hearts of all mankind;	Veni, Redemptor omnium,
Bid every strife and quarrel cease	Ut salvas tuos famulos
And fill the world with heaven's peace.	Peccati sibi conscios.
Rejoice! Rejoice! Emmanuel	Gaude! Gaude! Emmanuel,
Shall come to thee, O Israel!	Nascetur pro te Israel!

December 23: O God with Us (O Emmanuel)

All sing:

O Come, O come, Emmanuel,	Veni, veni, Emmanuel,
And ransom captive Israel,	Captivum solve Israel,
That mourns in lonely exile here	Qui gemit in exsilio,
Until the Son of God appear.	Privatus Dei Filio.
Rejoice! Rejoice! Emmanuel	Gaude! Gaude! Emmanuel,
Shall come to thee, O Israel!	Nascetur pro te Israel!

December 24

All sing:

O Come, O come, Emmanuel,	Veni, veni, Emmanuel,
And ransom captive Israel,	Captivum solve Israel,
That mourns in lonely exile here	Qui gemit in exsilio,
Until the Son of God appear.	Privatus Dei Filio.
Rejoice! Rejoice! Emmanuel	Gaude! Gaude! Emmanuel,
Shall come to thee, O Israel!	Nascetur pro te Israel!

Magnificat (Canticle of Mary)

Recited, chanted, or sung on each of the nine days.

> My soul proclaims the greatness of the Lord, my spirit rejoices in God my Savior, for he has looked with favor on his lowly servant.
>
> From this day all generations will call me blessed: the Almighty has done great things for me, and holy is his name.
>
> He has mercy on those who fear him in every generation.
>
> He has shown the strength of his arm, he has scattered the proud in their conceit.
>
> He has cast down the mighty from their thrones and has lifted up the lowly.
>
> He has filled the hungry with good things, and the rich he has sent away empty.
>
> He has come to the help of his servant Israel, for he has remembered his promise of mercy, the promise he made to our fathers, to Abraham and his children forever.
>
> Glory to the Father, and to the Son, and to the Holy Spirit,
>
> as it was in the beginning, is now, and will be forever. Amen. (cf. Lk 1:46–55)

All sing the O Antiphon for the day again, then move on to the closing prayers.

Closing Prayers

Recited on each of the nine days.

Leader 1: O Lord, hear my prayer.

All: And let my cry come to you.

Leader 1: Let us pray. Hasten, we beseech you, O Lord; do not delay; grant us the help of supernatural virtue, so that your coming will be a consolation to those who hope in your mercy. You who live and reign with God the Father in the unity of the Holy Spirit, God, world without end.

All: Amen.

Leader 1: Let us bless the Lord.

All: And give him thanks.

Leader 1: May the souls of the faithful departed,

All: Through the mercy of God, rest in peace. Amen.

Third Sunday of Advent
(Gaudete Sunday, Bambinelli Sunday)

COLLECT PRAYER

O God, who see how your people faithfully await the feast of the Lord's Nativity, enable us, we pray, to attain the joys of so great a salvation and to celebrate them always with solemn worship and glad rejoicing. Through our Lord Jesus Christ, your Son, who lives and reigns with you in the unity of the Holy Spirit, one God, for ever and ever. Amen.

Gaudete Introit[17]

The name Gaudete Sunday comes from the Latin word gaudete (rejoice), the first word of the Entrance Antiphon of this day's Mass.

Gaudete in Domino semper: iterum dico, gaudete. Modestia vestra nota sit omnibus hominibus: Dominus enim prope est. (Phil 4:4–5)

> Rejoice in the Lord always; again I say, Rejoice.…
> Indeed, the Lord is at hand. (Phil 4:4–5)

---

[17] Latin text: James Socías, *Daily Roman Missal*, 7th ed. (Woodridge, Ill.: James Socías for Midwest Theological Forum, 2012), 50. English text: *Roman Missal*, no. 17.

Admirabile Signum[18]

These are excerpts from an apostolic letter of Pope Francis on the meaning and importance of the nativity scene, given in Greccio, at the Shrine of the Nativity, on December 1, 2019. In many parts of the world, the nativity scene—also called a Christmas crèche—is traditionally a large tabletop display that can feature a whole village with many different characters in addition to the stable or cave and the Holy Family.

The enchanting image of the Christmas crèche, so dear to the Christian people, never ceases to arouse amazement and wonder. The depiction of Jesus' birth is itself a simple and joyful proclamation of the mystery of the Incarnation of the Son of God. The nativity scene is like a living Gospel rising up from the pages of sacred Scripture. As we contemplate the Christmas story, we are invited to set out on a spiritual journey, drawn by the humility of the God who became man in order to encounter every man and woman. We come to realize that so great is his love for us that he became one of us, so that we in turn might become one with him.

With this Letter, I wish to encourage the beautiful family tradition of preparing the nativity scene in the days before Christmas, but also the custom of setting it up in the workplace, in schools, hospitals, prisons and town squares. Great imagination and creativity is always shown in employing the most diverse materials to create small masterpieces of beauty. As children, we learn from our parents and grandparents to carry on this joyful tradition, which encapsulates a wealth of popular piety. It is my hope that this custom will never be lost and that, wherever it has fallen into disuse, it can be rediscovered and revived....

Why does the Christmas crèche arouse such wonder and move us so deeply? First, because it shows God's tender love: the Creator of the universe lowered himself to take up our littleness. The gift of life, in all its mystery, becomes all the more wondrous as we realize that the Son of Mary is the source and sustenance of all life. In Jesus, the Father has given us a brother who comes to seek us out whenever we

---

[18] Francis, apostolic letter *Admirabile Signum* (December 1, 2019), nos. 1, 3, 10, http://w2 .vatican.va/content/francesco/en/apost_letters/documents/papa-francesco-lettera-ap_2019 1201_admirabile-signum.html.

are confused or lost, a loyal friend ever at our side. He gave us his Son who forgives us and frees us from our sins.

Setting up the Christmas crèche in our homes helps us to relive the history of what took place in Bethlehem. Naturally, the Gospels remain our source for understanding and reflecting on that event. At the same time, its portrayal in the crèche helps us to imagine the scene. It touches our hearts and makes us enter into salvation history as contemporaries of an event that is living and real in a broad gamut of historical and cultural contexts.

In a particular way, from the time of its Franciscan origins, the nativity scene has invited us to "feel" and "touch" the poverty that God's Son took upon himself in the Incarnation. Implicitly, it summons us to follow him along the path of humility, poverty and self-denial that leads from the manger of Bethlehem to the cross. It asks us to meet him and serve him by showing mercy to those of our brothers and sisters in greatest need (cf. Mt 25:31–46)....

Standing before the Christmas crèche, we are reminded of the time when we were children, eagerly waiting to set it up. These memories make us all the more conscious of the precious gift received from those who passed on the faith to us. At the same time, they remind us of our duty to share this same experience with our children and our grandchildren. It does not matter how the nativity scene is arranged: it can always be the same or it can change from year to year. What matters is that it speaks to our lives. Wherever it is, and whatever form it takes, the Christmas crèche speaks to us of the love of God, the God who became a child in order to make us know how close he is to every man, woman and child, regardless of their condition.

Dear brothers and sisters, the Christmas crèche is part of the precious yet demanding process of passing on the faith. Beginning in childhood, and at every stage of our lives, it teaches us to contemplate Jesus, to experience God's love for us, to feel and believe that God is with us and that we are with him, his children, brothers and sisters all, thanks to that Child who is the Son of God and the Son of the Virgin Mary. And to realize that in that knowledge we find true happiness. Like Saint Francis, may we open our hearts to this simple grace, so that from our wonderment a humble prayer may arise: a prayer of thanksgiving to God, who wished to share with us his all, and thus never to leave us alone.

Blessing of a Christmas Manger or Nativity Scene[19]

In its present form the custom of displaying figures depicting the birth of Jesus Christ owes its origin to Saint Francis of Assisi, who made the Christmas crèche or manger for Christmas Eve 1223. When the manger is set up in the home, it is appropriate that it be blessed by a parent or another family member.

All make the sign of the cross.

Leader: Our help is in the name of the Lord.

All: Who made heaven and earth.

A reading from the Holy Gospel according to Saint Luke. (Lk 2:1–8, NAB)

In those days a decree went out from Caesar Augustus that the whole world should be enrolled. This was the first enrollment, when Quirinius was governor of Syria. So all went to be enrolled, each to his own town. And Joseph too went up from Galilee from the town of Nazareth to Judea, to the city of David that is called Bethlehem, because he was of the house and family of David, to be enrolled with Mary, his betrothed, who was with child. While they were there, the time came for her to have her child, and she gave birth to her firstborn son. She wrapped him in swaddling clothes and laid him in a manger, because there was no room for them in the inn.

Now there were shepherds in that region living in the fields and keeping the night watch over their flock.

The Gospel of the Lord.

All: Praise to you, Lord Jesus Christ.

The leader prays with hands joined:

Leader: God of every nation and people,
from the very beginning of creation
you have made manifest your love:
when our need for a Savior was great

---

[19] *Catholic Household Blessings and Prayers*, 78 (from *Book of Blessings*, nos. 1541, 1545, 1569). Used with permission.

you sent your Son to be born of the Virgin Mary.
To our lives he brings joy and peace,
justice, mercy, and love.

Lord,
bless all who look upon this manger;
may it remind us of the humble birth of Jesus,
and raise our thoughts to him,
who is God-with-us and Savior of all,
and who lives and reigns forever and ever.

All: Amen.

All make the sign of the cross.

After the blessing, the manger may be sprinkled with holy water.

December 24: Christmas Eve/ Saints Adam and Eve (Historical)

COLLECT PRAYER[20]

Come quickly, we pray, Lord Jesus, and do not delay, that those who trust in your compassion may find solace and relief in your coming. Who live and reign with God the Father in the unity of the Holy Spirit, one God, for ever and ever. Amen.

The New Adam and the New Eve[21]

From a treatise by Saint Irenaeus (+202).

The Lord, coming into his own creation in visible form, was sustained by his own creation which he himself sustains in being. His obedience on the tree of the cross reversed the disobedience at the tree in Eden; the good news of the truth announced by an angel to

---

[20] As far as I can tell, there has never been an official Mass for SS. Adam and Eve. This is the current Collect for daily Mass for December 24.

[21] Irenaeus, *Haer.* 5, 19; 20, 2; 21, 1, in *The Liturgy of the Hours: According to the Roman Rite*, vol. 1 (New York: Catholic Book Publishing Co., 1975), 244.

Mary, a virgin subject to a husband, undid the evil lie that seduced Eve, a virgin espoused to a husband.

As Eve was seduced by the word of an angel and so fled from God after disobeying his word, Mary in her turn was given the good news by the word of an angel, and bore God in obedience to his word. As Eve was seduced into disobedience to God, so Mary was persuaded into obedience to God; thus the Virgin Mary became the advocate of the virgin Eve.

A reading from the book of Genesis.   (Gen 2:4—3:24)

These are the generations of the heavens and the earth when they were created.

In the day that the LORD God made the earth and the heavens, when no plant of the field was yet in the earth and no herb of the field had yet sprung up—for the LORD God had not caused it to rain upon the earth, and there was no man to till the ground; but a mist went up from the earth and watered the whole face of the ground—then the LORD God formed man of dust from the ground, and breathed into his nostrils the breath of life; and man became a living soul. And the LORD God planted a garden in Eden, in the east; and there he put the man whom he had formed. And out of the ground the LORD God made to grow every tree that is pleasant to the sight and good for food, the tree of life also in the midst of the garden, and the tree of the knowledge of good and evil.

A river flowed out of Eden to water the garden, and there it divided and became four rivers. The name of the first is Pishon; it is the one which flows around the whole land of Havilah, where there is gold; and the gold of that land is good; bdellium and onyx stone are there. The name of the second river is Gihon; it is the one which flows around the whole land of Cush. And the name of the third river is Tigris, which flows east of Assyria. And the fourth river is the Euphrates.

The LORD God took the man and put him in the garden of Eden to till it and keep it. And the LORD God commanded the man, saying, "You may freely eat of every tree of the garden; but of the tree of the knowledge of good and evil you shall not eat, for in the day that you eat of it you shall die."

Then the LORD God said, "It is not good that the man should be alone; I will make him a helper fit for him." So out of the ground the

LORD God formed every beast of the field and every bird of the air, and brought them to the man to see what he would call them; and whatever the man called every living creature, that was its name. The man gave names to all cattle, and to the birds of the air, and to every beast of the field; but for the man there was not found a helper fit for him. So the LORD God caused a deep sleep to fall upon the man, and while he slept took one of his ribs and closed up its place with flesh; and the rib which the LORD God had taken from the man he made into a woman and brought her to the man. Then the man said,

> "This at last is bone of my bones
>   and flesh of my flesh;
> she shall be called Woman,
>   because she was taken out of Man."

Therefore a man leaves his father and his mother and clings to his wife, and they become one flesh. And the man and his wife were both naked, and were not ashamed.

Now the serpent was more subtle than any other wild creature that the LORD God had made. He said to the woman, "Did God say, 'You shall not eat of any tree of the garden'?" And the woman said to the serpent, "We may eat of the fruit of the trees of the garden; but God said, 'You shall not eat of the fruit of the tree which is in the midst of the garden, neither shall you touch it, lest you die.'" But the serpent said to the woman, "You will not die. For God knows that when you eat of it your eyes will be opened, and you will be like God, knowing good and evil." So when the woman saw that the tree was good for food, and that it was a delight to the eyes, and that the tree was to be desired to make one wise, she took of its fruit and ate; and she also gave some to her husband, and he ate. Then the eyes of both were opened, and they knew that they were naked; and they sewed fig leaves together and made themselves aprons.

And they heard the sound of the LORD God walking in the garden in the cool of the day, and the man and his wife hid themselves from the presence of the LORD God among the trees of the garden. But the LORD God called to the man, and said to him, "Where are you?" And he said, "I heard the sound of you in the garden, and I was afraid, because I was naked; and I hid myself." He said, "Who told you that you were naked? Have you eaten of the tree of which

I commanded you not to eat?" The man said, "The woman whom you gave to be with me, she gave me fruit of the tree, and I ate." Then the LORD God said to the woman, "What is this that you have done?" The woman said, "The serpent beguiled me, and I ate." The LORD God said to the serpent,

> "Because you have done this,
>> cursed are you above all cattle,
>> and above all wild animals;
> upon your belly you shall go,
>> and dust you shall eat
>> all the days of your life.
> I will put enmity between you and the woman,
>> and between your seed and her seed;
> he shall bruise your head,
>> and you shall bruise his heel."

To the woman he said,

> "I will greatly multiply your pain in childbearing;
>> in pain you shall bring forth children,
> yet your desire shall be for your husband,
>> and he shall rule over you."

And to Adam he said,

> "Because you have listened to the voice of your wife,
>> and have eaten of the tree
> of which I commanded you,
>> 'You shall not eat of it,'
> cursed is the ground because of you;
>> in toil you shall eat of it all the days of your life;
> thorns and thistles it shall bring forth to you;
>> and you shall eat the plants of the field.
> In the sweat of your face
>> you shall eat bread
> till you return to the ground,
>> for out of it you were taken;
> you are dust,
>> and to dust you shall return."

The man called his wife's name Eve, because she was the mother of all living. And the LORD God made for Adam and for his wife garments of skins, and clothed them.

Then the LORD God said, "Behold, the man has become like one of us, knowing good and evil; and now, lest he put forth his hand and take also of the tree of life, and eat, and live for ever"—therefore the LORD God sent him forth from the garden of Eden, to till the ground from which he was taken. He drove out the man; and at the east of the garden of Eden he placed the cherubim, and a flaming sword which turned every way, to guard the way to the tree of life.

The Word of the Lord.

All: Thanks be to God.

Blessing of a Christmas Tree[22]

From the Book of Blessings*: "The use of the Christmas tree is relatively modern. Its origins are found in the medieval mystery plays that depicted the tree of paradise and the Christmas light or candle that symbolized Christ, the Light of the world.*

"According to custom, the Christmas tree is set up just before Christmas and may remain in place until the Solemnity of Epiphany. . . .

"The lights of the tree are illuminated after the prayer of blessing.

"In the home the Christmas tree may be blessed by a parent or another family member, in connection with the evening meal on the Vigil of Christmas or at another suitable time on Christmas Day."

When all have gathered, a suitable song may be sung.

The leader makes the sign of the cross.

All: Amen.

Leader: Let us glorify Christ our light, who brings salvation and peace into our midst, now and forever.

All: Amen.

[22] *Book of Blessings*, Additional Blessings for Use in the United States, nos. 1570, 1571, 1573, 1574, 1581, 1595.

Leader: My brothers and sisters, amidst signs and wonders Christ Jesus was born in Bethlehem of Judea: his birth brings joy to our hearts and enlightenment to our minds. With this tree, decorated and adorned, may we welcome Christ among us; may its lights guide us to the perfect light.

A reading from the book of the prophet Ezekiel.
(Ezek 17:22–24, NAB)

> Thus says the Lord GOD:
> I, too, will pluck from the crest of the cedar
> the highest branch.
> From the top a tender shoot
> I will break off and transplant
> on a high, lofty mountain.
>
> On the mountain height of Israel
> I will plant it.
> It shall put forth branches and bear fruit,
> and become a majestic cedar.
> Every small bird will nest under it,
> all kinds of winged birds will dwell
> in the shade of its branches.
>
> Every tree of the field will know
> that I am the LORD.
> I bring low the high tree,
> lift high the lowly tree,
> Wither up the green tree,
> and make the dry tree bloom.
> As I, the LORD, have spoken, so will I do!

The Word of the Lord.

All: Thanks be to God.

The leader says the prayer with hands joined:

Leader: Lord our God,
we praise you for the light of creation:
the sun, the moon, and the stars of the night.

We praise you for the light of Israel:
the Law, the prophets, and the wisdom of the Scriptures.
We praise you for Jesus Christ, your Son:
he is Emmanuel, God-with-us, the Prince of Peace,
who fills us with the wonder of your love.

Lord God,
let your blessing come upon us
as we illumine this tree.
May the light and cheer it gives
be a sign of the joy that fills our hearts.
May all who delight in this tree
come to the knowledge and joy of salvation.
We ask this through Christ our Lord.

All: Amen.

The lights of the tree are then illuminated.

The leader concludes the rite by signing himself or herself with the sign of the cross and saying:

Leader: May the God of glory fill our hearts with peace and joy, now and for ever.

All: Amen.

All make the sign of the cross.

After the blessing, the tree may be sprinkled with holy water. End with a song.

O Tannenbaum[23]

1. O Tannenbaum, O Tannenbaum,
   How faithfully you blossom!
   Through summer's heat and winter's chill
   Your leaves are green and blooming still.
   O Tannenbaum, O Tannenbaum,
   How faithfully you blossom!

2. O Tannenbaum, O Tannenbaum,
   With what delight I see you!

[23] German text by Ernst Anschütz, 1824. English translation by John Rutter, 1989.

When winter days are dark and drear
You bring us hope for all the year.
O Tannenbaum, O Tannenbaum,
With what delight I see you!

3. O Tannenbaum, O Tannenbaum,
You bear a joyful message:
That faith and hope shall ever bloom
To bring us light in winter's gloom.
O Tannenbaum, O Tannenbaum,
You bear a joyful message!

Prayer before Baby Jesus in the Manger

The last thing we do before we go to bed on Christmas Eve is to place the baby Jesus in the manger of our nativity scene, say this prayer, and sing "Away in a Manger" and "Silent Night".

O Divine Redeemer Jesus Christ, prostrate before your crib, I believe you are the God of infinite Majesty, even though I see you here as a helpless babe. I humbly adore and thank you for having so humbled yourself for my salvation as to will to be born in a stable. I thank you for all you wish to suffer for me in Bethlehem, for your poverty and humility, for your nakedness, tears, cold, and sufferings.

Would that I could show you that tenderness which your Virgin Mother had toward you, and love you as she did. Would that I could praise you with the joy of the angels, that I could kneel before you with the faith of Saint Joseph, the simplicity of the shepherds.

Uniting myself with these first adorers at the crib, I offer you the homage of my heart, and I beg that you would be born spiritually in my soul. Make me reflect in some degree the virtues of your admirable nativity. Fill me with that spirit of renunciation, of poverty, of humility, which prompted you to assume the weakness of our nature, and to be born amid destitution and suffering. Grant that from this day forward, I may in all things seek your greater glory, and may enjoy that peace promised to men of good will. Amen.

SONG SUGGESTIONS: Silent Night; Away in a Manger

CHRISTMASTIDE BEGINS

December 25: THE NATIVITY OF THE LORD (Christmas) (Solemnity, Holy Day of Obligation)

COLLECT PRAYER

O God, who gladden us year by year as we wait in hope for our redemption, grant that, just as we joyfully welcome your Only Begotten Son as our Redeemer, we may also merit to face him confidently when he comes again as our Judge. Who lives and reigns with you in the unity of the Holy Spirit, one God, for ever and ever. Amen.

Urbi et Orbi Indulgence[24]

The papal Urbi et Orbi blessing, enhanced with a plenary indulgence (subject to the usual conditions), is given by the pope each Easter and Christmas from the central loggia of Saint Peter's Basilica in Rome, at noon (GMT+1). Since 1985 this indulgence has been granted not only to the people in Saint Peter's Square but also to those who, though unable to be physically present, "piously follow" as it is broadcast live by radio, television, or—since 2013— the Internet.[25]

The pope begins with an address, usually in Italian. The blessing is preceded by an announcement by the cardinal protodeacon, in Italian, which translates to:

His Holiness Pope N. grants a plenary indulgence in the form laid down by the Church to all the faithful present and to those who receive his blessing by radio, television, and the new communications media. Let us ask almighty God to grant the pope many years as leader of the Church and peace and unity to the Church throughout the world.

---

[24] Cappella Papale, "Domenica di Pasqua Risurrezione del Signore: Messa del giorno", booklet for Mass (Piazza San Pietro, March 27, 2016), 80–85, https://www.vatican.va/news _services/liturgy/libretti/2016/20160327-libretto-domenica-di-pasqua.pdf. See the introduction of this book for the usual conditions for indulgences.

[25] *Manual of Indulgences*, grant 4.

The blessing is performed in Latin:

Sancti Apostoli Petrus et Paulus: de quorum potestate et auctoritate confidimus, ipsi intercedant pro nobis ad Dominum.

All: Amen.

Precibus et meritis beatae Mariae semper Virginis, beati Michaelis Archangeli, beati Ioannis Baptistae et sanctorum Apostolorum Petri et Pauli et omnium Sanctorum, misereatur vestri omnipotens Deus; et dimissis omnibus peccatis vestris, perducat vos Iesus Christus ad vitam æternam.

All: Amen.

Indulgentiam, absolutionem, et remissionem omnium peccatorum vestrorum, spatium veræ et fructuosae pœnitentiae, cor semper paenitens, et emendationem vitae, gratiam et consolationem Sancti Spiritus; et finalem perseverantiam in bonis operibus tribuat vobis omnipotens et misericors Dominus.

All: Amen.

Et benedictio Dei omnipotentis, Patris, et Filii, et Spiritus Sancti, descendat super vos et maneat semper.

All: Amen.

English translation:

May the holy apostles Peter and Paul, in whose power and authority we trust, intercede for us before the Lord.

All: Amen.

Through the prayers and merits of Blessed Mary ever virgin, Saint Michael the archangel, Saint John the Baptist, the holy apostles Peter and Paul, and all the saints, may Almighty God have mercy on you and forgive all your sins, and may Jesus Christ bring you to everlasting life.

All: Amen.

May the almighty and merciful Lord grant you indulgence, absolution, and the remission of all your sins, a season of true and fruitful penance, a well-disposed heart, amendment of life, the grace and comfort of the Holy Spirit, and final perseverance in good works.

All: Amen.

And may the blessing of almighty God, the Father, and the Son, and the Holy Spirit, come down on you and remain with you forever.

All: Amen.

A reading from the Holy Gospel according to Saint Luke. (Lk 2:1–20)

In those days a decree went out from Caesar Augustus that the whole world should be enrolled. This was the first enrollment, when Quirinius was governor of Syria. So all went to be enrolled, each to his own city. And Joseph also went up from Galilee from the city of Nazareth, to Judea, to the city of David, which is called Bethlehem, because he was of the house and lineage of David, to be enrolled with Mary his betrothed, who was with child. While they were there, the time came for her to be delivered. And she gave birth to her first-born son and wrapped him in swaddling cloths, and laid him in a manger, because there was no place for them in the inn.

And in that region there were shepherds out in the field, keeping watch over their flock by night. And an angel of the Lord appeared to them, and the glory of the Lord shone around them, and they were filled with fear. And the angel said to them, "Be not be afraid; for behold, I bring you good news of a great joy which will come to all the people; for to you is born this day in the city of David a Savior, who is Christ the Lord. And this will be a sign for you: you will find a baby wrapped in swaddling cloths and lying in a manger." And suddenly there was with the angel a multitude of the heavenly host praising God and saying,

> "Glory to God in the highest, and on earth peace among men with whom he is pleased!"

When the angels went away from them into heaven, the shepherds said to one another, "Let us go over to Bethlehem to see this thing that has happened, which the Lord has made known to us." And they went in haste, and found Mary and Joseph, and the baby lying in a manger. And when they saw it they made known the saying which had been told them concerning this child; and all who heard it wondered at what the shepherds told them. But Mary kept all these things, pondering them in her heart. And the shepherds returned, glorifying and praising God for all they had heard and seen, as it had been told to them.

The Gospel of the Lord.

All: Praise to you, Lord Jesus Christ.

Gloria in excelsis Deo (Glory to God in the Highest)

This ancient hymn begins with the words that the angels sang at the annunciation to the shepherds. Early Christians added lines explaining the Holy Trinity, creating this confession of faith also called the Great Doxology.

Gloria in excelsis Deo et in terra pax hominibus bonae voluntatis. Laudamus te, benedicimus te, adoramus te, glorificamus te, gratias agimus tibi propter magnam gloriam tuam, Domine Deus, Rex caelestis, Deus Pater omnipotens.

Domine Fili unigenite, Iesu Christe, Domine Deus, Agnus Dei, Filius Patris, qui tollis peccata mundi, miserere nobis; qui tollis peccata mundi, suscipe deprecationem nostram. Qui sedes ad dexteram Patris, miserere nobis.

Quoniam tu solus Sanctus, tu solus Dominus, tu solus Altissimus, Iesu Christe, cum Sancto Spiritu: in gloria Dei Patris. Amen.

Glory to God in the highest, and on earth peace to people of good will. We praise you, we bless you, we adore you, we glorify you, we give you thanks for your great glory, Lord God, heavenly King, O God, almighty Father.

Lord Jesus Christ, Only Begotten Son, Lord God, Lamb of God, Son of the Father, you take away the sins of the world, have mercy on us; you take away the sins of the world, receive our prayer; you are seated at the right hand of the Father, have mercy on us.

For you alone are the Holy One, you alone are the Lord, you alone are the Most High, Jesus Christ, with the Holy Spirit, in the glory of God the Father. Amen.

CHRISTMAS SONG SUGGESTIONS: O Come, Little Children; Joy to the World; Angels We Have Heard on High; O Come, All Ye Faithful; Once in Royal David's City

December 26: Saint Stephen, the First Martyr (Feast)

COLLECT PRAYER

Grant, Lord, we pray, that we may imitate what we worship, and so learn to love even our enemies, for we celebrate the heavenly birthday of a man who knows how to pray even for his persecutors. Through our Lord Jesus Christ, your Son, who lives and reigns with you in the unity of the Holy Spirit, one God, for ever and ever. Amen.

A reading from the Acts of the Apostles.

(Acts 6:1–15; 7:51–60)

Now in these days when the disciples were increasing in number, the Hellenists murmured against the Hebrews because their widows were neglected in the daily distribution. And the Twelve summoned the body of the disciples and said, "It is not right that we should give up preaching the word of God to serve tables. Therefore, brethren, pick out from among you seven men of good repute, full of the Spirit and of wisdom, whom we may appoint to this duty. But we will devote ourselves to prayer and to the ministry of the word." And what they said pleased the whole multitude, and they chose Stephen, a man full of faith and of the Holy Spirit, and Philip, and Prochorus, and Nicanor, and Timon, and Parmenas, and Nicolaus, a proselyte of Antioch. These they set before the apostles, and they prayed and laid their hands upon them.

And the word of God increased; and the number of the disciples multiplied greatly in Jerusalem, and a great many of the priests were obedient to the faith.

And Stephen, full of grace and power, did great wonders and signs among the people. Then some of those who belonged to the synagogue of the Freedmen (as it was called), and of the Cyrenians, and of the Alexandrians, and of those from Cilicia and Asia, arose and disputed with Stephen. But they could not withstand the wisdom and the Spirit with which he spoke. Then they secretly instigated men, who said, "We have heard him speak blasphemous words against Moses and God." And they stirred up the people and the elders and the scribes, and they came upon him and seized him and brought him before the council, and set up false witnesses who said, "This man never ceases to speak words against this holy place and the law; for we have heard him say that this Jesus of Nazareth will destroy this place, and will change the customs which Moses delivered to us." And gazing at him, all who sat in the council saw that his face was like the face of an angel. . . .

"You stiff-necked people, uncircumcised in heart and ears, you always resist the Holy Spirit. As your fathers did, so do you. Which of the prophets did not your fathers persecute? And they killed those who announced beforehand the coming of the Righteous One, whom you have now betrayed and murdered, you who received the law as delivered by angels and did not keep it."

Now when they heard these things they were enraged, and they ground their teeth against him. But he, full of the Holy Spirit, gazed into heaven and saw the glory of God, and Jesus standing at the right hand of God; and he said, "Behold, I see the heavens opened, and the Son of man standing at the right hand of God." But they cried out with a loud voice and stopped their ears and rushed together upon him. Then they cast him out of the city and stoned him; and the witnesses laid down their garments at the feet of a young man named Saul. And as they were stoning Stephen, he prayed, "Lord Jesus, receive my spirit." And he knelt down and cried with a loud voice, "Lord, do not hold this sin against them." And when he had said this, he fell asleep.

The Word of the Lord.

All: Thanks be to God.

Prayer for Deacons and Other Ministers

Saint Stephen is a patron saint of deacons.

Heavenly Father, since the time of the apostles you have inspired the Church to commission certain members to assist in a special way in the pastoral mission of Christ. Bless the deacons and all other ordained and nonordained ministers, that they may be humble and faith-inspired in their service. We ask this through Christ our Lord. Amen.

SONG SUGGESTION: Good King Wenceslas

December 27: Saint John, Apostle and Evangelist (Feast)

COLLECT PRAYER

O God, who through the blessed Apostle John have unlocked for us the secrets of your Word, grant, we pray, that we may grasp with proper understanding what he has so marvelously brought to our ears. Through our Lord Jesus Christ, your Son, who lives and reigns with you in the unity of the Holy Spirit, one God, for ever and ever. Amen.

A reading from the Holy Gospel according to Saint John. (Jn 21:20–24)

Peter turned and saw following them the disciple whom Jesus loved, who had lain close to his breast at the supper and had said, "Lord, who is it that is going to betray you?" When Peter saw him, he said to Jesus, "Lord, what about this man?" Jesus said to him, "If it is my will that he remain until I come, what is that to you? Follow me!" The saying spread abroad among the brethren that this disciple was not to die; yet Jesus did not say to him that he was not to die, but, "If it is my will that he remain until I come, what is that to you?"

This is the disciple who is bearing witness to these things, and who has written these things; and we know that his testimony is true.

The Gospel of the Lord.

All: Praise to you, Lord Jesus Christ.

A reading from the book of Revelation.   (Rev 1:1–9)

The revelation of Jesus Christ, which God gave him to show to his servants what must soon take place; and he made it known by sending his angel to his servant John, who bore witness to the word of God and to the testimony of Jesus Christ, even to all that he saw.

Blessed is he who reads aloud the words of the prophecy, and blessed are those who hear, and who keep what is written therein; for the time is near.

John to the seven churches that are in Asia:

Grace to you and peace from him who is and who was and who is to come, and from the seven spirits who are before his throne, and from Jesus Christ the faithful witness, the first-born of the dead, and the ruler of kings on earth.

To him who loves us and has freed us from our sins by his blood and made us a kingdom, priests to his God and Father, to him be glory and dominion for ever and ever. Amen. Behold, he is coming with the clouds, and every eye will see him, every one who pierced him; and all tribes of the earth will wail on account of him. Even so. Amen.

"I am the Alpha and the Omega," says the Lord God, who is and who was and who is to come, the Almighty.

I John, your brother, who share with you in Jesus the tribulation and the kingdom and the patient endurance, was on the island called Patmos on account of the word of God and the testimony of Jesus.

The Word of the Lord.

All: Thanks be to God.

On Saint Peter and Saint John[26]

From a treatise by Saint Augustine (+430).

The Church recognizes two lives which Divinity himself has revealed and recommended. One is the life of faith, the other the life of vision; one the life of pilgrimage, the other life in the mansions of eternity; one the life of labor, the other the life of rest; one the life of the journey, the other the life of home; one the life of action, the other the life of contemplation. The one avoids evil and does good, the other knows no evil to avoid, but only a great good to enjoy. The one fights with the enemy, the other, having no enemy, reigns.

---

[26]Augustine, *Tract. 124*, 5, in Prosper Guéranger, *The Liturgical Year* (London: R & T Washbourne, 1918), quoted in Ed Masters, "Saint John, the Apostle and Evangelist", Regina, https://reginamag.com/saint-john-the-apostle/.

The one aids the needy, the other is where no needy are; the one forgives the trespasses of others that its own might be forgiven, the other has neither trespasses to forgive nor does anything which calls for forgiveness. The one is scourged with evils, lest it be made presumptuous by prosperity; the other possesses such a fullness of grace that it is without evil. Free from any temptation to pride, it adheres to the Supreme Good.

Wherefore one life is good, but as yet full of sorrows; the other is better, yea even blessed. The first is typified by the Apostle Peter, the other by John. The one life endures all labors up to the end of its allotted time, and there finds an end; the other, having fulfilled all things, stretches beyond the end of time, and in eternity finds no end. So, to Peter is said: "Follow me." Of the other, however; "If I wish him to remain until I come, what is that to thee? Follow thou me." What is the meaning of this? How much can I know of it? How much can I understand? What is it?—unless this: "You are to follow me, imitating me in suffering temporal evils. Let him remain until I come, bringing eternal rewards."

Drinking the Love of Saint John[27]

Wine is blessed and shared on this feast day. If possible, the wine is first blessed by a priest or deacon. At home, the prayer leader asks God's blessing on it, after which those present offer the wine to one another as the love of Saint John. Using a single cup, passed from one person to the next, is traditional, but each person can use his own cup if the group prefers. Traditionally, the wine left in the bottle is saved and a few drops added to other wines to spread the blessing throughout the year.

Leader: Our help is in the name of the Lord.

All: Who made heaven and earth.

Leader: Lord Jesus Christ, you did call yourself the vine and your holy apostles the branches; and out of all those who love you, you desired to make a good vineyard. Bless this wine and pour into it the might

---

[27] Helen McLoughlin, *Christmas to Candlemas in a Catholic Home* (Collegeville, Minn.: Liturgical Press, 1955), Catholic Culture, https://www.catholicculture.org/culture/liturgical year/prayers/view.cfm?id=519.

of your benediction so that everyone who drinks or takes of it, may through the intercession of your beloved disciple, the holy apostle and evangelist John, be freed from every disease or attack of illness and obtain health of body and soul.

Who lives and reigns forever.

All: Amen.

The wine may be sprinkled with holy water.

First person: I drink to you the love of Saint John.

He takes a drink of wine.

Second person: I thank you for the love of Saint John.

He takes a drink of wine.

The second person offers wine to the third. Repeat around the table until all have offered and received.

Prayer to Saint John[28]

Saint John, beloved disciple of Jesus, pray for us to be docile to those whom the Lord has put in authority over us, yet zealous in our love and service to God. In Jesus Christ's name, we pray. Amen.

Prayer for Priests[29]

Saint John is a patron saint of priests. This prayer for priests was composed by Richard Cardinal Cushing (+1970) of the Archdiocese of Boston.

O Jesus, I pray for your faithful and fervent priests; for your unfaithful and tepid priests; for your priests laboring at home or abroad in

---

[28] "St. John the Apostle", Catholic Exchange, December 2, 2019, https://catholic exchange.com/st-john-the-apostle-2. Used with permission.

[29] Richard Cardinal Cushing, "Litany of Prayers for Priests", Foundation of Prayer for Priests. Used with permission.

distant mission fields; for your tempted priests; for your lonely and desolate priests; for your young priests; for your dying priests; for the souls of your priests in purgatory. But above all, I recommend to you the priests dearest to me: the priest who baptized me; the priests who absolved me from my sins; the priests at whose Masses I assisted and who gave me your Body and Blood in Holy Communion; the priests who taught and instructed me; and all the priests to whom I am indebted in any other way, especially *(names here)*. O Jesus, keep them all close to your heart, and bless them abundantly in time and in eternity. Amen.

December 28: The Holy Innocents, Martyrs (Feast)

COLLECT PRAYER

O God, whom the Holy Innocents confessed and proclaimed on this day, not by speaking but by dying, grant, we pray, that the faith in you which we confess with our lips may also speak through our manner of life. Through our Lord Jesus Christ, your Son, who lives and reigns with you in the unity of the Holy Spirit, one God, for ever and ever. Amen.

A reading from the Holy Gospel according to Saint Matthew. (Mt 2:13–18)

Now when they had departed, behold, an angel of the Lord appeared to Joseph in a dream and said, "Rise, take the child and his mother, and flee to Egypt, and remain there till I tell you; for Herod is about to search for the child, to destroy him." And he rose and took the child and his mother by night, and departed to Egypt, and remained there until the death of Herod. This was to fulfil what the Lord had spoken by the prophet, "Out of Egypt have I called my son."

Then Herod, when he saw that he had been tricked by the Wise Men, was in a furious rage, and he sent and killed all the male children in Bethlehem and in all that region who were two years old or under, according to the time which he had ascertained from the Wise Men. Then was fulfilled what was spoken by the prophet Jeremiah:

"A voice was heard in Ramah,
wailing and loud lamentation,
Rachel weeping for her children;
she refused to be consoled,
because they were no more."

The Gospel of the Lord.

All: Praise to you, Lord Jesus Christ.

On the Holy Innocents[30]

From a homily by Saint Augustine (+430).

And while [Herod] thus persecutes Christ, he furnished an army [of martyrs] clothed in white robes of the same age as the Lord. Behold how this unrighteous enemy never could have so much profited these infants by his love as he did by his hate; for as much as iniquity abounded against them, so much did the grace of blessing abound on them. O blessed infants! He only will doubt of your crown in this your passion for Christ, who doubts that the baptism of Christ has a benefit for infants. He who at his birth had angels to proclaim him, the heavens to testify, and magi to worship him, could surely have prevented that these should not have died for him, had he not known that they died not in that death, but rather lived in higher bliss.

Altar Server's Prayer[31]

The Holy Innocents are patron saints of altar servers.

Open my mouth, O Lord, to bless your Holy Name. Cleanse my heart from all evil and distracting thoughts. Enlighten my understanding and inflame my will that I may serve more worthily at your holy altar. O Mary, Mother of Christ the High Priest, obtain for me

---

[30] Quoted in Thomas Aquinas, *Catena Aurea: Commentary on the Four Gospels, Collected Out of the Works of the Fathers* (Eugene, Ore.: Wipf and Stock, 2005), 82.

[31] Joseph De Silvestro, *National Altar Boy Handbook: A Handbook for Training Boys in Christ's Service through the Knights of the Altar* (Marseilles, Ill.: The Knights of the Altar, 1971), 35.

the most important grace of knowing my vocation in life. Grant me a true spirit of faith and humble obedience so that I may ever behold the priest as a representative of God and be willing to follow him in the Way, the Truth, and the Life of Christ. Amen.

SONG SUGGESTIONS: *Coventry Carol; All Glory, Laud, and Honor*

Sunday after Christmas
(or December 30 if Christmas is a Sunday):
The Holy Family of Jesus, Mary, and Joseph (Feast)

COLLECT PRAYER

O God, who were pleased to give us the shining example of the Holy Family, graciously grant that we may imitate them in practicing the virtues of family life and in the bonds of charity, and so, in the joy of your house, delight one day in eternal rewards. Through our Lord Jesus Christ, your Son, who lives and reigns with you in the unity of the Holy Spirit, one God, for ever and ever. Amen.

A reading from the Holy Gospel according to Saint Luke.
(Lk 2:39–52)

And when they had performed everything according to the law of the Lord, they returned into Galilee, to their own city, Nazareth. And the child grew and became strong, filled with wisdom; and the favor of God was upon him.

Now his parents went to Jerusalem every year at the feast of the Passover. And when he was twelve years old, they went up according to custom; and when the feast was ended, as they were returning, the boy Jesus stayed behind in Jerusalem. His parents did not know it, but supposing him to be in the company they went a day's journey, and they sought him among their kinsfolk and acquaintances; and when they did not find him, they returned to Jerusalem, seeking him. After three days they found him in the temple, sitting among the teachers, listening to them and asking them questions; and all who heard him were amazed at his understanding and his answers. And when they saw him they were astonished; and his mother said to him,

"Son, why have you treated us so? Behold, your father and I have been looking for you anxiously." And he said to them, "How is it that you sought me? Did you not know that I must be in my Father's house?" And they did not understand the saying which he spoke to them. And he went down with them and came to Nazareth, and was obedient to them; and his mother kept all these things in her heart. And Jesus increased in wisdom and in stature, and in favor with God and man.

The Gospel of the Lord.

All: Praise to you, Lord Jesus Christ.

See also Prayer to the Holy Family and Consecration to the Holy Family, p. 142.

4

January

The month of the Holy Name of Jesus

Prayer after Blessing before Meals: The Golden Arrow

This prayer is said to have been revealed by Jesus in a vision to a Carmelite nun of Tours in 1843 as a reparation for blasphemy.

May the most holy, most sacred, most adorable, most mysterious and unutterable Name of God be always praised, blessed, loved, adored, and glorified in heaven, on earth, and under the earth, by all the creatures of God, and by the Sacred Heart of our Lord Jesus Christ in the Most Holy Sacrament of the altar. Amen.

Vigil of January 1
(December 31, New Year's Eve)

Te Deum

Dating from the fourth century, the Latin hymn Te Deum is traditionally chanted, recited, or sung in thanksgiving at the end of an undertaking (for a partial indulgence) anytime during the year. It is specifically recommended on December 31. A plenary indulgence is offered when this prayer is recited publicly, which means in a church, family, group of friends, or religious community, on the last day of the year.[1] It is historically attributed to Saint Ambrose.

---

[1] *Manual of Indulgences*, grant 26.1.2. See the introduction of this book for the usual conditions for indulgences.

You are God: we praise you;
You are the Lord: we acclaim you;
You are the eternal Father:
All creation worships you.
To you all angels, all the powers of heaven,
Cherubim and seraphim, sing in endless praise:
   Holy, holy, holy, Lord God of power and might,
   Heaven and earth are full of your glory.
The glorious company of apostles praise you.
The noble fellowship of prophets praise you.
The white-robed army of martyrs praise you.
Throughout the world, the holy Church acclaims you:
   Father of majesty unbounded,
   Your true and only Son, worthy of all worship,
   And the Holy Spirit, advocate and guide.
You, Christ, are the King of Glory,
The eternal Son of the Father.
When you became man to set us free,
You did not spurn the Virgin's womb.
You overcame the sting of death,
And opened the kingdom of heaven to all believers.
You are seated at God's right hand in glory.
We believe that you will come and be our judge.
Come then, Lord, and help your people,
Bought with the price of your own blood,
And bring us with your saints to glory everlasting.

Leader: Save your people, Lord, and bless your inheritance.

All: Govern and uphold them now and always.

Leader: Day by day we bless you.

All: We praise your name forever.

Leader: Keep us today, Lord, from all sin.

All: Have mercy on us, Lord, have mercy.

Leader: Lord, show us your love and mercy,

All: For we put our trust in you.

Leader: In you, Lord, is our hope:

All: And we shall never hope in vain. Amen.

January 1: SOLEMNITY OF MARY, THE HOLY MOTHER OF GOD
(Solemnity, Holy Day of Obligation)

COLLECT PRAYER

O God, who through the fruitful virginity of Blessed Mary bestowed on the human race the grace of eternal salvation, grant, we pray, that we may experience the intercession of her, through whom we were found worthy to receive the author of life, our Lord Jesus Christ, your Son. Who lives and reigns with you in the unity of the Holy Spirit, one God, for ever and ever. Amen.

Come, Holy Ghost, Creator Blest (*Veni Creator Spiritus*)

While the Te Deum is for the ending of things, the Veni Creator Spiritus *is for the beginning of things. A plenary indulgence is available (subject to the usual conditions) when it is recited or sung on the first day of the year (and on Pentecost, to celebrate the beginning of the Church).*[2] *It's believed to have been written by Frankish Benedictine monk Rabanus Maurus, archbishop of Mainz, in the ninth century. In its nineteenth-century English translation by Father Edward Caswall, it's known as "Come, Holy Ghost, Creator Blest".*

1. Come, Holy Ghost, Creator blest,
   And in our hearts take up thy rest;
   Come with thy grace and heav'nly aid
   To fill the hearts which thou hast made,
   To fill the hearts which thou hast made.

---

[2] *Manual of Indulgences*, grant 26.1.1. See the introduction of this book for the usual conditions for indulgences.

2. O Comforter, to thee we cry,
   Thou heav'nly gift of God most high,
   Thou font of life and fire of love,
   And sweet anointing from above,
   And sweet anointing from above.

3. Praise be to thee, Father and Son,
   And Holy Spirit, with them one;
   And may the Son on us bestow
   The gifts that from the Spirit flow,
   The gifts that from the Spirit flow.

See also Litany of Loreto, p. 52.

January 3: The Most Holy Name of Jesus (Optional Memorial)

COLLECT PRAYER

O God, who founded the salvation of the human race on the Incarnation of your Word, give your peoples the mercy they implore, so that all may know there is no other name to be invoked but the Name of your Only Begotten Son. Who lives and reigns with you in the unity of the Holy Spirit, one God, for ever and ever. Amen.

Bible Passages about the Holy Name of Jesus

And at the end of eight days, when he was circumcised, he was called Jesus, the name given by the angel before he was conceived in the womb. (Lk 2:21)

Therefore God has highly exalted him and bestowed on him the name which is above every name, that at the name of Jesus every knee should bow, in heaven and on earth and under the earth, and every tongue confess that Jesus Christ is Lord, to the glory of God the Father. (Phil 2:9–11)

And whatever you do, in word or deed, do everything in the name of the Lord Jesus, giving thanks to God the Father through him. (Col 3:17)

Quick Prayers of Reparation upon Taking or Hearing Another Take the Name of the Lord in Vain

Father, forgive them; for they know not what they do. (Lk 23:34)
Blessed be the name of the LORD. (Job 1:21)

Litany of the Holy Name of Jesus[3]

Believed to have been composed in the fifteenth century by Saint Bernardine of Siena and his student Saint John of Capistrano, this litany was approved for public recitation by Pope Leo XIII in 1886. A partial indulgence is available for its recitation at any time.

Leader: Lord, have mercy;

All: Lord, have mercy.

Leader: Christ, have mercy;

All: Christ, have mercy.

Leader: Lord, have mercy;

All: Lord, have mercy.

The leader announces each name of Jesus.

All reply: have mercy on us.

Leader: God our Father in heaven, *have mercy on us.*

God the Son, Redeemer of the world, *have mercy on us.*
God the Holy Spirit, *have mercy on us.*
Holy Trinity, one God, *have mercy on us.*
Jesus, Son of the living God, *have mercy on us.*

---

[3] *Manual of Indulgences*, grant 22. See the introduction of this book for the usual conditions for indulgences.

Jesus, splendor of the Father, *have mercy on us.*
Jesus, brightness of everlasting light, *have mercy on us.*
Jesus, king of glory, *have mercy on us.*
Jesus, dawn of justice, *have mercy on us.*
Jesus, Son of the Virgin Mary, *have mercy on us.*
Jesus, worthy of our love, *have mercy on us.*
Jesus, worthy of our wonder, *have mercy on us.*
Jesus, mighty God, *have mercy on us.*
Jesus, father of the world to come, *have mercy on us.*
Jesus, prince of peace, *have mercy on us.*
Jesus, all-powerful, *have mercy on us.*
Jesus, pattern of patience, *have mercy on us.*
Jesus, model of obedience, *have mercy on us.*
Jesus, gentle and humble of heart, *have mercy on us.*
Jesus, lover of chastity, *have mercy on us.*
Jesus, lover of us all, *have mercy on us.*
Jesus, God of peace, *have mercy on us.*
Jesus, author of life, *have mercy on us.*
Jesus, model of goodness, *have mercy on us.*
Jesus, seeker of souls, *have mercy on us.*
Jesus, our God, *have mercy on us.*
Jesus, our refuge, *have mercy on us.*
Jesus, father of the poor, *have mercy on us.*
Jesus, treasure of the faithful, *have mercy on us.*
Jesus, Good Shepherd, *have mercy on us.*
Jesus, the true light, *have mercy on us.*
Jesus, eternal wisdom, *have mercy on us.*
Jesus, infinite goodness, *have mercy on us.*
Jesus, our way and our life, *have mercy on us.*
Jesus, joy of angels, *have mercy on us.*
Jesus, king of patriarchs, *have mercy on us.*
Jesus, teacher of apostles, *have mercy on us.*
Jesus, master of evangelists, *have mercy on us.*
Jesus, courage of martyrs, *have mercy on us.*
Jesus, light of confessors, *have mercy on us.*
Jesus, purity of virgins, *have mercy on us.*
Jesus, crown of all saints, *have mercy on us.*

The leader announces each petition.

All reply: Jesus, save your people.

Lord, be merciful; *Jesus, save your people.*
From all evil, *Jesus, save your people.*
From every sin, *Jesus, save your people.*
From the snares of the devil, *Jesus, save your people.*
From your anger, *Jesus, save your people.*
From the spirit of infidelity, *Jesus, save your people.*
From everlasting death, *Jesus, save your people.*
From neglect of your Holy Spirit, *Jesus, save your people.*
By the mystery of your Incarnation, *Jesus, save your people.*
By your birth, *Jesus, save your people.*
By your childhood, *Jesus, save your people.*
By your hidden life, *Jesus, save your people.*
By your public ministry, *Jesus, save your people.*
By your agony and crucifixion, *Jesus, save your people.*
By your abandonment, *Jesus, save your people.*
By your grief and sorrow, *Jesus, save your people.*
By your death and burial, *Jesus, save your people.*
By your rising to new life, *Jesus, save your people.*
By your return in glory to the Father, *Jesus, save your people.*
By your gift of the Holy Eucharist, *Jesus, save your people.*
By your joy and glory, *Jesus, save your people.*

Leader: Christ, hear us;

All: Christ, hear us.

Leader: Lord Jesus, hear our prayer;

All: Lord Jesus, hear our prayer.

Leader: Lamb of God, you take away the sins of the world;

All: Have mercy on us.

Leader: Lamb of God, you take away the sins of the world;

All: Have mercy on us.

Leader: Lamb of God, you take away the sins of the world;

All: Have mercy on us.

Leader: Let us pray.
As we venerate the Most Holy Name of Jesus,
mercifully grant us, Lord,
that, savoring its sweetness in this life,
we may be filled with everlasting joy
in our heavenly homeland.
Through Christ our Lord.
All: Amen.

January 4: Saint Elizabeth Ann Seton, Religious (Memorial)

COLLECT PRAYER

O God, who crowned with the gift of true faith Saint Elizabeth Ann Seton's burning zeal to find you, grant by her intercession and example that we may always seek you with diligent love and find you in daily service with sincere faith. Through our Lord Jesus Christ, your Son, who lives and reigns with you in the unity of the Holy Spirit, one God, for ever and ever. Amen.

Saint Elizabeth Ann Seton Prayer for Students[4]

O God, you called Elizabeth Ann Seton to be an instrument of
  your loving mercy.
Despite loss and sorrow, she was an example of hope and love.
Inspire us with your Blessed Sacrament to live our life for
  others.
We ask this in the name of Jesus Christ, our Lord and teacher.
  Amen.

---

[4] "Saint Elizabeth Ann Seton Prayers for Students and Teachers", Ave Maria Press, https://www.avemariapress.com/engagingfaith/st-elizabeth-ann-seton-prayers-for. Copyright Ave Maria Press®, Inc., P.O. Box 428, Notre Dame, Ind., 46556. Used with permission of the publisher.

Saint Elizabeth Ann Seton Prayer for Teachers[5]

Holy Father, you called Elizabeth Ann Seton to educate your children. Inspire us, by her example, to find your will in the present moment. Through her prayers, may we learn to teach others how to love like you. We ask this in the name of Jesus Christ, our Lord and teacher. Amen.

Prayer of Saint Elizabeth Ann Seton

O Father, the first rule of our dear Savior's life was to do your will. Let his will of the present moment be the first rule of our daily life and work, with no other desire but for its most full and complete accomplishment. Help us to follow it faithfully, so that doing what you wish we will be pleasing to you. Amen.

January 5: Saint John Neumann, Bishop (Memorial)

COLLECT PRAYER

O God, who called the Bishop Saint John Neumann, renowned for his charity and pastoral service, to shepherd your people in America, grant by his intercession that, as we foster the Christian education of youth and are strengthened by the witness of brotherly love, we may constantly increase the family of your Church. Through our Lord Jesus Christ, your Son, who lives and reigns with you in the unity of the Holy Spirit, one God, for ever and ever. Amen.

Prayer of Saint John Neumann[6]

Lord, grant that not one of those whom thou hast confided to me be lost through my fault. O my Jesus, help me to sanctify my children!

---

[5] Ibid.

[6] Johann Berger and Eugene Grimm, *Life of Right Rev. John N. Neumann, D.D., of the Congregation of the Most Holy Redeemer: Fourth Bishop of Philadelphia* (New York: Benziger Bros., 1884), 164.

O holy Mother of my Lord and my God, pray for me and my flock! Holy guardian angels of my dear children, teach me how to act toward them in order to instill into their hearts principles of pure faith and the love of God! Amen.

Prayer for Catholic Schools[7]

Saint John Neumann, you helped organize Catholic education in the United States. Please watch over all Catholic schools and help them be a model of Christianity in their actions as well as their words. Amen.

January 6 (or the Sunday after January 1): THE EPIPHANY OF THE LORD (Solemnity)

COLLECT PRAYER

May the splendor of your majesty, O Lord, we pray, shed its light upon our hearts, that we may pass through the shadows of this world and reach the brightness of our eternal home. Through our Lord Jesus Christ, your Son, who lives and reigns with you in the unity of the Holy Spirit, one God, for ever and ever. Amen.

A reading from the Holy Gospel according to Saint Matthew. (Mt 2:1–12)

Now when Jesus was born in Bethlehem of Judea in the days of Herod the king, behold, Wise Men from the East came to Jerusalem, saying, "Where is he who has been born king of the Jews? For we have seen his star in the East, and have come to worship him." When Herod the king heard this, he was troubled, and all Jerusalem with him; and assembling all the chief priests and scribes of the people, he inquired of them where the Christ was to be born. They told him, "In Bethlehem of Judea; for so it is written by the prophet:

---

[7] "Our Patron Saint", St. John Neumann Academy (Blacksburg, Va.), https://www .stjohnneumannacademy.org/apex/f?p=200:10:2436532010147506.

'And you, O Bethlehem, in the land of Judah,
are by no means least among the rulers of Judah;
for from you shall come a ruler
who will govern my people Israel.' "

Then Herod summoned the Wise Men secretly and ascertained from them what time the star appeared; and he sent them to Bethlehem, saying, "Go and search diligently for the child, and when you have found him bring me word, that I too may come and worship him." When they had heard the king they went their way; and behold, the star which they had seen in the East went before them, till it came to rest over the place where the child was. When they saw the star, they rejoiced exceedingly with great joy; and going into the house they saw the child with Mary his mother, and they fell down and worshiped him. Then, opening their treasures, they offered him gifts, gold and frankincense and myrrh. And being warned in a dream not to return to Herod, they departed to their own country by another way.

The Gospel of the Lord.

All: Praise to you, Lord Jesus Christ.

SONG SUGGESTION: We Three Kings of Orient Are

Chalking the Door for Epiphany[8]

The feast of Epiphany is traditionally associated with house blessings. In some places, it is common for priests to visit the homes of their parishioners in the days close to Epiphany to bless their homes. It is also permissible for the faithful to ask God's blessing on their own homes. A common way of doing this is to use blessed chalk to write above the home's entrance: 20 + C + M + B + 22 (or whatever is the current year).

The letters C, M, and B have two meanings. They are the initials of the traditional names of the three magi: Caspar, Melchior, and Balthazar. They

---

[8] Adapted from Daryl Moresco, "Chalking the Door: An Epiphany House Blessing 2016", January 1, 2016, Order of Carmelites, http://www.carmelites.net/news/chalking -door-epiphany-house-blessing-2015/.

also abbreviate the Latin words Christus mansionem benedicat, *"May Christ bless the house." The* + *signs represent the cross, and 2022 is the year. The chalking can be done on or around the feast of Epiphany.*

On Epiphany many parishes hand out blessed chalk[9] for house blessings. If this isn't the case at your parish, you can bring chalk to church and ask the priest to bless it for you. If this is not possible, the head of your household can ask God's blessing on the chalk with the following prayer. If your chalk is already blessed you can skip this part.

Leader: Our help is in the name of the Lord.

All: Who made heaven and earth.

Leader: The Lord shall watch over your going out and your coming in.

All: From this time forth for evermore.

Leader: Let us pray. Loving God, bless this chalk which you have created, that it may be helpful to your people; and grant that through the invocation of your Most Holy Name that we who use it in faith to write upon the door of our home the names of your holy ones Caspar, Melchior, and Balthazar, may receive health of body and protection of soul for all who dwell in or visit our home; through Jesus Christ our Lord.

All: Amen.

Using blessed chalk, mark the lintel of your front door, inside or out, or front porch step, as follows: 20 + C + M + B + 22 (or current year).

Leader: The three wise men, Caspar, Melchior, and Balthazar, followed the star of God's Son, who became human two thousand twenty-one years (*or whatever number of years corresponds to one less than the calendar year*) ago. May Christ bless our home and remain with us throughout the new year.

All: Amen.

Leader: Visit, O blessed Lord, this home with the gladness of your presence. Bless all who live or visit here with the gift of your love;

[9] Chalk blessed by a priest is a sacramental. You may save it to use year after year. When you wish to dispose of it, as with other sacramentals, bury it instead of throwing it away.

and grant that we may manifest your love to each other and to all whose lives we touch. May we grow in grace and in the knowledge and love of you; guide, comfort, and strengthen us in peace, O Jesus Christ, now and forever.

All: Amen.

Sunday after Epiphany (or January 9): The Baptism of the Lord (Feast)

COLLECT PRAYER

Almighty ever-living God, who, when Christ had been baptized in the River Jordan and as the Holy Spirit descended upon him, solemnly declared him your beloved Son, grant that your children by adoption, reborn of water and the Holy Spirit, may always be well pleasing to you. Through our Lord Jesus Christ, your Son, who lives and reigns with you in the unity of the Holy Spirit, one God, for ever and ever. Amen.

A reading from the Holy Gospel according to Saint Matthew. (Mt 3:13–17)

Then Jesus came from Galilee to the Jordan to John, to be baptized by him. John would have prevented him, saying, "I need to be baptized by you, and do you come to me?" But Jesus answered him, "Let it be so now; for thus it is fitting for us to fulfil all righteousness." Then he consented. And when Jesus was baptized, he went up immediately from the water, and behold, the heavens were opened and he saw the Spirit of God descending like a dove, and alighting on him; and lo, a voice from heaven, saying, "This is my beloved Son, with whom I am well pleased."

The Gospel of the Lord.

All: Praise to you, Lord Jesus Christ.

See also Renewal of Baptismal Promises, p. 353.

ORDINARY TIME BEGINS

January 20: Saint Sebastian, Martyr (Optional Memorial)

COLLECT PRAYER

Grant us, we pray, O Lord, a spirit of fortitude, so that, taught by the glorious example of your Martyr Saint Sebastian, we may learn to obey you rather than men. Through our Lord Jesus Christ, your Son, who lives and reigns with you in the unity of the Holy Spirit, one God, for ever and ever. Amen.

For Courage in the Time of Battle[10]

Saint Sebastian was a third-century member of the Roman army and is a patron saint of soldiers.

O Prince of Peace, we humbly ask your protection
for all our men and women in military service.
Give them unflinching courage to defend
with honor, dignity, and devotion
the rights of all who are imperiled
by injustice and evil.
Be their rock, their shield, and their stronghold
and let them draw their strength from you.
For you are God, for ever and ever. Amen.

January 21: Saint Agnes, Virgin and Martyr (Memorial)

COLLECT PRAYER

Almighty ever-living God, who choose what is weak in the world to confound the strong, mercifully grant, that we, who celebrate the

[10] "Prayer for Troops", no. 9, United States Council of Catholic Bishops, https://www.usccb.org/prayer-and-worship/prayers-and-devotions/prayers/prayer-for-troops.

heavenly birthday of your Martyr Saint Agnes, may follow her constancy in the faith. Through our Lord Jesus Christ, your Son, who lives and reigns with you in the unity of the Holy Spirit, one God, for ever and ever. Amen.

Prayer to Saint Agnes

O glorious Saint Agnes, by the living faith that animated you from your tender years and rendered you so pleasing to God that you merited a martyr's crown: obtain for us the grace to keep our holy faith pure within us and to profess ourselves Christians in both word and work. May our open confession of Jesus before men cause him to bear a favorable witness to us before his eternal Father. Amen.

January 22 (or January 23 if the 22nd is a Sunday): Day of Prayer for the Legal Protection of Unborn Children in the United States

Observed as a particular day of prayer for the full restoration of the legal guarantee of the right to life, and of penance for violations to the dignity of the human person committed through acts of abortion, we are called to participate as individuals through the penitential practices of prayer, fasting, and giving alms, and also together by joining in special events like the Walk for Life that observe the anniversary of the legal decision Roe v. Wade, *which made abortion legal in the United States.*

COLLECT PRAYER

God our Creator, we give thanks to you, who alone have the power to impart the breath of life as you form each of us in our mother's womb; grant, we pray, that we, whom you have made stewards of creation, may remain faithful to this sacred trust and constant in safeguarding the dignity of every human life. Through our Lord Jesus Christ, your Son, who lives and reigns with you in the unity of the Holy Spirit, one God, for ever and ever. Amen.

A reading from the book of Psalms. (Ps 139:1–6, 13–16)

O LORD, you have searched me and known me!

You know when I sit down and when I rise up; you discern my thoughts from afar.

You search out my path and my lying down, and are acquainted with all my ways.

Even before a word is on my tongue, behold, O LORD, you know it altogether.

You beset me behind and before, and lay your hand upon me.

Such knowledge is too wonderful for me; it is high, I cannot attain it.

For you formed my inward parts, you knitted me together in my mother's womb.

I praise you, for I am wondrously made. Wonderful are your works!

You know me right well; my frame was not hidden from you, when I was being made in secret, intricately wrought in the depths of the earth.

Your eyes beheld my unformed substance; in your book were written, every one of them,

the days that were formed for me, when as yet there was none of them.

The Word of the Lord.

All: Thanks be to God.

Prayer for the Unborn[11]

Pope Benedict XVI led this prayer at the conclusion of a prayer vigil for the unborn at the Vatican in 2010.

Lord Jesus, you who faithfully visit and fulfill with your Presence the Church and the history of men; you who in the miraculous Sacrament of your Body and Blood render us participants in divine life and

---

[11] Benedict XVI, Prayer Vigil for the Unborn, St. Peter's Basilica (November 27, 2010). Translated by Vatican Radio.

allow us a foretaste of the joy of eternal life; we adore and bless you. Prostrated before you, source and lover of life, truly present and alive among us, we beg you.

Reawaken in us respect for every unborn life, make us capable of seeing in the fruit of the maternal womb the miraculous work of the Creator, open our hearts to generously welcoming every child that comes into life.

Bless all families, sanctify the union of spouses, render fruitful their love.

Accompany the choices of legislative assemblies with the light of your Spirit, so that peoples and nations may recognize and respect the sacred nature of life, of every human life.

Guide the work of scientists and doctors, so that all progress contributes to the integral well-being of the person, and no one endures suppression or injustice.

Give creative charity to administrators and economists, so they may realize and promote sufficient conditions so that young families can serenely embrace the birth of new children.

Console the married couples who suffer because they are unable to have children, and in your goodness provide for them.

Teach us all to care for orphaned or abandoned children, so they may experience the warmth of your charity, the consolation of your divine heart.

Together with Mary, your Mother, the great believer, in whose womb you took on our human nature, we wait to receive from you, our only true God and Savior, the strength to love and serve life, in anticipation of living forever in you, in communion with the Blessed Trinity. Amen.

Our Lady of Guadalupe, patroness of the unborn, pray for us!

January 23: Saint Vincent, Deacon and Martyr (Optional Memorial)

COLLECT PRAYER

Almighty ever-living God, mercifully pour out your Spirit upon us, so that our hearts may possess the strong love by which the Martyr

Saint Vincent triumphed over all bodily torments. Through our Lord Jesus Christ, your Son, who lives and reigns with you in the unity of the Holy Spirit, one God, for ever and ever. Amen.

A reading from the Holy Gospel according to Saint John. (Jn 2:1–5)

On the third day there was a marriage at Cana in Galilee, and the mother of Jesus was there; Jesus also was invited to the marriage, with his disciples. When the wine failed, the mother of Jesus said to him, "They have no wine." And Jesus said to her, "O woman, what have you to do with me? My hour has not yet come." His mother said to the servants, "Do whatever he tells you."

The Gospel of the Lord.

All: Praise to you, Lord Jesus Christ.

Blessing for Products of Nature[12]

There is a fun legend that says Saint Vincent of Saragossa's donkey got a case of the nibbles while in a vineyard and so winemakers learned that grapevines must be pruned. Therefore, Saint Vincent is the patron saint of vineyards, grapes, and winemakers. We use this blessing for grapes and wine for the feast day.

All make the sign of the cross.

Leader: Brothers and sisters, let us bless and praise the Lord, the fountain of all goodness. Blessed be God now and forever.

All: Amen.

A reading from the First Letter of Saint Paul to Timothy. (1 Tim 4:4–5, NAB)

For everything created by God is good, and nothing is to be rejected when it is received with thanksgiving, for it is made holy by the invocation of God in prayer.

---

[12] *Book of Blessings*, nos. 1989, 1993, 2000.

Leader: Let us pray.
Blessed are you, O God,
Creator of the universe,
Who have made all things good
and given the earth for us to cultivate.
Grant that we may always use created things gratefully
and share your gifts with those in need,
out of the love of Christ our Lord,
who lives and reigns with you forever and ever.
All: Amen.

All make the sign of the cross.

After the blessing, the wine and grapes may be sprinkled with holy water, and all may conclude with a suitable song.

See The Doxology (hymn), p. 326.

January 25: The Conversion of Saint Paul the Apostle (Feast)

COLLECT PRAYER

O God, who taught the whole world through the preaching of the blessed Apostle Paul, draw us, we pray, nearer to you through the example of him whose conversion we celebrate today, and so make us witnesses to your truth in the world. Through our Lord Jesus Christ, your Son, who lives and reigns with you in the unity of the Holy Spirit, one God, for ever and ever. Amen.

A reading from the Acts of the Apostles. (Acts 9:1–22)

But Saul, still breathing threats and murder against the disciples of the Lord, went to the high priest and asked him for letters to the synagogues at Damascus, so that if he found any belonging to the Way, men or women, he might bring them bound to Jerusalem. Now as he journeyed he approached Damascus, and suddenly a light from heaven flashed about him. And he fell to the ground and heard a voice saying to him, "Saul, Saul, why do you persecute me?" And he said, "Who are you, Lord?" And he said, "I am Jesus, whom you are persecuting; but rise and enter the city, and you will be told what you are to do." The men who were traveling with him stood speechless, hearing the voice but seeing no one. Saul arose from the ground; and when his eyes were opened, he could see nothing; so they led him by the hand and brought him into Damascus. And for three days he was without sight, and neither ate nor drank.

Now there was a disciple at Damascus named Ananias. The Lord said to him in a vision, "Ananias." And he said, "Here I am, Lord." And the Lord said to him, "Rise and go to the street called Straight, and inquire in the house of Judas for a man of Tarsus named Saul; for behold, he is praying, and he has seen a man named Ananias come in and lay his hands on him so that he might regain his sight." But Ananias answered, "Lord, I have heard from many about this man, how much evil he has done to thy saints at Jerusalem; and here he has authority from the chief priests to bind all who call upon your name." But the Lord said to him, "Go, for he is a chosen instrument of mine to carry my name before the Gentiles and kings and the sons of Israel; for I will show him how much he must suffer for the sake of my name." So Ananias departed and entered the house. And laying his hands on him he said, "Brother Saul, the Lord Jesus who appeared to you on the road by which you came, has sent me that you may regain your sight and be filled with the Holy Spirit." And immediately something like scales fell from his eyes and he regained his sight. Then he rose and was baptized, and took food and was strengthened.

For several days he was with the disciples at Damascus. And in the synagogues immediately he proclaimed Jesus, saying, "He is the Son of God." And all who heard him were amazed, and said, "Is not this the man who made havoc in Jerusalem of those who called on this name? And he has come here for this purpose, to bring them bound before the chief priests." But Saul increased all the more in strength, and confounded the Jews who lived in Damascus by proving that Jesus was the Christ.

The Word of the Lord.

All: Thanks be to God.

Prayer for the Missions[13]

Saint Paul is a patron saint of missionaries. He spent about thirty years as a missionary himself, sailing around the Mediterranean basin with various companions and visiting all the major cities of his time.

O God, who would have all his children to be saved and to come to the knowledge of the truth, send forth, we beseech you, laborers into your harvest and grant them with all confidence to preach the Word; that everywhere your Gospel may be heard and glorified, and that all nations may know you, the one True God, and him whom you have sent, Jesus Christ, your Son, our Lord. Amen.

Queen of the apostles, and all you angels and saints of God, pray the Lord of the harvest to send laborers into the harvest and to spare his people, that we may all rejoice with him and the Father and the Holy Spirit forever and ever. Amen.

January 28: Saint Thomas Aquinas, Priest and Doctor of the Church (Memorial)

COLLECT PRAYER

O God, who made Saint Thomas Aquinas outstanding in his zeal for holiness and his study of sacred doctrine, grant us, we pray, that we may understand what he taught and imitate what he accomplished. Through our Lord Jesus Christ, your Son, who lives and reigns with you in the unity of the Holy Spirit, one God, for ever and ever. Amen.

A Student's Prayer

Saint Thomas Aquinas (+1274) is a patron saint of schools, universities, scholars, academics, students, theologians, philosophers, and pencil makers. He composed this prayer.

---

[13] "Prayer for the Missions", CatholiCity, the Mary Foundation, https://www.catholicity.com/prayer/prayer-for-the-missions.html. Used with permission.

Come, Holy Spirit, divine Creator, true source of light and fountain of wisdom! Pour forth your brilliance upon my dense intellect, dissipate the darkness which covers me, that of sin and of ignorance. Grant me a penetrating mind to understand, a retentive memory, method and ease in learning, the lucidity to comprehend, and abundant grace in expressing myself. Guide the beginning of my work, direct its progress, and bring it to successful completion. This I ask through Jesus Christ, true God and true man, living and reigning with you and the Father, forever and ever. Amen.

Prayer for Chastity

Saint Thomas Aquinas is also a patron saint of chastity, for having heroically persevered in chastity in the face of temptation. He composed this prayer.

Dearest Jesus! I know well that every perfect gift, and above all others that of chastity, depends upon the most powerful assistance of your providence, and that without you a creature can do nothing. Therefore, I pray you to defend, with your grace, chastity and purity in my soul as well as in my body. And if I have ever received through my senses any impression that could stain my chastity and purity, may you, who are the Supreme Lord of all my powers, take it from me, that I may with an immaculate heart advance in your love and service, offering myself chaste all the days of my life on the most pure altar of your divinity. Amen.

SONG SUGGESTIONS: Pange lingua gloriosi; Tantum ergo; Adoro te devote *(all composed by Saint Thomas Aquinas); or their English translations.*

Seven Sundays of Saint Joseph

(This devotion begins seven Sundays before the solemnity of Saint Joseph on March 19. That means the first Sunday falls at the end of January or the beginning of February, and the Sundays continue into March. See appendix B for a list of start dates.)

The Seven Sundays of Saint Joseph is a devotion that dates back to the seventeenth century, when tradition holds that Saint Joseph appeared to two shipwrecked monks and advised them to pray seven Our Fathers and Hail Marys in honor of his sorrows. Blessed Gennaro Sarnelli (+1744) is credited with popularizing the practice of honoring Saint Joseph's sorrows and including the seven joys as well. The considerations included here are from Pope Saint John Paul II's Apostolic Exhortation on the Person and Mission of Saint Joseph in the Life of Christ and of the Church Redemptoris Custos *(Guardian of the Redeemer).*[14]

To pray the devotion:

1. *Announce the week's sorrow and joy.*
2. *Recite the introductory prayer and read the scripture reading and the consideration.*
3. *Pray one Our Father, one Hail Mary, and one Glory Be.*
4. *Conclude by praying the Litany of Saint Joseph (p. 187).*

First Sunday

His sorrow when he decided to leave the Blessed Virgin; his joy when the angel told him the mystery of the Incarnation.

Introductory Prayer

O chaste spouse of Mary, great was the trouble and anguish of your heart when you were considering quietly sending away your inviolate spouse; yet your joy was unspeakable, when the surpassing mystery of the Incarnation was made known to you by the angel.

By this sorrow and this joy, we beseech you to comfort our souls, both now and in the sorrows of our final hour, with the joy of a good life and a holy death after the pattern of your own life and death in the arms of Jesus and Mary. Amen.

---

[14]John Paul II, apostolic exhortation *Redemptoris Custos* (August 15, 1989), http://www.vatican.va/content/john-paul-ii/en/apost_exhortations/documents/hf_jp-ii_exh_1508 1989_redemptoris-custos.html.

Reading

A reading from the Holy Gospel according to Saint Matthew.
(Mt 1:18–25)

Now the birth of Jesus Christ took place in this way. When his Mother Mary had been betrothed to Joseph, before they came together she was found to be with child of the Holy Spirit; and her husband Joseph, being a just man and unwilling to put her to shame, resolved to send her away quietly.

But as he considered this, behold, an angel of the Lord appeared to him in a dream, saying, "Joseph, son of David, do not fear to take Mary your wife, for that which is conceived in her is of the Holy Spirit; she will bear a son, and you shall call his name Jesus, for he will save his people from their sins."

All this took place to fulfill what the Lord had spoken by the prophet: "Behold, a virgin shall conceive and bear a son, and his name shall be called Emmanuel" (which means, God with us).

When Joseph woke from sleep, he did as the angel of the Lord commanded him; he took his wife, but knew her not until she had borne a son; and he called his name Jesus.

The Gospel of the Lord.

All: Praise to you, Lord Jesus Christ.

Consideration   *(Redemptoris Custos,* no. 3)

There is a strict parallel between the "annunciation" in Matthew's text and the one in Luke. The divine messenger introduces Joseph to the mystery of Mary's motherhood. While remaining a virgin, she who by law is his "spouse" has become a mother through the power of the Holy Spirit. And when the Son in Mary's womb comes into the world, he must receive the name Jesus....

Joseph is visited by the messenger as "Mary's spouse," as the one who in due time must give this name to the Son to be born of the Virgin of Nazareth who is married to him. It is to Joseph, then, that the messenger turns, entrusting to him the responsibilities of an earthly father with regard to Mary's Son.

"When Joseph woke from sleep, he did as the angel of the Lord commanded him and took Mary as his wife" (cf. Mt 1:24). He took her in all the mystery of her motherhood. He took her together with the Son who had come into the world by the power of the Holy Spirit. In this way he showed a readiness of will like Mary's with regard to what God asked of him through the angel.

Pray one Our Father, one Hail Mary, and one Glory Be. Conclude by praying the Litany of Saint Joseph (p. 187).

Second Sunday

His sorrow when he saw Jesus born in poverty; his joy when the angels announced Jesus' birth.

Introductory Prayer

O most blessed patriarch, glorious Saint Joseph, who were chosen to be the foster father of the Word made flesh, your sorrow at seeing the Child Jesus born in such poverty was suddenly changed into heavenly exultation when you heard the angelic hymn and beheld the glories of that resplendent night.

By this sorrow and this joy, we implore you to obtain for us the grace to pass over from life's pathway to hear angelic songs of praise and to rejoice in the shining splendor of celestial glory. Amen.

Reading

A reading from the Holy Gospel according to Saint Luke. (Lk 2:1–20)

In those days a decree went out from Caesar Augustus that all the world should be enrolled. This was the first enrollment, when Quirinius was governor of Syria. And all went to be enrolled, each to his own city. And Joseph also went up from Galilee, from the city of Nazareth, to Judaea, to the city of David, which is called Bethlehem, because he was of the house and lineage of David, to be enrolled with Mary, his betrothed, who was with child. And while they were there, the time came for her to be delivered. And she gave birth to her first-born son and wrapped him in swaddling cloths, and laid him in a manger, because there was no place for them in the inn. And in that region there were shepherds out in the field, keeping watch over their flock by night. And an angel of the Lord appeared to them, and the glory of the Lord shone around them, and they were filled with fear.

And the angel said to them, "Be not afraid; for behold, I bring you good news of a great joy which will come to all the people; for to you is born this day in the city of David a Savior, who is Christ the Lord. And this will be a sign for you: you will find a baby wrapped in swaddling cloths and lying in a manger." And suddenly there was with the angel a multitude of the heavenly host praising God and saying, "Glory to God in the highest, and on earth peace among men with whom he is pleased!"

When the angels went away from them into heaven, the shepherds said to one another, "Let us go over to Bethlehem and see this thing that has happened, which the Lord has made known to us." And they went with haste, and found Mary and Joseph, and the baby lying in a manger. And when they saw it they made known the saying which had been told them concerning this child; and all who heard it wondered at what the shepherds told them. But Mary kept all these things, pondering them in her heart. And the shepherds returned, glorifying and praising God for all they had heard and seen, as it had been told them.

The Gospel of the Lord.

All: Praise to you, Lord Jesus Christ.

Consideration   *(Redemptoris Custos, nos. 9, 10)*

Journeying to Bethlehem for the census in obedience to the orders of legitimate authority, Joseph fulfilled for the child the significant task of officially inserting the name "Jesus, son of Joseph of Nazareth" (cf. Jn 1:45) in the registry of the Roman Empire. This registration clearly shows that Jesus belongs to the human race as a man among men, a citizen of this world, subject to laws and civil institutions, but also "savior of the world." ...

As guardian of the mystery "hidden for ages in the mind of God," which begins to unfold before his eyes "in the fullness of time,"

Joseph, together with Mary, is a privileged witness to the birth of the Son of God into the world on Christmas night in Bethlehem....

Joseph was an eyewitness to this birth, which took place in conditions that, humanly speaking, were embarrassing—a first announcement of that "self-emptying" (cf. Phil 2:5–8) which Christ freely accepted for the forgiveness of sins. Joseph also witnessed the adoration of the shepherds who arrived at Jesus' birthplace after the angel had brought them the great and happy news (cf. Lk 2:15–16). Later he also witnessed the homage of the magi who came from the East (cf. Mt 2:11).

Pray one Our Father, one Hail Mary, and one Glory Be. Conclude by praying the Litany of Saint Joseph (p. 187).

Third Sunday

His sorrow when he saw Jesus' blood shed in circumcision; his joy in giving him the name Jesus.

Introductory Prayer

O glorious Saint Joseph, who faithfully obeyed the law of God, your heart was pierced at the sight of the most precious blood that was shed by the infant Savior during his circumcision, but the name of Jesus gave you new life and filled you with quiet joy.

By this sorrow and this joy, obtain for us the grace to be freed from all sin during life and to die rejoicing, with the Holy Name of Jesus in our hearts and on our lips. Amen.

Reading

A reading from the Holy Gospel according to Saint Luke. (Lk 2:21)

And at the end of eight days, when he was circumcised, he was called Jesus, the name given by the angel before he was conceived in the womb.

The Gospel of the Lord.

All: Praise to you, Lord Jesus Christ.

Consideration *(Redemptoris Custos, nos. 11–12)*

A son's circumcision was the first religious obligation of a father, and with this ceremony (cf. Lk 2:21) Joseph exercised his right and duty with regard to Jesus.

The principle which holds that all the rites of the Old Testament are a shadow of the reality (cf. Heb 9:9f.; 10:1) serves to explain why Jesus would accept them. As with all the other rites, circumcision too is "fulfilled" in Jesus. God's covenant with Abraham, of which circumcision was the sign (cf. Gen 17:13), reaches its full effect and perfect realization in Jesus, who is the "yes" of all the ancient promises (cf. 2 Cor 1:20).

At the circumcision Joseph names the child "Jesus." This is the only name in which there is salvation (cf. Acts 4:12). Its significance had been revealed to Joseph at the moment of his "annunciation": "You shall call the child Jesus, for he will save his people from their sins" (cf. Mt 1:21). In conferring the name, Joseph declares his own legal fatherhood over Jesus, and in speaking the name he proclaims the child's mission as Savior.

Pray one Our Father, one Hail Mary, and one Glory Be. Conclude by praying the Litany of Saint Joseph (p. 187).

Fourth Sunday

His sorrow when he heard the prophecy of Simeon; his joy when he learned that many would be saved through the sufferings of Jesus.

Introductory Prayer

O most faithful Saint Joseph, who shared the mysteries of our redemption, the prophecy of Simeon, touching the sufferings of Jesus and Mary, caused you to shudder with mortal dread but at the same time filled you with a blessed joy for the salvation and glorious resurrection that would be attained by countless souls.

By this sorrow and this joy, obtain for us that we may be of the number of those who, through the merits of Jesus and the intercession of Mary the Virgin Mother, are predestined to a glorious resurrection. Amen.

Reading

A reading from the Holy Gospel according to Saint Luke.
(Lk 2:22–35)

And when the time came for their purification according to the law of Moses, they brought him up to Jerusalem to present him to the Lord (as it is written in the law of the Lord, "Every male that opens the womb shall be called holy to the Lord") and to offer a sacrifice according to what is said in the law of the Lord, "a pair of turtledoves, or two young pigeons."

Now there was a man in Jerusalem, whose name was Simeon, and this man was righteous and devout, looking for the consolation of Israel, and the Holy Spirit was upon him. And it had been revealed to him by the Holy Spirit that he should not see death before he had seen the Lord's Christ. And inspired by the Spirit he came into the Temple; and when the parents brought in the child Jesus, to do for him according to the custom of the law, he took him up in his arms and blessed God and said,

> "Lord, now let your servant depart in peace,
> according to your word;
> for my eyes have seen your salvation
> which you have prepared in the presence of all peoples,
> a light for revelation to the Gentiles,
> and for glory to your people Israel."

And his father and his mother marveled at what was said about him; and Simeon blessed them and said to Mary his mother, "Behold, this child is set for the fall and rising of many in Israel, and for a sign that is spoken against (and a sword will pierce through your own soul also), that thoughts out of many hearts may be revealed."

The Gospel of the Lord.

All: Praise to you, Lord Jesus Christ.

Consideration   (*Redemptoris Custos*, no. 13)

This rite, to which Luke refers (2:22ff.), includes the ransom of the first-born and sheds light on the subsequent stay of Jesus in the Temple at the age of twelve.

The ransoming of the first-born is another obligation of the father, and it is fulfilled by Joseph. Represented in the first-born is the people of the covenant, ransomed from slavery in order to belong to God. Here too, Jesus—who is the true "price" of ransom (cf. 1 Cor 6:20; 7:23; 1 Pet 1:19)—not only "fulfills" the Old Testament rite, but at the same time transcends it, since he is not a subject to be redeemed, but the very author of redemption.

The gospel writer notes that "his father and his mother marveled at what was said about him" (Lk 2:23), in particular at what Simeon said in his canticle to God, when he referred to Jesus as the "salvation which you have prepared in the presence of all peoples, a light for revelation to the Gentiles, and for glory to your people Israel" and as a "sign that is spoken against" (cf. Lk 2:30–34).

Pray one Our Father, one Hail Mary, and one Glory Be. Conclude by praying the Litany of Saint Joseph (p. 187).

Fifth Sunday

His sorrow when he had to flee to Egypt; his joy in being always with Jesus and Mary.

Introductory Prayer

O most watchful guardian of the Son of God, glorious Saint Joseph, great was your toil in supporting and waiting upon the Son of God, especially during the flight into Egypt! Yet, how you rejoiced to have God himself always near you.

By this sorrow and this joy, obtain for us the grace that would keep us safe from the devil, especially the help we need to flee from dangerous situations. May we serve Jesus and Mary, and for them alone may we live and happily die. Amen.

Reading

A reading from the Holy Gospel according to Saint Matthew. (Mt 2:13–15)

Now when they had departed, behold, an angel of the Lord appeared to Joseph in a dream and said, "Rise, take the child and his mother, and flee to Egypt, and remain there till I tell you; for Herod is about to search for the child, to destroy him." And he rose and took the child and his mother by night, and departed to Egypt, and remained there until the death of Herod. This was to fulfill what the Lord had spoken by the prophet, "Out of Egypt have I called my son."

The Gospel of the Lord.

All: Praise to you, Lord Jesus Christ.

Consideration   (*Redemptoris Custos*, no. 14)

A very important event took place before the return to Galilee, an event in which divine providence once again had recourse to Joseph. We read: "Now when [the magi] had departed, behold, an angel of the Lord appeared to Joseph in a dream and said, 'Rise, take the child and his mother, and flee to Egypt, and remain there till I tell you; for Herod is about to search for the child, to destroy him'" (Mt 2:13). Herod learned from the magi who came from the East about the birth of the "king of the Jews" (Mt 2:2). And when the magi departed, he "sent and killed all the male children in Bethlehem and in all that region who were two years old or under" (Mt 2:16). By killing them all, he wished to kill the new-born "king of the Jews" whom he had heard about. And so, Joseph, having been warned in a dream, "took the child and his mother by night, and departed to Egypt, and remained there until the death of Herod. This was to ful-fill what the Lord had spoken by the prophet, 'Out of Egypt have I called my son'" (Mt 2:14–15; cf. Hos 11:1).

And so Jesus' way back to Nazareth from Bethlehem passed through Egypt. Just as Israel had followed the path of the exodus "from the condition of slavery" in order to begin the Old Covenant, so Joseph, guardian and cooperator in the providential mystery of God, even in exile watched over the one who brings about the New Covenant.

Pray one Our Father, one Hail Mary, and one Glory Be. Conclude by pray-ing the Litany of Saint Joseph (p. 187).

Sixth Sunday

His sorrow when he was afraid to return to his homeland; his joy on being told by the angel to go to Nazareth.

Introductory Prayer

O glorious Saint Joseph, you marveled to see the King of heaven obedient to your commands. Your consolation in bringing Jesus out of the land of Egypt was troubled by your fear of Archelaus. Nevertheless, being assured by an angel, you lived in gladness at Nazareth with Jesus and Mary.

By this sorrow and this joy, obtain for us that our hearts may be delivered from harmful fears, so that we may rejoice in peace of conscience and may live with Jesus and Mary, and, like you, may die in their company. Amen.

Reading

A reading from the Holy Gospel according to Saint Matthew and Saint Luke.   (Mt 2:19–23; Lk 2:40)

But when Herod died, behold, an angel of the Lord appeared in a dream to Joseph in Egypt, saying, "Rise, take the child and his mother, and go to the land of Israel, for those who sought the child's life are dead." And he rose and took the child and his mother, and went to the land of Israel. But when he heard that Archelaus reigned over Judaea in place of his father Herod, he was afraid to go there, and being warned in a dream he withdrew to the district of Galilee. And he went and dwelt in a city called Nazareth, that what was spoken by the prophets might be fulfilled, "He shall be called a Nazarene."

And the child grew and became strong, filled with wisdom; and the favor of God was upon him.

The Gospel of the Lord.

All: Praise to you, Lord Jesus Christ.

Consideration   (*Redemptoris Custos*, nos. 21–22)

This bond of charity was the core of the Holy Family's life, first in the poverty of Bethlehem, then in their exile in Egypt, and later in the house of Nazareth. The Church deeply venerates this Family, and proposes it as the model of all families. Inserted directly in the mystery of the Incarnation, the Family of Nazareth has its own special mystery. And in this mystery, as in the Incarnation, one finds a true fatherhood: the human form of the family of the Son of God, a true human family, formed by the divine mystery. In this family, Joseph is the father: his fatherhood is not one that derives from begetting offspring; but neither is it an "apparent" or merely "substitute" fatherhood. Rather, it is one that fully shares in authentic human fatherhood and the mission of a father in the family....

Work was the daily expression of love in the life of the Family of Nazareth. The Gospel specifies the kind of work Joseph did in order to support his family: he was a carpenter. This simple word sums up Joseph's entire life.... Having learned the work of his presumed father, [Jesus] was known as "the carpenter's son." If the Family of Nazareth is an example and model for human families, in the order of salvation and holiness, so too, by analogy, is Jesus' work at the side of Joseph the carpenter. In our own day, the Church has emphasized this by instituting the liturgical memorial of St. Joseph the Worker on May 1. Human work, and especially manual labor, receive special prominence in the Gospel. Along with the humanity of the Son of God, work too has been taken up in the mystery of the Incarnation, and has also been redeemed in a special way. At the workbench where he plied his trade together with Jesus, Joseph brought human work closer to the mystery of the Redemption.

Pray one Our Father, one Hail Mary, and one Glory Be. Conclude by praying the Litany of Saint Joseph (p. 187).

Seventh Sunday

His sorrow when he lost the Child Jesus; his joy in finding him in the temple.

Introductory Prayer

O glorious Saint Joseph, pattern of all holiness, when you lost the Child Jesus, you sought him sorrowing for the space of three days, until with great joy you found him again in the temple, sitting in the midst of the doctors.

By this sorrow and this joy, we ask you, with our hearts upon our lips, to keep us from ever having the misfortune of losing Jesus through mortal sin. Grant also that we always may seek him with unceasing sorrow, when we commit a serious sin, until we find him again, ready to show us his great mercy in the sacrament of reconciliation. Amen.

Reading

A reading from the Holy Gospel according to Saint Luke. (Lk 2:41–50)

Now his parents went to Jerusalem every year at the feast of the Passover. And when he was twelve years old, they went up according to custom; and when the feast was ended, as they were returning, the boy Jesus stayed behind in Jerusalem. His parents did not know it, but supposing him to be in the company, they went a day's journey, and they sought him among their kinsfolk and acquaintances; and when they did not find him, they returned to Jerusalem, seeking him. After three days they found him in the temple, sitting among the teachers, listening to them and asking them questions; and all who heard him were amazed at his understanding and his answers. And when they saw him they were astonished; and his mother said to him, "Son, why have you treated us so? Behold, your father and I have been looking for you anxiously."

And he said to them, "How is it that you sought me? Did you not know that I must be in my Father's house?" And they did not understand the saying which he spoke to them.

The Gospel of the Lord.

All: Praise to you, Lord Jesus Christ.

Consideration (*Redemptoris Custos*, nos. 15–16)

Joseph, of whom Mary had just used the words "your father," heard this answer. That, after all, is what all the people said and thought: Jesus was the son (as was supposed) of Joseph (Lk 3:23). Nonetheless, the reply of Jesus in the Temple brought once again to the mind of his "presumed father" what he had heard on that night twelve years earlier: "Joseph ... do not fear to take Mary your wife, for that which is conceived in her is of the Holy Spirit." From that time onwards he knew that he was a guardian of the mystery of God, and it was precisely this mystery that the twelve-year-old Jesus brought to mind: "I must be in my Father's house."

The growth of Jesus "in wisdom and in stature, and in favor with God and man" (Lk 2:52) took place within the Holy Family under the eyes of Joseph, who had the important task of "raising" Jesus, that is, feeding, clothing and educating him in the Law and in a trade, in keeping with the duties of a father.

In the Eucharistic Sacrifice, the Church venerates the memory of Mary the ever Virgin Mother of God and the memory of St. Joseph, because "he fed him whom the faithful must eat as the bread of eternal life."

For his part, Jesus "was obedient to them" (Lk 2:51), respectfully returning the affection of his "parents." In this way he wished to sanctify the obligations of the family and of work, which he performed at the side of Joseph.

Pray one Our Father, one Hail Mary, and one Glory Be. Conclude by praying the Litany of Saint Joseph (p. 187).

5

February

Prayer after Blessing before Meals:
Prayer to the Holy Family[1]

Lord Jesus Christ, who, being made subject to Mary and Joseph, did consecrate domestic life by your ineffable virtues; grant that we, with the assistance of both, may be taught by the example of your Holy Family and may attain to its everlasting fellowship. Who lives and reigns, world without end. Amen.

Consecration to the Holy Family[2]

A plenary indulgence is granted to the members of a family on the day it is first consecrated to the Holy Family, if they devoutly recite the duly approved prayer before an image of Jesus, Mary, and Joseph. If at all possible, the consecration should be performed by a priest or deacon. On the anniversary of the consecration, the prayer can be recited again for a partial indulgence.[3]

O Jesus, our most loving Redeemer, who having come to enlighten the world with your teaching and example, willed to pass the greater part of your life in humility and subjection to Mary and Joseph in the poor home in Nazareth, thus sanctifying the Family that was to be an example for all Christian families, graciously receive our family as it dedicates and consecrates itself to you this day. Defend us, guard us, and establish among us your holy fear, true peace, and concord in Christian love: in order that, by conforming ourselves to the divine

---

[1] *Raccolta*, no. 276.

[2] Ibid., no. 706.

[3] *Manual of Indulgences*, grant 1. See the introduction of this book for the usual conditions for indulgences.

pattern of your family, we may be able, all of us without exception, to attain to eternal happiness.

Mary, dear Mother of Jesus and Mother of us, by your kindly intercession make this our humble offering acceptable in the sight of Jesus, and obtain for us his graces and blessings.

O Saint Joseph, most holy guardian of Jesus and Mary, assist us by your prayers in all our spiritual and temporal necessities, so that we may be enabled to praise our divine Savior Jesus, together with Mary and you, for all eternity.

Our Father, Hail Mary, Glory Be (three times each).

February 1: Saint Brigid of Ireland (Optional Memorial)

COLLECT PRAYER

Almighty ever-living God, direct our actions according to your good pleasure, that in the name of your beloved Son we may abound in good works. Through our Lord Jesus Christ, your Son, who lives and reigns with you in the unity of the Holy Spirit, one God, for ever and ever. Amen.

Saint Brigid's House Prayer

May Saint Brigid's prayers bless the house wherein we dwell. Bless every fireside, every wall and door. Bless every heart that beats beneath its roof. Bless every hand that toils to bring it joy. Bless every foot that walks its portals through. May Saint Brigid's prayers bless the house that shelters us. Amen.

Blessing of Cheese and Butter[4]

Saint Brigid is the patron saint of dairy maids. She is said to have given away to a poor man the butter she had churned for her master, only to have the butter miraculously restore itself before she could get in trouble!

[4]J. H. Schlarman, trans., *With the Blessing of the Church* (Des Moines, Iowa: National Catholic Rural Life Conference, 1946), Eternal Word Television Network, https://www.ewtn.com/catholicism/library/with-the-blessing-of-the-church-11899. This work contains translations of various blessings in the *Roman Ritual.*

O Lord, almighty God, deign to bless and sanctify this cheese (or butter), which you have produced from the fat of animals, that whoever of your faithful people eat of it may be filled with every heavenly blessing and your grace, and may abound in good works. Through Christ our Lord. Amen.

February 2: Candlemas (The Presentation of the Lord) (Feast)

COLLECT PRAYER

Almighty ever-living God, we humbly implore your majesty that, just as your Only Begotten Son was presented on this day in the Temple in the substance of our flesh, so, by your grace, we may be presented to you with minds made pure. Through our Lord Jesus Christ, your Son, who lives and reigns with you in the unity of the Holy Spirit, one God, for ever and ever. Amen.

A reading from the Holy Gospel according to Saint Luke. (Lk 2:22–38)

And when the time came for their purification according to the law of Moses, they brought him up to Jerusalem to present him to the Lord (as it is written in the law of the Lord, "Every male that opens the womb shall be called holy to the Lord") and to offer a sacrifice according to what is said in the law of the Lord, "a pair of turtledoves, or two young pigeons." Now there was a man in Jerusalem, whose name was Simeon, and this man was righteous and devout, looking for the consolation of Israel, and the Holy Spirit was upon him. And it had been revealed to him by the Holy Spirit that he should not see death before he had seen the Lord's Christ. And inspired by the Spirit he came into the temple; and when the parents brought in the child Jesus, to do for him according to the custom of the law, he took him up in his arms and blessed God and said,

> "Lord, now let your servant depart in peace,
> according to your word;
> for my eyes have seen your salvation
> which you have prepared in the presence of all peoples,
> a light for revelation to the Gentiles,
> and for glory to your people Israel."

And his father and his mother marveled at what was said about him; and Simeon blessed them and said to Mary his mother,

"Behold, this child is set for the fall and rising of many in Israel,
and for a sign that is spoken against
(and a sword will pierce through your own soul also),
that thoughts out of many hearts may be revealed."

And there was a prophetess, Anna, the daughter of Phanu-el, of the tribe of Asher; she was of a great age, having lived with her husband seven years from her virginity, and as a widow till she was eighty-four. She did not depart from the temple, worshiping with fasting and prayer night and day. And coming up at that very hour she gave thanks to God, and spoke of him to all who were looking for the redemption of Jerusalem.

The Gospel of the Lord.

All: Praise to you, Lord Jesus Christ.

Prayer for the Lighting of Candles[5]

Jesus is the light of the world, so this is the day when the Church blesses candles for use on the altar throughout the year. Traditionally, families bring their own candles to church to be blessed by a priest or deacon on this day and then use them in their homes. Candles with at least 51 percent beeswax are required for use on the altar. Beeswax candles are also preferred, but not required, for sacramental use in the home. This prayer can be used when lighting a candle for prayer, devotion, study, or meals, whether or not the candle has been blessed.

My Lord Jesus Christ, Son of the living God, I humbly beseech you to scatter the darkness of my mind and to give me lively faith, firm hope, and burning love. Grant, O my God, that I may know you well and may do all things in your light and in conformity to your holy will. Amen.

See also Nunc Dimittis (Canticle of Simeon), p. 330.

SONG SUGGESTION: This Little Light of Mine

---

[5] *Raccolta*, no. 106.

ORDINARY TIME BEGINS

Marian Antiphon II: Ave Regina Caelorum

This is the Marian antiphon sung, chanted, or recited after Compline (Night Prayer) during Ordinary Time after Candlemas and through Lent, until the Easter Vigil. By an unknown author, it has been in use since at least the twelfth century.

Ave regina caelorum, ave domina angelorum: salve radix, salve porta, ex qua mundo lux est orta: Gaude Virgo, gloriosa, super omnes speciosa, vale o valde decora, et pro nobis Christum exora.

Hail, Queen of Heaven, hail Lady of the Angels. Hail, root, hail the door through which the Light of the world is risen. Rejoice, glorious Virgin, beautiful above all. Hail, O very fair one, and plead for us to Christ.[6]

February 3: Saint Blaise, Bishop and Martyr (Optional Memorial)

COLLECT PRAYER

Hear, O Lord, the supplications your people make under the patronage of the Martyr Saint Blaise, and grant that they may rejoice in peace in this present life, and find help for life eternal. Through our Lord Jesus Christ, your Son, who lives and reigns with you in the unity of the Holy Spirit, one God, for ever and ever. Amen.

Blessing of Throats[7]

Saint Blaise is remembered for—among many holy acts—having miraculously healed a boy who was choking on a fishbone. Therefore, the traditional Catholic practice for his feast day is the blessing of the throats. The blessing is

---

[6] English translation by Rudolph Masciantonio, president of the Philadelphia Latin Liturgy Association. Lucy E. Carroll, "Singing the Four Seasonal Marian Anthems", *Adoremus Bulletin*, September 15, 2007, https://adoremus.org/2007/09/15/singing-the-four-seasonal-marian-anthems/.

[7] *Book of Blessings*, Shorter Rite of the Blessing of Throats, nos. 1651, 1652, 1655.

given by touching the throat of each person present with two candles blessed on Candlemas, which have been tied together in the middle to form a cross. It's best to have the blessing given by a priest or deacon in a church, but if that's not possible, this shorter version of the blessing of throats is authorized for use by laypeople and in homes.

All make the sign of the cross.

Leader: Our help is in the name of the Lord.

All: Who made heaven and earth.

A reading from the Holy Gospel according to Saint Mark.
(Mk 16:15–20, NAB)

They will place their hands on the sick and they will recover. Jesus said to the eleven, "Go into the whole world and proclaim the gospel to every creature. Whoever believes and is baptized will be saved; whoever does not believe will be condemned. These signs will accompany those who believe: in my name they will drive out demons, they will speak new languages. They will pick up serpents with their hands, and if they drink any deadly thing, it will not harm them. They will lay hands on the sick, and they will recover."

A lay minister touches the throat of each person with the crossed candles and, without making the sign of the cross, says the prayer of blessing.

Through the intercession of Saint Blaise, bishop and martyr, may God deliver you from every disease of the throat and from every other illness: In the name of the Father, and of the Son, and of the Holy Spirit.

Each person responds: Amen.

The blessing may conclude with a suitable song.

See The Doxology (hymn), p. 326.

February 5: Saint Agatha, Virgin and Martyr (Memorial)

COLLECT PRAYER

May the Virgin Martyr Saint Agatha implore your compassion for us, O Lord, we pray, for she found favor with you by the courage of her martyrdom and the merit of her chastity. Through our Lord Jesus Christ, your Son, who lives and reigns with you in the unity of the Holy Spirit, one God, for ever and ever. Amen.

For Healing of Breast Cancer

Saint Agatha endured many tortures for her Christian faith, including having her breasts cut off. She was then sent to prison, where Saint Peter the apostle appeared to her and healed her wounds. She is a patron saint of people suffering from breast cancer, and of nurses.

Saint Agatha, woman of valor, from your own suffering we have been moved to ask your prayers for those of us who suffer from breast cancer. We place [name(s)] before you and ask you to intercede on [her/their] behalf. From where you stand in the health of life eternal—all wounds healed, and all tears wiped away—pray for [name(s)], and for all of us. Pray that God will give us his holy benediction of health and healing.

We remember that you were a victim of torture and that you learned, firsthand, of human cruelty and inhumanity. We ask you to pray for our entire world. Ask God to enlighten us with a genius for peace and understanding. Ask him to send us his spirit of serenity, and ask him to help us share that peace with all we meet. From what you learned from your own path of pain, ask God to give us the grace we need to remain holy in difficulties, not allowing our anger or our bitterness to overtake us. Pray that we will be more peaceful and more charitable. And from your holy place in Christ's mystical body, the Church, pray that we, in our place and time, will, together, create a world of justice and peace. Amen.

Prayer for Nurses

O merciful Father, who have wonderfully fashioned man in your own image, and have made his body to be a temple of the Holy Spirit, sanctify, we pray you, our nurses and all those whom you have called to study and practice the arts of healing the sick and the prevention of disease and pain. Strengthen them in body and soul, and bless their work, that they may give comfort to those for whose salvation your Son became man, lived on this earth, healed the sick, and suffered and died on the cross. Amen.

February 6: Saint Paul Miki and Companions, Martyrs (Memorial)

COLLECT PRAYER

O God, strength of all the Saints, who through the Cross were pleased to call the Martyrs Saint Paul Miki and companions to life, grant, we pray, that by their intercession we may hold with courage even until death to the faith that we profess. Through our Lord Jesus Christ, your Son, who lives and reigns with you in the unity of the Holy Spirit, one God, for ever and ever. Amen.

Saint Paul Miki's Words from the Cross[8]

I am a true Japanese. The only reason for my being killed is that I have taught the doctrine of Christ. I certainly did teach the doctrine of Christ. I thank God it is for this reason I die. I believe that I am telling only the truth before I die. I know you believe me and I want to say to you all once again: Ask Christ to help you to become happy. I obey Christ. After Christ's example I forgive my persecutors. I do not hate them. I ask God to have pity on all, and I hope my blood will fall on my fellow men as a fruitful rain.

Prayer for Courage

God our Father, source of strength for all your saints, you led Paul Miki and his companions through the suffering of the cross to the joy of eternal life. May their prayers give us courage to be loyal until

---

[8] "Saint Paul Miki and Companions", Franciscan Media, https://www.franciscanmedia.org /saint-paul-miki-and-companions/. From Leonard Foley and Patrick McCloskey, *Saint of the Day: The Definitive Guide to the Saints* (Cincinnati, Ohio: Franciscan Media, 2018).

death in professing our faith. Through Jesus Christ, your Son, who lives and reigns with you in the unity of the Holy Spirit, one God, forever and ever. Amen.

February 8: Saint Josephine Bakhita, Virgin (Optional Memorial)

COLLECT PRAYER

O God, who led Saint Josephine Bakhita from abject slavery to the dignity of being your daughter and a bride of Christ, grant, we pray, that by her example we may show constant love for the Lord Jesus crucified, remaining steadfast in charity and prompt to show compassion. Through our Lord Jesus Christ, your Son, who lives and reigns with you in the unity of the Holy Spirit, one God, for ever and ever. Amen.

Prayer to Saint Josephine Bakhita[9]

Saint Josephine Bakhita, you were sold into slavery as a child
and endured untold hardship and suffering.
Once liberated from your physical enslavement,
you found true redemption in your encounter with Christ and his
    Church.
O Saint Bakhita, assist all those who are trapped in a state of slavery;
intercede with God on their behalf
so that they will be released from their chains of captivity.
Those whom man enslaves, let God set free.
Provide comfort to survivors of slavery
and let them look to you as an example of hope and faith.
Help all survivors find healing from their wounds.
We ask for your prayers and intercessions for those enslaved among
    us.
Amen.

[9] Migration and Refugee Services, United States Conference of Catholic Bishops, "Prayer to St. Josephine Bakhita", prayer card (2011), https://www.usccb.org/about/migration-and-refugee-services/national-migration-week/upload/M7-266-Josephine-Bakhita-Prayer-Card.pdf.

Words of Saint Josephine Bakhita[10]

If I were to meet those who kidnapped me, and even those who tortured me, I would kneel and kiss their hands. For, if these things had not happened, I would not have been a Christian and a religious today.

February 11: Our Lady of Lourdes (Optional Memorial)

COLLECT PRAYER

Grant us, O merciful God, protection in our weakness, that we, who keep the Memorial of the Immaculate Mother of God, may, with the help of her intercession, rise up from our iniquities. Through our Lord Jesus Christ, your Son, who lives and reigns with you in the unity of the Holy Spirit, one God, for ever and ever. Amen.

Prayer to Be Said When Using Lourdes Water

Blessed be the Holy and Immaculate Conception of the Blessed Virgin Mary, Mother of God.
Our Lady of Lourdes, pray for us. Mother, have mercy on us.
Our Lady of Lourdes, heal us for the greater glory of the Holy Trinity.
Our Lady of Lourdes, heal us for the greater glory of our Lord Jesus Christ.
Our Lady of Lourdes, heal the sick, convert sinners.
Health of the sick, help of the suffering, pray for us.
Mary, conceived without sin, pray for us who have recourse to you.
Saint Bernadette, pray for us! Amen.

Pilgrim's Prayer of Saint James

We like to make a family pilgrimage twice a year, usually in February in honor of Our Lady of Lourdes, and in May in honor of the month of Our

[10] Pontifical University Urbaniana, "Goodness and Missionary Zeal", http://www.vatican.va/spirit/documents/spirit_20010112_bakhita_en.html.

Lady. This ancient prayer is associated with the Camino de Santiago de Compostela pilgrimage in Spain and makes an excellent start to any pilgrimage. It's also appropriate for the feast of Saint James the Greater on July 25.

O God, who brought your servant Abraham out of the land of the Chaldeans, protecting him in his wandering across the desert, we ask that you watch over us, your servants, as we walk in the love of your name to *(destination)*.

> Be for us our companion on the walk,
> Our guide at the crossroads,
> Our breath in our weariness,
> Our protection in danger,
> Our home on the Camino,
> Our shade in the heat,
> Our light in the darkness,
> Our consolation in our discouragements,
> And our strength in our intentions,

so that with your guidance we may arrive safe and sound at the end of the road and, enriched with grace and virtue, return safely to our homes, filled with joy.

In the name of Jesus Christ our Lord. Amen.

Saint James the apostle, pray for us.

Mary, Mother of God, pray for us.

See also Litany of Loreto, p. 52; Immaculate Mary (hymn), p. 241; Rosary, p. 363.

February 14: Saints Cyril, Monk, and Methodius, Bishop (Optional Memorial) / Saint Valentine (Historical)

COLLECT PRAYER

O God, who enlightened the Slavic peoples through the brothers Saints Cyril and Methodius, grant that our hearts may grasp the words of your teaching, and perfect us as a people of one accord in true faith and right confession. Through our Lord Jesus Christ, your Son, who lives and reigns with you in the unity of the Holy Spirit, one God, for ever and ever. Amen.

COLLECT PRAYER[11]

Grant, we beseech you, almighty God: that we, who celebrate the heavenly birthday of blessed Valentine, your martyr, may, through his intercession, be strengthened in the love of your name. Through our Lord Jesus Christ, your Son, who lives and reigns with you in the unity of the Holy Spirit, one God, for ever and ever. Amen.

A reading from the First Letter of Saint Paul to the Corinthians. (1 Cor 13)

If I speak in the tongues of men and of angels, but have not love, I am a noisy gong or a clanging cymbal. And if I have prophetic powers, and understand all mysteries and all knowledge, and if I have all faith, so as to remove mountains, but have not love, I am nothing. If I give away all I have, and if I deliver my body to be burned, but have not love, I gain nothing.

Love is patient and kind; love is not jealous or boastful; it is not arrogant or rude. Love does not insist on its own way; it is not irritable or resentful; it does not rejoice at wrong, but rejoices in the right. Love bears all things, believes all things, hopes all things, endures all things.

Love never ends; as for prophecies, they will pass away; as for tongues, they will cease; as for knowledge, it will pass away. For our knowledge is imperfect and our prophecy is imperfect; but when the perfect comes, the imperfect will pass away. When I was a child, I spoke like a child, I thought like a child, I reasoned like a child; when I became a man, I gave up childish ways. For now we see in a mirror dimly, but then face to face. Now I know in part; then I shall understand fully, even as I have been fully understood. So faith, hope, love abide, these three; but the greatest of these is love.

SONG SUGGESTIONS: *Love Divine, All Loves Excelling; The King of Love*

---

[11] Gaspar Lefebvre, *Saint Andrew Daily Missal* (1945).

February 22: The Chair of Saint Peter the Apostle (Feast)

COLLECT PRAYER

Grant, we pray, almighty God, that no tempests may disturb us, for you have set us fast on the rock of the Apostle Peter's confession of faith. Through our Lord Jesus Christ, your Son, who lives and reigns with you in the unity of the Holy Spirit, one God, for ever and ever. Amen.

A reading from the Holy Gospel according to Saint Matthew. (Mt 16:13–19)

Now when Jesus came into the district of Caesarea Philippi, he asked his disciples, "Who do men say that the Son of man is?" And they said, "Some say John the Baptist, others say Elijah, and others Jeremiah or one of the prophets." He said to them, "But who do you say that I am?" Simon Peter replied, "You are the Christ, the Son of the living God." And Jesus answered him, "Blessed are you, Simon Bar-Jona! For flesh and blood has not revealed this to you, but my Father who is in heaven. And I tell you, you are Peter, and on this rock I will build my Church, and the gates of Hades shall not prevail against it. I will give you the keys of the kingdom of heaven, and whatever you bind on earth shall be bound in heaven, and whatever you loose on earth shall be loosed in heaven."

The Gospel of the Lord.

All: Praise to you, Lord Jesus Christ.

Prayer for the Pope

In 2012 Pope Benedict XVI described the Chair of Saint Peter as "a symbol of the special mission of Peter and his Successors to tend Christ's flock, keeping it united in faith and in charity".[12] This is a special day to pray for the pope and his mission.

[12] Benedict XVI, Angelus Message (February 19, 2012), http://www.vatican.va/content/benedict-xvi/en/angelus/2012/documents/hf_ben-xvi_ang_20120219.html.

Lord, source of eternal life and truth, give to your shepherd, Pope *(name)*, a spirit of courage and right judgment, a spirit of knowledge and love. By governing with fidelity those entrusted to his care may he, as successor to the apostle Peter and vicar of Christ, build your Church into a sacrament of unity, love, and peace for all the world. We ask this through our Lord Jesus Christ, your Son, who lives and reigns with you and the Holy Spirit, one God, forever and ever. Amen.

See also On Saint Peter and Saint John, p. 100.

Forty-seven Days before Easter: Fat Tuesday (Mardi Gras, Shrove Tuesday)

In anticipation of the solemn days of Lent to come, in our family we observe Fat Tuesday (Mardi Gras in French and Shrove Tuesday in much of the English-speaking world outside the United States). We celebrate with food and treats and fun. At the end of the evening's festive activities comes the beautiful and meaningful (but still awfully fun) tradition of burying the Alleluia.

Burying the Alleluia

During the penitential season of Lent, the joyful declaration of "Alleluia" (Praise the Lord in Hebrew) is omitted from all liturgies. It will return triumphantly at Easter, when the Resurrection is proclaimed. We can "bury the Alleluia" as a symbolic gesture on the eve of Lent, to focus ourselves on the somberness of the season about to begin.

The depositio *(discontinuance) of the Alleluia during Lent is a tradition that dates back to at least the medieval era.[13] Thirteenth-century bishop William Duranti wrote in his commentaries on the Divine Office: "We part from the alleluia as from a beloved friend, whom we embrace many times and kiss on the mouth, head, and hand, before we leave him."[14]*

---

[13] In earlier eras the burial of the Alleluia would take place on the eve of Septuagesima Sunday, the ninth Sunday before Easter, which began a three-week period of pre-Lent preparation.

[14] Francis X. Weiser, *Handbook of Christian Feasts and Customs* (New York: Harcourt, Brace and Company, 1952), https://archive.org/stream/WeiserChristianFeastsandCustoms/Weiser--ChristianFeastsandCustoms_djvu.txt.

A family can create a symbolic Alleluia by writing the word on wood, fabric, or paper. After kissing it goodbye, if desired, place it in a bag or box. Holding the bag or box wide open while singing an Alleluia hymn (such as the refrain from "Ye Sons and Daughters") everyone parades to a burial spot and says a prayer of farewell.

Alleluia Farewell Prayer[15]

Stay with us today, Alleluia, and tomorrow you shall part.
When the morning rises, you shall go your way.
Alleluia, alleluia.
The mountains and hills shall rejoice, Alleluia, while they await your
     glory.
You go, Alleluia; may your way be blessed, until you shall return
     with joy.
Alleluia, alleluia, alleluia.

After the last three Alleluias are said (or shouted), the bag or box is closed to trap them inside. It is buried in the ground, and the spot is marked. (The spot must be well marked so that the Alleluia can be dug up on Easter morning.) A verse or two from a Lenten hymn such as "The Glory of These Forty Days" makes an excellent end to the ceremony.

The Glory of These Forty Days

This is a 1906 translation by Maurice F. Bell (1862–1947) of the sixth-century Latin hymn Clarum decus jejunii, *attributed to Pope Saint Gregory the Great (540–604). It is traditionally sung at Matins (prayer during the night) during Lent.*

1. The glory of these forty days
   we celebrate with songs of praise,
   for Christ, through whom all things were made,
   himself has fasted and has prayed.

2. Alone and fasting Moses saw
   the loving God who gave the law,
   and to Elijah, fasting, came
   the steeds and chariots of flame.

---

[15] Ibid.

3. So Daniel trained his mystic sight,
   delivered from the lions' might,
   and John, the Bridegroom's friend, became
   the herald of Messiah's name.

4. Then grant us, Lord, like them to be
   full oft in fast and prayer with thee;
   our spirits strengthen with thy grace,
   and give us joy to see thy face.

5. O Father, Son and Spirit blest,
   to thee be every prayer addressed,
   who art in threefold name adored,
   from age to age, the only Lord.

6

Movable Feasts: Lent

Lent begins on Ash Wednesday, which is a movable holy day in February or March, forty-six days before Easter Sunday (see appendix B for dates in upcoming years).

Prayer after Blessing before Meals I: Counting to Forty

In our home during Lent, we count to forty after grace before we eat. This is a small sacrifice the family can make together, and a reminder that it is Lent. It's also how all our kids have learned to count past twenty.

or

Prayer after Blessing before Meals: The Jesus Prayer

Lord Jesus Christ, Son of God, have mercy on me, a sinner. Amen.

Forty-Six Days before Easter: Ash Wednesday

Ash Wednesday is a day of required fasting and abstinence. The spring Ember Days—voluntary days of fasting and abstinence—fall on the Wednesday, Friday, and Saturday the week after Ash Wednesday.[1] This season's days are offered for the flower harvest and recall our baptism. Saturday is also offered as a day of prayer for priests and for vocations. See Ember Days

---

[1] For more on Ember Days, vigils, and general fasting and abstinence requirements and recommendations, see appendix A of *The Catholic All Year Compendium.*

Prayer, p. 57; Farmer's Prayer, p. 235; Blessing for the Products of Nature, p. 124; Prayer for Priests, p. 102; Prayer for Vocations, p. 357.

COLLECT

Grant, O Lord, that we may begin with holy fasting this campaign of Christian service, so that, as we take up battle against spiritual evils, we may be armed with weapons of self-restraint. Through our Lord Jesus Christ, your Son, who lives and reigns with you in the unity of the Holy Spirit, one God, for ever and ever. Amen.

Prayer for Fasting

Lord, give us grace to inaugurate with holy fasting the defenses of Christian warfare, so that we who are to fight against spiritual wickedness, may be helped and strengthened by self-denial. Amen.

A reading from the book of the prophet Joel.
(Joel 2:12–19, NAB)

> Even now, says the LORD,
>   return to me with your whole heart,
>   with fasting, and weeping, and mourning;
> Rend your hearts, not your garments,
>   and return to the LORD, your God.
> For gracious and merciful is he,
>   slow to anger, rich in kindness,
>   and relenting in punishment.
> Perhaps he will again relent
>   and leave behind him a blessing,
> Offerings and libations
>   for the LORD, your God.
>
> Blow the trumpet in Zion!
>   proclaim a fast,
>   call an assembly;
> Gather the people,
>   notify the congregation;

Assemble the elders,
   gather the children
   and the infants at the breast;
Let the bridegroom quit his room
   and the bride her chamber.
Between the porch and the altar
   let the priests, the ministers of the LORD, weep,
And say, "Spare, O LORD, your people,
   and make not your heritage a reproach,
   with the nations ruling over them!
Why should they say among the peoples,
   'Where is their God?'"

Then the LORD was stirred to concern for his land
   and took pity on his people.

The Word of the Lord.

All: Thanks be to God.

A reading from the Holy Gospel according to Saint Matthew.
(Mt 6:16–21)

"And when you fast, do not look dismal, like the hypocrites, for they disfigure their faces that their fasting may be seen by men. Truly, I say to you, they have their reward. But when you fast, anoint your head and wash your face, that your fasting may not be seen by men but by your Father who is in secret; and your Father who sees in secret will reward you.

"Do not lay up for yourselves treasures on earth, where moth and rust consume and where thieves break in and steal, but lay up for yourselves treasures in heaven, where neither moth nor rust consumes and where thieves do not break in and steal. For where your treasure is, there will your heart be also."

The Gospel of the Lord.

All: Praise to you, Lord Jesus Christ.

LENT SONG SUGGESTIONS: Stabat Mater; *Forty Days and Forty Nights*; Parce Domine

Fridays in Lent

Prayer to Our Lord Jesus Christ Crucified
(*En ego, O bone et dulcissime Iesu*)[2]

The Manual of Indulgences *states: "A plenary indulgence is granted to the faithful who on any of the Fridays of Lent devoutly recite after Communion the prayer* En ego, O bone et dulcissime Iesu *before a crucifix."*[3]

Behold, O good and loving Jesus, that I cast myself on my knees before you, and with the greatest fervor of spirit, I pray and beseech you to instill into my heart ardent sentiments of faith, hope, and charity, with true repentance for my sins and a most firm purpose of amendment. With deep affection and sorrow I ponder intimately and contemplate in my mind your five wounds, having before my eyes what the prophet David had already put in your mouth about yourself, O good Jesus: They have pierced my hands and my feet; they have numbered all my bones (Ps 21:17–18).

Stations of the Cross

The Stations of the Cross are a devotion dating back to the late Middle Ages, in which pilgrims to the Holy Land would follow the "Way of the Cross" in Jerusalem, tracing Jesus' actual path to Mount Calvary. Eventually, the Franciscans in Europe began to build replica paths of a varying number of stations along the roads to churches. In the eighteenth century Pope Clement XII fixed the number of stations at fourteen and gave permission for them to be installed within churches.

According to the 2006 Manual of Indulgences,[4] *an indulgence (subject to the usual conditions) is granted to the faithful who make the Way of the Cross any day of the year. To make the Way of the Cross is defined as "to meditate devoutly on the Lord's Passion and Death". To make the indulgence*

---

[2] *Roman Missal*, Thanksgiving after Mass.

[3] *Manual of Indulgences*, grant 8.1.2. See the introduction of this book for the usual conditions for indulgences.

[4] *Manual of Indulgences*, grant 13.2. See the introduction of this book for the usual conditions for indulgences.

plenary (or full), the pious exercise must be made before stations of the Way of the Cross legitimately erected. For the erection of the Way of the Cross, fourteen crosses are required. (It is customary to add fourteen images, which represent the stations of Jerusalem.) In common practice, praying the Stations of the Cross includes a reading and vocal prayers at each station. However, nothing more is required than a pious meditation on the Passion and death of the Lord. A movement from one station to the next is required if possible.

These meditations are adapted from those composed by Saint Alphonsus Liguori (+1787).

Make the sign of the cross and, with a contrite heart, form the intention of gaining an indulgence, for yourself or the soul of another.

Opening Prayer

All: My Lord Jesus Christ,
you have made this journey to die for me with unspeakable love;
and I have so many times ungratefully abandoned you. But now I
    love you with all my heart;
and, because I love you, I am sincerely sorry for ever having offended
    you.
Pardon me, my God, and permit me to accompany you on this journey.
You go to die for love of me;
I want, my beloved Redeemer, to die for love of you.
My Jesus, I will live and die always united to you. Amen.

First Station: Pilate Condemns Jesus to Die

Leader: We adore you, O Christ, and we praise you. *Genuflect.*
All: Because by your holy cross you have redeemed the world. *Rise.*

A reading from the Holy Gospel according to Saint Mark.
(Mk 15:1–5, 15)

And as soon as it was morning the chief priests, with the elders and scribes, and the whole council held a consultation; and they bound Jesus and led him away and delivered him to Pilate. And Pilate asked him, "Are you the King of the Jews?" And he answered him, "You have said so." And the chief priests accused him of many things. And Pilate again asked him, "Have you no answer to make? See how many charges they bring against you." But Jesus made no further answer, so that Pilate wondered. Wishing to satisfy the crowd, Pilate released for them Barabbas; and having scourged Jesus, he delivered him to be crucified.

The Gospel of the Lord.

All: Praise to you, Lord Jesus Christ.

Meditation: Consider how Jesus Christ, after being scourged and crowned with thorns, was unjustly condemned by Pilate to die on the cross.

Prayer: My adorable Jesus, it was not Pilate; no, it was my sins that condemned you to die. I beseech you, by the merits of this sorrowful journey, to assist my soul on its journey to eternity.

Leader: O my Jesus, I repent of having offended you. Grant that I may love you always;

All: And then do with me as you will.

Stabat Mater

Stabat Mater dolorósa,	At the cross her station keeping,
juxta Crucem lacrimósa,	stood the mournful Mother weeping,
dum pendébat Fílius.	close to Jesus to the last.

Second Station: Jesus Accepts His Cross

Leader: We adore you, O Christ, and we praise you. *Genuflect.*

All: Because by your holy cross you have redeemed the world. *Rise.*

A reading from the Holy Gospel according to Saint John. (Jn 19:6, 15–17)

When the chief priests and the officers saw him, they cried out, "Crucify him, crucify him!" Pilate said to them, "Take him yourselves and crucify him, for I find no crime in him." They cried out, "Away with him, away with him, crucify him!" Pilate said to them, "Shall I crucify your King?" The chief priests answered, "We have no king but Caesar." Then he handed him over to them to be crucified. So they took Jesus, and he went out, bearing his own cross, to the place called the place of a skull, which is called in Hebrew Golgotha.

The Gospel of the Lord.

All: Praise to you, Lord Jesus Christ.

Meditation: Consider that Jesus, in making this journey with the cross on his shoulders, thought of us, and offered for us, to his Father, the death that he was about to undergo.

Prayer: My most beloved Jesus, I embrace all the tribulations that you have destined for me until death. I beseech you, by the merits of the pain you suffered in carrying your cross, to give me the necessary help to carry mine with perfect patience and resignation.

Leader: O my Jesus, I repent of having offended you. Grant that I may love you always;

All: And then do with me as you will.

Stabat Mater

Cuius ánimam geméntem, contristátam et doléntem pertransívit gládius.	Through her heart, his sorrow sharing, all his bitter anguish bearing, now at length the sword has passed.

Third Station: Jesus Falls the First Time

Leader: We adore you, O Christ, and we praise you. *Genuflect.*

All: Because by your holy cross you have redeemed the world. *Rise.*

A reading from the book of the prophet Isaiah.   (Is 63:2–5)

Why is your apparel red,
  and your garments like his who treads in the wine press?
"I have trodden the wine press alone,
  and from the peoples no one was with me;
I trod them in my anger
  and trampled them in my wrath;
their lifeblood is sprinkled upon my garments,
  and I have stained all my clothing.
For the day of vengeance was in my heart,
  and my year of redemption has come.
I looked, but there was no one to help;
  I was appalled, but there was no one to uphold;

so my own arm brought me victory,
and my wrath upheld me."

The Word of the Lord.

All: Thanks be to God.

Meditation: Consider the first fall of Jesus. Loss of blood from the scourging and crowning with thorns had so weakened him that he could hardly walk; and yet he had to carry that great load upon his shoulders. As the soldiers struck him cruelly, he fell several times under the heavy cross.

Prayer: My beloved Jesus, it was not the weight of the cross but the weight of my sins which made you suffer so much. By the merits of this first fall, save me from falling into mortal sin.

Leader: O my Jesus, I repent of having offended you. Grant that I may love you always;

All: And then do with me as you will.

Stabat Mater

O quam tristis et afflícta,   O how sad and sore distressed
fuit illa benedícta,   was that Mother, highly blest,
Mater Unigéniti!   of the sole-begotten one.

Fourth Station: Jesus Meets His Mother, Mary

Leader: We adore you, O Christ, and we praise you. *Genuflect*.

All: Because by your holy cross you have redeemed the world. *Rise*.

A reading from the book of Lamentations.   (Lam 2:13)

What can I say for you, to what compare you,
    O daughter of Jerusalem?
What can I liken to you, that I may comfort you,
    O virgin daughter of Zion?
For vast as the sea is your ruin;
    who can restore you?

The Word of the Lord.

All: Thanks be to God.

A reading from the Holy Gospel according to Saint John. (Jn 16:22)

So you have sorrow now, but I will see you again and your hearts will rejoice, and no one will take your joy from you.

The Gospel of the Lord.

All: Praise to you, Lord Jesus Christ.

Meditation: Consider how the Son met his Mother on his way to Calvary. Jesus and Mary gazed at each other, and their looks became as so many arrows to wound those hearts which loved each other so tenderly.

Prayer: My most loving Jesus, by the pain you suffered in this meeting, grant me the grace of being truly devoted to your most holy Mother. And you, my Queen, who was overwhelmed with sorrow, obtain for me by your prayers a tender and a lasting remembrance of the Passion of your divine Son.

Leader: O my Jesus, I repent of having offended you. Grant that I may love you always;

All: And then do with me as you will.

Stabat Mater

Quae mœrébat et dolébat,
pia Mater, dum vidébat
nati pœnas ínclyti.

Christ above in torment hangs.
She beneath beholds the pangs
of her dying glorious son.

Fifth Station: Simon Helps Carry the Cross

Leader: We adore you, O Christ, and we praise you. *Genuflect*.

All: Because by your holy cross you have redeemed the world. *Rise*.

A reading from the Holy Gospel according to Saint Matthew. (Mt 27:30–32)

And they spat upon him, and took the reed and struck him on the head. And when they had mocked him, they stripped him of the robe, and put his own clothes on him, and led him away to crucify him. As they were marching out, they came upon a man of Cyrene, Simon by name; this man they compelled to carry his cross.

The Gospel of the Lord.

All: Praise to you, Lord Jesus Christ.

A reading from the Letter of Saint Paul to the Galatians.
(Gal 6:2)

Bear one another's burdens, and so fulfil the law of Christ.

The Word of the Lord.

All: Thanks be to God.

Meditation: Consider how weak and weary Jesus was. At each step he was at the point of expiring. Fearing that he would die on the way when they wished him to die the infamous death of the cross, they forced Simon of Cyrene to help carry the cross after our Lord.

Prayer: My beloved Jesus, I will not refuse the cross, like Simon: I accept it and embrace it. I accept in particular the death that is destined for me with all the pains that may accompany it. I unite it to your death, and I offer it to you.

Leader: O my Jesus, I repent of having offended you. Grant that I may love you always;

All: And then do with me as you will.

Stabat Mater

Quis est homo qui non fleret,	Is there one who would not weep,
Matrem Christi si vidéret	whelmed in miseries so deep,
in tanto supplício?	Christ's dear Mother to behold?

Sixth Station: Veronica Wipes the Face of Jesus

Leader: We adore you, O Christ, and we praise you. *Genuflect*.

All: Because by your holy cross you have redeemed the world. *Rise*.

A reading from the book of Sirach. (Sir 6:14–16)

A faithful friend is a sturdy shelter:
    he that has found one has found a treasure.
There is nothing so precious as a faithful friend,
    and no scales can measure his excellence.
A faithful friend is an elixir of life;
    and those who fear the Lord will find him.

The Word of the Lord.

All: Thanks be to God.

A reading from the book of the prophet Isaiah.   (Is 52:14)

> As many were astonished at him—
>> his appearance was so marred, beyond human semblance,
>> and his form beyond that of the sons of men.

The Word of the Lord.

All: Thanks be to God.

Meditation: Consider the compassion of the holy woman Veronica. Seeing Jesus in such distress, his face bathed in sweat and blood, she presented him with her veil. Jesus wiped his face and left upon the cloth the image of his sacred countenance.

Prayer: My beloved Jesus, your face was beautiful before you began this journey; but now it no longer appears beautiful and is disfigured with wounds and blood. By the merits of your Passion, restore the beauty of grace to my soul, gained in baptism but disfigured by sin.

Leader: O my Jesus, I repent of having offended you. Grant that I may love you always;

All: And then do with me as you will.

Stabat Mater

Quis non posset contristári,	Can the human heart refrain
Christi Matrem contemplári,	from partaking in her pain,
doléntem cum Fílio?	in that Mother's pain untold?

Seventh Station: Jesus Falls the Second Time

Leader: We adore you, O Christ, and we praise you. *Genuflect.*

All: Because by your holy cross you have redeemed the world. *Rise.*

A reading from the book of the prophet Isaiah.   (Is 53:4–6)

> Surely he has borne our griefs
>> and carried our sorrows;

yet we esteemed him stricken,
 struck down by God, and afflicted.
But he was wounded for our transgressions,
 he was bruised for our iniquities;
upon him was the chastisement that made us whole,
 and with his stripes we are healed.
All we like sheep have gone astray;
 we have turned every one to his own way;
and the LORD has laid on him
 the iniquity of us all.

The Word of the Lord.

All: Thanks be to God.

A reading from the Letter of Saint Paul to the Hebrews.
(Heb 4:15)

For we have not a high priest who is unable to sympathize with our weaknesses, but one who in every respect has been tempted as we are, yet without sinning.

The Word of the Lord.

All: Thanks be to God.

Meditation: Consider how the second fall of Jesus under his cross renews the pain in all the wounds of our afflicted Lord.

Prayer: My most gentle Jesus, how many times you have forgiven me; and how many times I have fallen again and begun again to offend you! By the merits of this second fall, give me the grace to persevere in your love until death. Grant that in all my temptations, I may always have recourse to you.

Leader: O my Jesus, I repent of having offended you. Grant that I may love you always;

All: And then do with me as you will.

Stabat Mater

Eja, Mater, fons amóris,	O thou Mother! Fount of love!
me sentíre vim dolóris	Touch my spirit from above,
fac, ut tecum lúgeam.	make my heart with thine accord.

Eighth Station: Jesus Meets the Women of Jerusalem

Leader: We adore you, O Christ, and we praise you. *Genuflect.*

All: Because by your holy cross you have redeemed the world. *Rise.*

A reading from the Holy Gospel according to Saint Luke.
(Lk 23:27–31)

And there followed him a great multitude of the people, and of women who bewailed and lamented him. But Jesus turning to them said, "Daughters of Jerusalem, do not weep for me, but weep for yourselves and for your children. For behold, the days are coming when they will say, 'Blessed are the barren, and the wombs that never bore, and the breasts that never nursed!' Then they will begin to say to the mountains, 'Fall on us'; and to the hills, 'Cover us.' For if they do this when the wood is green, what will happen when it is dry?"

The Gospel of the Lord.

All: Praise to you, Lord Jesus Christ.

Meditation: Consider how the women wept with compassion seeing Jesus so distressed and dripping with blood as he walked along. Jesus said to them, "Do not weep for me, but rather for your children."

Prayer: My Jesus, laden with sorrows, I weep for the sins which I have committed because of the displeasure they have caused you, who have loved me with an infinite love. It is your love, more than the fear of punishment, which makes me weep for my sins.

Leader: O my Jesus, I repent of having offended you. Grant that I may love you always;

All: And then do with me as you will.

Stabat Mater

Fac, ut árdeat cor meum,	Make me feel as thou hast felt;
in amándo Christum Deum,	make my soul to glow and melt
ut sibi compláceam.	with the love of Christ my Lord.

Ninth Station: Jesus Falls the Third Time

Leader: We adore you, O Christ, and we praise you. *Genuflect.*

All: Because by your holy cross you have redeemed the world. *Rise.*

A reading from the book of Psalms. (Ps 119:25–28)

> My soul clings to the dust;
>> revive me according to your word!
> When I told of my ways, you answered me;
>> teach me your statutes!
> Make me understand the way of your precepts,
>> and I will meditate on your wondrous works.
> My soul melts away for sorrow;
>> strengthen me according to your word!

The Word of the Lord.

All: Thanks be to God.

A reading from the Letter of Saint Paul to the Philippians. (Phil 2:5–8)

Have this mind among yourselves, which was in Christ Jesus, who, though he was in the form of God, did not count equality with God a thing to be grasped, but emptied himself, taking the form of a servant, being born in the likeness of men. And being found in human form he humbled himself and became obedient unto death, even death on a cross.

The Word of the Lord.

All: Thanks be to God.

Meditation: Consider how Jesus Christ fell for the third time. He was extremely weak, and the cruelty of his executioners was excessive; they tried to hasten his steps though he hardly had strength to move.

Prayer: My outraged Jesus, by the weakness you suffered in going to Calvary, give me enough strength to overcome my desire for human respect and my corrupt passions.

Leader: O my Jesus, I repent of having offended you. Grant that I may love you always;

All: And then do with me as you will.

Stabat Mater

Sancta Mater, istud agas,	Holy Mother, pierce me through;
crucifíxi fige plagas	In my heart each wound renew
cordi meo válide.	of my Savior crucified.

Tenth Station: Jesus Is Stripped of His Clothes

Leader: We adore you, O Christ, and we praise you. *Genuflect.*

All: Because by your holy cross you have redeemed the world. *Rise.*

A reading from the Holy Gospel according to Saint John.
(Jn 19:23–25)

When the soldiers had crucified Jesus they took his garments and made four parts, one for each soldier; also his tunic. But the tunic was without seam, woven from top to bottom; so they said to one another, "Let us not tear it, but cast lots for it to see whose it shall be." This was to fulfil the Scripture,

"They parted my garments among them, and for my clothing they cast lots."

So the soldiers did this. But standing by the cross of Jesus were his mother, and his mother's sister, Mary the wife of Clopas, and Mary Magdalene.

The Gospel of the Lord.

All: Praise to you, Lord Jesus Christ.

Meditation: Consider how violently was Jesus' torn and lacerated body stripped of clothing by his executioners. Have pity for your Savior so cruelly treated and tell him:

Prayer: My innocent Jesus, by the torment you suffered in being stripped of your garments, help me to strip myself of all attachment for the things of earth, that I may place all my love in you who are so worthy of my love.

Leader: O my Jesus, I repent of having offended you. Grant that I may love you always;

All: And then do with me as you will.

Stabat Mater

Tui Nati vulneráti,	Let me share with thee his pain,
tam dignáti pro me pati,	who for all my sins was slain,
pœnas mecum dívide.	who for me in torments died.

Eleventh Station: Jesus Is Nailed to the Cross

Leader: We adore you, O Christ, and we praise you. *Genuflect.*

All: Because by your holy cross you have redeemed the world. *Rise.*

A reading from the Holy Gospel according to Saint Luke.
(Lk 23:33–38)

And when they came to the place which is called The Skull, there they crucified him, and the criminals, one on the right and one on the left. And Jesus said, "Father, forgive them; for they know not what they do." And they cast lots to divide his garments. And the people stood by, watching; but the rulers scoffed at him, saying, "He saved others; let him save himself, if he is the Christ of God, his Chosen One!" The soldiers also mocked him, coming up and offering him vinegar, and saying, "If you are the King of the Jews, save yourself!" There was also an inscription over him, "This is the King of the Jews."

The Gospel of the Lord.

All: Praise to you, Lord Jesus Christ.

Meditation: Consider how Jesus, after being thrown down upon the cross, stretched out his arms and offered to his eternal Father the sacrifice of his life for our salvation. They nailed his hands and feet, and then, raising the cross, left him to die in anguish.

Prayer: My despised Jesus, nail my heart to the cross, that it may always remain there to love you and never leave you again.

Leader: O my Jesus, I repent of having offended you. Grant that I may love you always;

All: And then do with me as you will.

Stabat Mater

Fac me tecum pie flere,	Let me mingle tears with thee,
crucifixo condolére,	mourning him who mourned for
donec ego víxero.	me,
	all the days that I may live.

Twelfth Station: Jesus Dies on the Cross

Leader: We adore you, O Christ, and we praise you. *Genuflect.*

All: Because by your holy cross you have redeemed the world. *Rise.*

A reading from the Holy Gospel according to Saint John.
(Jn 19:26–30)

When Jesus saw his mother, and the disciple whom he loved standing near, he said to his mother, "Woman, behold, your son!" Then
he said to the disciple, "Behold, your mother!" And from that hour
the disciple took her to his own home. After this Jesus, knowing that
all was now finished, said (to fulfill the scripture), "I thirst." A bowl
full of vinegar stood there; so they put a sponge full of the vinegar
on hyssop and held it to his mouth. When Jesus had received the
vinegar, he said, "It is finished"; and he bowed his head and gave
up his spirit.

The Gospel of the Lord.

All: Praise to you, Lord Jesus Christ.

Meditation: Consider how Jesus, after three hours of agony on the
cross, is finally overwhelmed with suffering and, abandoning himself
to the weight of his body, bows his head and dies.

Prayer: My dying Jesus, I devoutly kiss the cross on which you would
die for love of me. Your death is my hope. By the merits of your
death, give me the grace to die embracing your feet and burning with
love of you.

Leader: O my Jesus, I repent of having offended you. Grant that I may
love you always;

All: And then do with me as you will.

Stabat Mater

Juxta Crucem tecum stare,	By the cross with thee to stay,
et me tibi sociáre,	there with thee to weep and pray,
in planctu desídero.	is all I ask of thee to give.

Thirteenth Station: Jesus Is Taken Down from the Cross

Leader: We adore you, O Christ, and we praise you. *Genuflect.*

All: Because by your holy cross you have redeemed the world. *Rise.*

A reading from the Holy Gospel according to Saint John. (Jn 19:32–37)

So the soldiers came and broke the legs of the first, and of the other who had been crucified with him; but when they came to Jesus and saw that he was already dead, they did not break his legs. But one of the soldiers pierced his side with a spear, and at once there came out blood and water. He who saw it has borne witness—his testimony is true, and he knows that he tells the truth—that you also may believe. For these things took place that the Scripture might be fulfilled: "Not a bone of him will be broken." And again another Scripture says: "They shall look on him whom they have pierced."

The Gospel of the Lord.

All: Praise to you, Lord Jesus Christ.

Meditation: Consider how, after our Lord had died, he was taken down from the cross by two of his disciples, Joseph and Nicodemus, and placed in the arms of his afflicted Mother. She received him with unutterable tenderness.

Prayer: O Mother of Sorrows, for the love of your Son, accept me as your servant and pray to him for me; and you, my Redeemer, since you have died for me, allow me to love you, for I desire only you and nothing more.

Leader: O my Jesus, I repent of having offended you. Grant that I may love you always;

All: And then do with me as you will.

Stabat Mater

Fac, ut portem Christi mortem,	Let me, to my latest breath,
passiónis fac consórtem,	in my body bear the death
et plagas recólere.	of that dying Son of thine.

Fourteenth Station: Jesus Is Placed in the Tomb

Leader: We adore you, O Christ, and we praise you. *Genuflect.*

All: Because by your holy cross you have redeemed the world. *Rise.*

A reading from the Holy Gospel according to Saint John.
(Jn 19:38–42)

After this, Joseph of Arimathea, who was a disciple of Jesus, but secretly, for fear of the Jews, asked Pilate that he might take away the body of Jesus, and Pilate gave him leave. So he came and took away his body. Nicodemus also, who had at first come to him by night, came bringing a mixture of myrrh and aloes, about a hundred pounds' weight. They took the body of Jesus, and bound it in linen cloths with the spices, as is the burial custom of the Jews. Now in the place where he was crucified there was a garden, and in the garden a new tomb where no one had ever been laid. So because of the Jewish day of Preparation, as the tomb was close at hand, they laid Jesus there.

The Gospel of the Lord.

All: Praise to you, Lord Jesus Christ.

Meditation: Consider how the disciples carried the body of Jesus to its burial, while his holy Mother went with them and arranged it in the sepulcher with her own hands. They then closed the tomb, and all departed.

Prayer: Jesus, I kiss the stone that closes you in. I beg that I may be raised gloriously on the last day, to be united with you in heaven, to praise you and love you forever.

Leader: O my Jesus, I repent of having offended you. Grant that I may love you always;

All: And then do with me as you will.

Stabat Mater

Christe, cum sit hinc exíre,	Christ, when thou shalt call me hence,
da per Matrem me veníre	be thy Mother my defense,
ad palmam victóriæ.	be thy cross my victory.

Fourth Sunday of Lent
(Laetare Sunday, Mothering Sunday)

Laetare Sunday is observed as Mother's Day in many historically Catholic countries.

COLLECT PRAYER

O God, who through your Word reconcile the human race to yourself in a wonderful way, grant, we pray, that with prompt devotion and eager faith the Christian people may hasten toward the solemn celebrations to come. Through our Lord Jesus Christ, your Son, who lives and reigns with you in the unity of the Holy Spirit, one God, for ever and ever. Amen.

A reading from the book of the prophet Isaiah. (Is 66:10)

Rejoice with Jerusalem, and be glad for her,
    all you who love her;
rejoice with her in joy,
    all you who mourn over her.

The Word of the Lord.

All: Thanks be to God.

Prayer for Mothers

O almighty and eternal God, Lord of both the living and the dead, your tender mercy embraces all men foreknown to be yours by faith and a good life. Through the intercession of the Most Blessed Virgin Mary our Mother, and of all the saints, grant your merciful pardon to all mothers for whom we pray, whether they still are living in this world or have departed from this flesh into the world to come.

Especially, dear Lord, grant the requests I now make of you for my own beloved mother. *(List requests.)* Amen.

Fifth Sunday of Lent / Passion Sunday (Historical)

COLLECT PRAYER[5]

By your help, we beseech you, Lord our God, may we walk eagerly in that same charity with which, out of love for the world, your Son handed himself over to death. Through our Lord Jesus Christ, your Son, who lives and reigns with you in the unity of the Holy Spirit, one God, for ever and ever. Amen.

Veiling of Statues

It is a long tradition of the Catholic Church to veil images of Christ and the saints beginning on the Fifth Sunday of Lent. This day was historically known as Passion Sunday, and the tradition is based on the Gospel reading for the day (see below). The title of Passion Sunday is no longer in use after the 1969 revisions of the liturgical calendar (the Sixth Sunday of Lent is now known as Palm Sunday of the Passion of the Lord), but the practice of veiling statues is still in practice in all forms of the liturgy. The rubrics of the third edition of the Roman Missal *state: "In the Dioceses of the United States, the practice of covering crosses and images throughout the church from this Sunday may be observed. Crosses remain covered until the end of the Celebration of the Lord's Passion on Good Friday, but images remain covered until the beginning of the Easter Vigil."[6]*

Images should be covered with lightweight, unadorned cloth, usually purple. Stained-glass windows and Stations of the Cross remain uncovered. In our home we cover our main crucifixes and religious images (but not all religious knick-knacks). It's interesting how much attention they command by being covered!

A reading from the Gospel according to Saint John. (Jn 8:59)

So they took up stones to throw at him; but Jesus hid himself and went out of the temple.

---

[5] *Roman Missal*, Fifth Sunday of Lent.
[6] Ibid.

The Gospel of the Lord.

All: Praise to you, Lord Jesus Christ.

SONG SUGGESTION: There Is a Green Hill Far Away

Confession

To remain in good standing with the Church, Catholics are required to make a good confession to a priest at least once per year. Many great saints recommend partaking of the mercy of the sacrament much more frequently than that—monthly or even weekly—even if we haven't committed mortal sins. The week before Holy Week is a good time in which to go to confession during Lent, to prepare our souls for the joy of the Easter season. For an Examination of Conscience, see p. 371.

7

March

The month of Saint Joseph

Prayer after Blessing before Meals: Prayer to Saint Joseph[1]

Joseph, son of David, and husband of Mary; we honor you, guardian of the Redeemer, and we adore the child you named Jesus. Saint Joseph, patron of the universal Church, pray for us, that like you we may live totally dedicated to the interests of the Savior. Amen.

March 7: Saints Perpetua and Felicity, Martyrs (Optional Memorial)

COLLECT PRAYER

O God, at the urging of whose love the Martyrs Saints Perpetua and Felicity defied their persecutors and overcame the torment of earth, grant, we ask, by their prayers, that we may ever grow in your love. Through our Lord Jesus Christ, your Son, who lives and reigns with you in the unity of the Holy Spirit, one God, for ever and ever. Amen.

The Passion of Saints Perpetua and Felicity

Perpetua was a Roman citizen of African Berber descent, a young wife and mother of an infant son. Felicity was her servant, and eight months pregnant.

---

[1] "St. Joseph Rosary", a devotion of the Oblates of St. Joseph, Holy Spouses Province, U.S.A., https://osjusa.org/prayers/st-joseph-rosary/. Used with permission.

They were catechumens, preparing to be received into the Church, and were imprisoned together for refusing to renounce Christianity. A diary written by Perpetua herself from jail in the year 203 exists and is considered by scholars to be authentic. An introduction and description of her martyrdom was added by an unknown witness, perhaps Tertullian. The following is an exerpt.

There were apprehended many young catechumens, including Felicity, a servant, and Perpetua, nobly born, reared, and educated, wedded honorably; having a father and mother and two brothers, and a son, a child at the breast; and she herself was about twenty-two years of age....

Now dawned the day of their victory, and they went forth from the prison into the amphitheatre as it were into heaven, cheerful and bright of countenance; if they trembled at all, it was for joy, not for fear. Perpetua followed behind, glorious of presence, as a true spouse of Christ and darling of God; at whose piercing look all cast down their eyes. Felicity likewise, rejoicing that she had borne a child in safety, that she might fight with the beasts, came now from blood to blood, from the midwife to the gladiator, to wash after her travail in a second baptism.

For the women, the devil had made ready a most savage cow, prepared for this purpose against all custom; for even in this beast he would mock their femininity. Perpetua was first thrown, and fell upon her loins. Next, looking for a pin, she likewise pinned up her dishevelled hair; for it was not meet that a martyr should suffer with hair dishevelled, lest she should seem to grieve in her glory. So she stood up; and when she saw Felicity smitten down, she went up and gave her a hand and raised her up. And both of them stood up together and, the hardness of the people being now subdued, were called back to the Gate of Life.

Having faced and suffered the beasts, those who were still living gave each other the kiss of peace. Then, not moving and in silence, received the sword....

O most valiant and blessed martyrs! O truly called and elected unto the glory of Our Lord Jesus Christ! Which glory he that magnifies, honors and adores, ought to read these witnesses likewise, as being no less than the old, unto the Church's edification; that these new wonders also may testify that one and the same Holy Spirit works ever until now, and with him God the Father Almighty, and his Son

Jesus Christ Our Lord, to whom is glory and power unending for ever and ever. Amen.[2]

March 9: Saint Frances of Rome, Religious (Optional Memorial)

COLLECT PRAYER

O God, who have given us in Saint Frances of Rome a singular model of both married and monastic life, grant us perseverance in your service, that in every circumstance of life we may see and follow you. Through our Lord Jesus Christ, your Son, who lives and reigns with you in the unity of the Holy Spirit, one God, for ever and ever. Amen.

Words of Saint Frances of Rome

Sometimes she must leave God at the altar to find him in her housekeeping.

Kitchen Prayer

Written by Klara Munkres (+1971), a retired schoolteacher from Savannah, Missouri, this poem is an example of the universal call to holiness and the sanctification of everyday work.

> Lord of all pots and pans and things,
> Since I've not time to be
> A saint by doing lovely things or
> Watching late with thee
> Or dreaming in the dawn light or

---

[2] *The Passion of SS. Perpetua and Felicity,* trans. Walter Shewring (London: Sheed and Ward, 1931), Internet Archive, https://archive.org/stream/passionofssperpeooperp/passionofssper peooperp_djvu.txt. Perpetua's diary is available online in its entirety in the original Latin and translated into English. This excerpt from the witness' testimony has been condensed and modernized by me.

Storming heaven's gates,
Make me a saint by getting meals and
Washing up the plates.

Although I must have Martha's hands,
I have a Mary mind
And when I black the boots and shoes,
Thy sandals, Lord, I find.
I think of how they trod the earth,
What time I scrub the floor.
Accept this meditation, Lord,
I haven't time for more.

Warm all the kitchen with thy love,
And light it with thy peace.
Forgive me all my worrying and make
My grumbling cease.
Thou who didst love to give men food,
In room or by the sea,
Accept this service that I do,
I do it unto thee.

March 17: Saint Patrick, Bishop (Optional Memorial)

COLLECT PRAYER

O God, who chose the Bishop Saint Patrick to preach your glory
to the peoples of Ireland, grant, through his merits and intercession,
that those who glory in the name of Christian may never cease to
proclaim your wondrous deeds to all. Through our Lord Jesus Christ,
your Son, who lives and reigns with you in the unity of the Holy
Spirit, one God, for ever and ever. Amen.

Saint Patrick's Breastplate

According to tradition, this prayer was composed by Saint Patrick in A.D. *433*
as a request for divine protection as he prepared to fight for souls, successfully

converting the Irish king Laoghaire and his subjects from paganism to Christianity. (The term breastplate refers to a piece of armor worn in battle.) It makes an excellent morning prayer for every day but is especially appropriate for the feast.

I arise today
Through a mighty strength, the invocation of the Trinity,
Through belief in the Threeness,
Through confession of the Oneness
toward the Creator.

I arise today
Through the strength of Christ's birth with his baptism,
Through the strength of his crucifixion with his burial,
Through the strength of his Resurrection with his Ascension,
Through the strength of his descent for the judgment of doom.

I arise today
Through the strength of the love of cherubim,
In the obedience of angels,
In the service of archangels,
In the hope of resurrection to meet with reward,
In the prayers of patriarchs,
In the predictions of prophets,
In the preaching of apostles,
In the faith of confessors,
In the innocence of holy virgins,
In the deeds of righteous men.

I arise today, through
The strength of heaven,
The light of the sun,
The radiance of the moon,
The splendor of fire,
The speed of lightning,
The swiftness of wind,
The depth of the sea,
The stability of the earth,
The firmness of rock.

I arise today, through
God's strength to pilot me,

God's might to uphold me,
God's wisdom to guide me,
God's eye to look before me,
God's ear to hear me,
God's word to speak for me,
God's hand to guard me,
God's shield to protect me,
God's host to save me
From snares of devils,
From temptation of vices,
From everyone who shall wish me ill,
Afar and near.

I summon today
All these powers between me and those evils,
Against every cruel and merciless power
That may oppose my body and soul,
Against incantations of false prophets,
Against black laws of pagandom,
Against false laws of heretics,
Against craft of idolatry,
Against spells of smiths and wizards,
Against every knowledge that corrupts man's body and soul;
Christ for my guardianship today
Against poison, against burning,
Against drowning, against wounding,
That there may come to me a multitude of rewards.

Christ with me,
Christ before me,
Christ behind me,
Christ in me,
Christ over me,
Christ to the right of me,
Christ to the left of me,
Christ in lying down,
Christ in sitting,
Christ in rising up,
Christ in the heart of every person who may think of me,
Christ in the mouth of every person who may speak of me,

Christ in every eye which may look on me,
Christ in every ear which may hear me.

I arise today
Through a mighty strength, the invocation of the Trinity,
Through belief in the Threeness,
Through confession of the Oneness
of the Creator of creation. Amen.

An Irish Long-Life Toast

May you live as long as you want,
And never want as long as you live.
May you live to be a hundred years,
With one extra year to repent.

May God grant you many years to live,
For sure he must be knowing
The earth has saints all too few
And heaven is overflowing.

Here's to a long life and a merry one
A quick death and an easy one
A pretty girl and an honest one
A cold beer and another one!

March 19: SAINT JOSEPH, SPOUSE OF THE BLESSED VIRGIN MARY (Solemnity)

COLLECT PRAYER

Grant, we pray, almighty God, that by Saint Joseph's intercession your Church may constantly watch over the unfolding of the mysteries of human salvation, whose beginnings you entrusted to his faithful care. Through our Lord Jesus Christ, your Son, who lives and reigns with you in the unity of the Holy Spirit, one God, for ever and ever. Amen.

Litany of Saint Joseph[3]

The Litany of Saint Joseph was approved by Pope Pius X in 1909. A partial indulgence is available for its recitation at any time.

Leader: Lord, have mercy;
All: Lord, have mercy.
Leader: Christ, have mercy;
All: Christ, have mercy.
Leader: Lord, have mercy;
All: Lord, have mercy.
Leader: God our Father in heaven,
All: Have mercy on us.
Leader: God the Son, Redeemer of the world,
All: Have mercy on us.
Leader: God the Holy Spirit,
All: Have mercy on us.
Leader: Holy Mary,
All: Pray for us.

The leader announces each title of Saint Joseph.

All reply: pray for us.

Saint Joseph, *pray for us.*
Noble son of the House of David, *pray for us.*
Light of patriarchs, *pray for us.*
Husband of the Mother of God, *pray for us.*
Guardian of the Virgin, *pray for us.*
Foster father of the Son of God, *pray for us.*
Faithful guardian of Christ, *pray for us.*
Head of the Holy Family, *pray for us.*
Joseph, chaste and just, *pray for us.*
Joseph, prudent and brave, *pray for us.*
Joseph, obedient and loyal, *pray for us.*

[3] *Manual of Indulgences*, grant 22. See the introduction of this book for the usual conditions for indulgences.

Pattern of patience, *pray for us.*
Lover of poverty, *pray for us.*
Model of workers, *pray for us.*
Example to parents, *pray for us.*
Guardian of virgins, *pray for us.*
Pillar of family life, *pray for us.*
Comfort of the troubled, *pray for us.*
Hope of the sick, *pray for us.*
Patron of the dying, *pray for us.*
Terror of evil spirits, *pray for us.*
Protector of the Church, *pray for us.*

Leader: Lamb of God, you take away the sins of the world;

All: Have mercy on us.

Leader: Lamb of God, you take away the sins of the world;

All: Have mercy on us.

Leader: Lamb of God, you take away the sins of the world;

All: Have mercy on us.

Leader: God made him master of his household.

All: And put him in charge of all that he owned.

Leader: Let us pray. Almighty God, in your infinite wisdom and love you chose Joseph to be the husband of Mary, the Mother of your Son. As we enjoy his protection on earth, may we have the help of his prayers in heaven. We ask this through Christ our Lord.

All: Amen.

Newland Family Saint Joseph Prayer[4]

Mary Reed Newland was the author of many influential twentieth-century books on Catholic family life and liturgical living in the home. This was a favorite family prayer.

O glorious Saint Joseph, spouse of the Immaculate Virgin, obtain for me a pure, humble, and charitable mind, and perfect resignation to

---

[4] Mary Reed Newland, *The Year and Our Children: Catholic Family Celebrations for Every Season* (Manchester, N.H.: Sophia Institute, 2007), 146. Used with permission.

the Divine Will. Be my guide, father, and model through life, that I may merit to die as you did, in the arms of Jesus and Mary. Amen.

See also To You O Blessed Joseph, p. 368; Flos Carmeli, p. 277; In the Hour of Our Death, p. 358; Prayer to Saint Joseph, p. 180; Seven Sundays of Saint Joseph, p. 128; Thanksgiving Prayer for a Newborn Child, p. 354.

March 24: Saint Catherine of Sweden (Optional Memorial)

COLLECT PRAYER[5]

O God, the exaltation of the lowly, who willed that blessed Saint Catherine of Sweden should excel in the beauty of her charity and patience, grant, through her merits and intercession, that, carrying our cross each day, we may persevere in love for you. Through our Lord Jesus Christ, your Son, who lives and reigns with you in the unity of the Holy Spirit, one God, for ever and ever. Amen.

Miscarriage Prayer[6]

Saint Catherine of Sweden is invoked as the patroness against miscarriage and of women who have suffered miscarriage, stillbirth, and infant loss. This is an excerpt from a prayer written by Mother Angelica (+2016), a Poor Clare nun and founder of the Eternal Word Television Network (EWTN). In this meditation, God speaks to the grieving mother.

Why, my child—do you ask "why"? Well, I will tell you why.

You see, the child lives. Instead of the wind, he hears the sound of angels singing before my throne. Instead of the beauty that passes, he sees everlasting beauty—he sees my face. He was created and lived a short time, so the image of his parents imprinted on his face may stand before me as their personal intercessor. He knows secrets of heaven unknown to men on earth. He laughs with a special joy

[5] *Roman Missal*, Commons for Holy Women, no. V.2.
[6] Mother M. Angelica, "Miscarriage Prayer", Eternal Word Television Network, https://www.ewtn.com/catholicism/devotions/miscarriage-prayer-351.

that only the innocent possess. My ways are not the ways of man. I create for my kingdom, and each creature fills a place in that kingdom that could not be filled by another. He was created for my joy and his parents' merits. He has never seen pain or sin. He has never felt hunger or pain. I breathed a soul into a seed, made it grow, and called it forth.

Blessing of Parents after a Miscarriage or Stillbirth[7]

This rite from the Book of Blessings *can be led by a priest or deacon, or by a friend or member of the family.*

In times of death and grief the Christian turns to the Lord for consolation and strength. This is especially true when a child dies before birth. This blessing is provided to assist the parents in their grief and console them with the blessing of God.

All make the sign of the cross.

Leader: Our help is in the name of the Lord.

All: Who made heaven and earth.

A reading from the book of Lamentations.
(Lam 3:17–18, 21–24, NAB)

My soul is deprived of peace,
I have forgotten what happiness is;
I tell myself my future is lost,
all that I hoped for from the LORD.
But I will call this to mind,
as my reason to have hope:
The favors of the LORD are not exhausted,
his mercies are not spent;
They are renewed each morning,
so great is his faithfulness.
My portion is the LORD, says my soul;
therefore I will hope in him.

---

[7] *Book of Blessings*, nos. 279, 297, 298, 300.

The Word of the Lord.

All: Thanks be to God.

A minister who is a priest or deacon says the prayer of blessing with hands outstretched over the parents; a lay minister says the prayer of blessing with hands joined.

Leader: Compassionate God,
soothe the hearts of N. and N.,
and grant that through the prayers of Mary,
who grieved by the Cross of her Son,
you may enlighten their faith,
give hope to their hearts,
and peace to their lives.
Lord,
grant mercy to all the members of this family
and comfort them with the hope
that one day we will all live with you,
with your Son Jesus Christ, and the Holy Spirit,
forever and ever.
All: Amen.

See also Eternal Rest Prayer, p. 335.

March 25: THE ANNUNCIATION OF THE LORD (Solemnity)

The Annunciation falls on March 25, exactly nine months before the birth of Jesus Christ at Christmas. In some years the solemnity is moved to a different day, because of rules governing liturgical celebrations. The Church considers Masses for the Sundays of Lent, anytime in Holy Week, and anytime during the Easter Octave (through Divine Mercy Sunday) to be so important that even this Marian feast cannot displace one of them. So, when the Annunciation falls on a Sunday in Lent (before Palm Sunday), it is transferred to the following Monday. If it falls on Palm Sunday or on any day in Holy Week or Easter Week, it is transferred to Low Monday, the Monday after the Sunday after Easter.

COLLECT PRAYER

O God, who willed that your Word should take on the reality of human flesh in the womb of the Virgin Mary, grant, we pray, that we, who confess our Redeemer to be God and man, may merit to become partakers even in his divine nature. Who lives and reigns with you in the unity of the Holy Spirit, one God, for ever and ever. Amen.

SONG SUGGESTION: The Angel Gabriel from Heaven Came

See also the reading from the Holy Gospel according to Saint Luke (Lk 1:26–38), p. 71, and the Angelus, p. 361. (The Angelus is traditionally recited at noon each day, and sometimes also at six in the morning and six in the evening, and is based on the angel Gabriel's message to Mary, and her reply.)

8

Movable Feasts: Holy Week

This is the week of the liturgical year most dedicated to prayer and devotional activities. Parishes offer unique and moving liturgies throughout the week. For those of us unable to attend some or all of them, there are at many at-home liturgical living practices that can help us enter into the spirit of Holy Week at home.

Sixth Sunday of Lent: Palm Sunday

COLLECT PRAYER

Almighty ever-living God, who as an example of humility for the human race to follow caused our Savior to take flesh and submit to the Cross, graciously grant that we may heed his lesson of patient suffering and so merit a share in his Resurrection. Who lives and reigns with you in the unity of the Holy Spirit, one God, for ever and ever. Amen.

A reading from the Holy Gospel according to Saint Mark. (Mk 11:1–11)

And when they drew near to Jerusalem, to Bethphage and Bethany, at the Mount of Olives, he sent two of his disciples, and said to them, "Go into the village opposite you, and immediately as you enter it you will find a colt tied, on which no one has ever sat; untie it and bring it. If any one says to you, 'Why are you doing this?' say, 'The Lord has need of it and will send it back here immediately.'" And they went away, and found a colt tied at the door out in the open street; and they untied it. And those who stood there said to them, "What are you doing, untying the colt?" And they told them what Jesus had said; and they let them go. And they brought the colt to Jesus, and threw their garments on it; and he sat upon it. And many spread their garments on the road, and others spread leafy branches which they had cut from the fields. And those who went before and those who followed cried out, "Hosanna! Blessed is he who comes in the name of the Lord! Blessed is the kingdom of our father David that is coming! Hosanna in the highest!"

And he entered Jerusalem, and went into the temple; and when he had looked round at everything, as it was already late, he went out to Bethany with the Twelve.

The Gospel of the Lord.

All: Praise to you, Lord Jesus Christ.

Reverence for Blessed Palms

When palms are blessed, they become sacramentals, which the Catechism tells us "are sacred signs which bear a resemblance to the sacraments. . . . By them men are disposed to receive the chief effect of the sacraments, and various occasions in life are rendered holy."[1] Sacramentals should be treated with respect and never be thrown away. Blessed palms may be disposed of by burning or burial at home or can be returned to church before the next Ash Wednesday, so they can be used to create sacramental ashes.

SONG SUGGESTION: All Glory, Laud, and Honor

Holy Week: Monday and Tuesday

A reading from the Holy Gospel according to Saint Mark. (Mk 11:12–25; 14:3–9)

On the following day, when they came from Bethany, he was hungry. And seeing in the distance a fig tree in leaf, he went to see if he could find anything on it. When he came to it, he found nothing but

---

[1] CCC 1667, quoting Vatican II, *Sacrosanctum Concilium* (December 4, 1963), no. 60.

leaves, for it was not the season for figs. And he said to it, "May no one ever eat fruit from you again." And his disciples heard it. And they came to Jerusalem. And he entered the temple and began to drive out those who sold and those who bought in the temple, and he overturned the tables of the money-changers and the seats of those who sold pigeons; and he would not allow any one to carry anything through the temple. And he taught, and said to them, "Is it not written, 'My house shall be called a house of prayer for all the nations'? But you have made it a den of robbers." And the chief priests and the scribes heard it and sought a way to destroy him; for they feared him, because all the multitude was astonished at his teaching. And when evening came they went out of the city.

As they passed by in the morning, they saw the fig tree withered away to its roots. And Peter remembered and said to him, "Master, look! The fig tree which you cursed has withered." And Jesus answered them, "Have faith in God. Truly, I say to you, whoever says to this mountain, 'Be taken up and cast into the sea,' and does not doubt in his heart, but believes that what he says will come to pass, it will be done for him. Therefore I tell you, whatever you ask in prayer, believe that you receive it, and you will. And whenever you stand praying, forgive, if you have anything against any one; so that your Father also who is in heaven may forgive you your trespasses."

And while he was at Bethany in the house of Simon the leper, as he sat at table, a woman came with an alabaster jar of ointment of pure nard, very costly, and she broke the jar and poured it over his head. But there were some who said to themselves indignantly, "Why was the ointment thus wasted? For this ointment might have been sold for more than three hundred denarii, and given to the poor." And they reproached her. But Jesus said, "Let her alone; why do you trouble her? She has done a beautiful thing to me. For you always have the poor with you, and whenever you will, you can do good to them; but you will not always have me. She has done what she could; she has anointed my body beforehand for burying. And truly, I say to you, wherever the gospel is preached in the whole world, what she has done will be told in memory of her."

The Gospel of the Lord.

All: Praise to you, Lord Jesus Christ.

A reading from the Holy Gospel according to Saint John.
(Jn 12:23–25)

Jesus answered them, "The hour has come for the Son of man to be glorified. Truly, truly, I say to you, unless a grain of wheat falls into the earth and dies, it remains alone; but if it dies, it bears much fruit. He who loves his life loses it, and he who hates his life in this world will keep it for eternal life."

The Gospel of the Lord.

All: Praise to you, Lord Jesus Christ.

Holy Week: Spy Wednesday

COLLECT PRAYER

O God, who willed your Son to submit for our sake to the yoke of the Cross, so that you might drive from us the power of the enemy, grant us, your servants, to attain the grace of the resurrection. Through our Lord Jesus Christ, your Son, who lives and reigns with you in the unity of the Holy Spirit, one God, for ever and ever. Amen.

A reading from the Holy Gospel according to Saint Matthew.
(Mt 26:14–16)

Then one of the Twelve, who was called Judas Iscariot, went to the chief priests and said, "What will you give me if I deliver him to you?" And they paid him thirty pieces of silver. And from that moment he sought an opportunity to betray him.

The Gospel of the Lord.

All: Praise to you, Lord Jesus Christ.

A reading from the book of Psalms. (Ps 55:12–14, 20–23)

It is not an enemy who taunts me—
    then I could bear it;
it is not an adversary who deals insolently with me—
    then I could hide from him.

But it is you, my equal,
    my companion, my familiar friend.
We used to hold sweet converse together;
    within God's house we walked in fellowship.

My companion stretched out his hand against his friends,
    he violated his covenant.
His speech was smoother than butter, yet war was in his heart;
    his words were softer than oil,
yet they were drawn swords.

Cast your burden on the LORD,
    and he will sustain you;
he will never permit
    the righteous to be moved.
But you, O God, will cast them down
    into the lowest pit;
men of blood and treachery
    shall not live out half their days.
But I will trust in you.

The Word of the Lord.

All: Thanks be to God.

Tenebrae

Latin for "darkness", Tenebrae is a service observed on Wednesday, Thursday, and Friday of Holy Week. It features a unique triangular candelabra called a hearse. In the hearse are fifteen candles, usually fourteen darker natural wax candles and one white candle. The fourteen candles represent followers of Jesus; the white candle represents Jesus.

Fourteen readings are proclaimed; after each, one candle in the hearse is extinguished, symbolizing Jesus' followers abandoning him one by one. At the end, just the white Christ candle is left burning. It is removed from the hearse and placed on the altar, then hidden under the altar. The services end with a strepitus (loud noise) made by slamming a book shut or stamping on the floor, symbolizing the earthquake that followed Christ's death. This takes place in total darkness. Then the last candle is returned, representing the light of Christ returning.

A family-friendly interpretation of this practice is to recite the final prayers of the service—the Benedictus, Christus factus est, Psalm 51, and the Our Father—after dinner on one or each of the evenings of Spy Wednesday, Holy Thursday, and Good Friday, extinguishing candles as you go. Fifteen candles of any color or type will work, and if you can't get your teenage son to build you a Tenebrae hearse out of copper piping, as I did, you can arrange your candles in a line or circle in the center of the table. The readings below are numbered for the fourteen "follower" candles. The Christ candle is hidden under the table or taken out of the room; then all can bang their hands or utensils on the table for thirty seconds or so. The Christ candle is then returned, admired, and extinguished, and the service ends.

Benedictus

The prophecy of Zechariah after the birth of his son, John the Baptist, recorded in Luke 1:67–79.

1. Blessed be the Lord, the God of Israel; he has come to his people and set them free.
   He has raised up for us a mighty savior, born of the house of his servant David.
   Through his holy prophets he promised of old that he would save us from our enemies,
   from the hands of all who hate us.

2. He promised to show mercy to our fathers and to remember his holy covenant.
   This was the oath he swore to our father Abraham:
   to set us free from the hands of our enemies, free to worship him without fear,
   holy and righteous in his sight all the days of our life.

3. You, my child, shall be called the prophet of the Most High;
   for you will go before the Lord to prepare his way,
   to give his people knowledge of salvation by the forgiveness of their sins.
   In the tender compassion of our God the dawn from on high shall break upon us,

to shine on those who dwell in darkness and the shadow of death,
And to guide our feet into the way of peace.

4. Glory to the Father and to the Son and to the Holy Spirit,
as it was in the beginning, is now, and will be forever. Amen.

Christus factus est

From Philippians 2:8–9.

5. And being found in human form he humbled himself and became
obedient unto death, even death on a cross. Therefore God has
highly exalted him and bestowed on him the name which is above
every name.

Miserere

*Psalm 51, also called the Miserere after its opening word in Latin, is used in
the Liturgy of the Hours to express repentance for sin.*

6. Have mercy on me, O God, according to your merciful love;
according to your abundant mercy blot out my transgressions.
Wash me thoroughly from my iniquity, and cleanse me from my
sin!

7. For I know my transgressions, and my sin is ever before me.
Against you, you only, have I sinned, and done that which is evil
in your sight,
so that you are justified in your sentence and blameless in your
judgment.
Behold, I was brought forth in iniquity, and in sin did my mother
conceive me.

8. Behold, you desire truth in the inward being; therefore teach me
wisdom in my secret heart.
Purge me with hyssop, and I shall be clean; wash me, and I shall
be whiter than snow.
Make me hear joy and gladness; let the bones which you have
broken rejoice.
Hide your face from my sins, and blot out all my iniquities.

9. Create in me a clean heart, O God, and put a new and right spirit within me.

   Cast me not away from your presence, and take not your holy Spirit from me.

   Restore to me the joy of your salvation, and uphold me with a willing spirit.

   Then I will teach transgressors your ways, and sinners will return to you.

10. Deliver me from bloodguilt, O God, O God of my salvation, and my tongue will sing aloud of your deliverance.

    O Lord, open my lips, and my mouth shall show forth your praise.

    For you take no delight in sacrifice; were I to give a burnt offering, you would not be pleased.

11. The sacrifice acceptable to God is a broken spirit; a broken and contrite heart, O God, you will not despise.

12. Do good to Zion in your good pleasure; rebuild the walls of Jerusalem,

    then will you delight in right sacrifices, in burnt offerings and whole burnt offerings;

    then bulls will be offered on your altar.

Our Father

13. Our Father, who art in heaven, hallowed be thy name.
    Thy kingdom come. Thy will be done, on earth as it is in heaven.

14. Give us this day our daily bread, and forgive us our trespasses, as we forgive those who trespass against us.
    And lead us not into temptation, but deliver us from evil. Amen.

Holy Week: Holy Thursday

COLLECT PRAYER

O God, who have called us to participate in this most sacred Supper, in which your Only Begotten Son, when about to hand himself over to death, entrusted to the Church a sacrifice new for all eternity, the banquet of his love, grant, we pray, that we may draw from so great a mystery, the fullness of charity and of life. Through our Lord Jesus Christ, your Son, who lives and reigns with you in the unity of the Holy Spirit, one God, for ever and ever. Amen.

A reading from the Holy Gospel according to Saint John. (Jn 13:1–20)

Now before the feast of the Passover, when Jesus knew that his hour had come to depart out of this world to the Father, having loved his own who were in the world, he loved them to the end. And during supper, when the devil had already put it into the heart of Judas Iscariot, Simon's son, to betray him, Jesus, knowing that the Father had given all things into his hands, and that he had come from God and was going to God, rose from supper, laid aside his garments, and tied a towel around himself. Then he poured water into a basin, and began to wash the disciples' feet, and to wipe them with the towel that was tied around him. He came to Simon Peter; and Peter said to him, "Lord, do you wash my feet?" Jesus answered him, "What I am doing you do not know now, but afterward you will understand." Peter said to him, "You shall never wash my feet." Jesus answered him, "If I do not wash you, you have no part in me." Simon Peter said to him, "Lord, not my feet only but also my hands and my head!" Jesus said to him, "He who has bathed does not need to wash, except for his feet, but he is clean all over; and you are clean, but not all of you." For he knew who was to betray him; that was why he said, "You are not all clean."

When he had washed their feet, and taken his garments, and resumed his place, he said to them, "Do you know what I have done to you? You call me Teacher and Lord; and you are right, for so I am. If I then, your Lord and Teacher, have washed your feet, you also ought to wash one another's feet. For I have given you an example, that you also should do as I have done to you. Truly, truly, I say to you, a servant is not greater than his master; nor is he who is sent greater than he who sent him. If you know these things, blessed are you if you do them. I am not speaking of you all; I know whom I have chosen; it is that the Scripture may be fulfilled, 'He who ate my bread has lifted his heel against me.' I tell you this now, before it takes place, that when it does take place you may believe that I am he. Truly, truly, I say to you, he who receives any one whom I send receives me; and he who receives me receives him who sent me."

The Gospel of the Lord.

All: Praise to you, Lord Jesus Christ.

A reading from the Holy Gospel according to Saint Matthew. (Mt 26:17–29)

Now on the first day of Unleavened Bread the disciples came to Jesus, saying, "Where will you have us prepare for you to eat the Passover?" He said, "Go into the city to such a one, and say to him, 'The Teacher says, My time is at hand; I will keep the Passover at your house with my disciples.'" And the disciples did as Jesus had directed them, and they prepared the Passover. When it was evening, he sat at table with the twelve disciples; and as they were eating, he said, "Truly, I say to you, one of you will betray me." And they were very sorrowful, and began to say to him one after another, "Is it I, Lord?" He answered, "He who has dipped his hand in the dish with me, will betray me. The Son of man goes as it is written of him, but woe to that man by whom the Son of man is betrayed! It would have been better for that man if he had not been born." Judas, who betrayed him, said, "Is it I, Master?" He said to him, "You have said so."

Now as they were eating, Jesus took bread, and blessed, and broke it, and gave it to the disciples and said, "Take, eat; this is my body." And he took a chalice, and when he had given thanks he gave it to them, saying, "Drink of it, all of you; for this is my blood of the covenant, which is poured out for many for the forgiveness of sins. I tell you I shall not drink again of this fruit of the vine until that day when I drink it new with you in my Father's kingdom."

The Gospel of the Lord.

All: Praise to you, Lord Jesus Christ.

Tantum ergo

A plenary indulgence is granted to the faithful who piously sing or recite the verses of the Tantum ergo *after the Mass of the Lord's Supper on Holy Thursday.*

Tantum ergo sacraméntum
Venerémur cérnui:
Et antíquum documéntum
Novo cedat rítui:
Præstet fides suppleméntum
Sénsuum deféctui.

Genitóri, Genitóque
Laus et jubilátio,
Salus, honor, virtus quoque
Sit et benedíctio:
Procedénti ab utróque
Compar sit laudátio.
Amen. (*In other than Lent and the Triduum, add*: Alleluia.)

Leader: Panem de caelo praestitisti eis. (*In other than Lent and the Triduum, add*: Alleluia.)

All: Omne delectamentum in se habentem. (*In other than Lent and the Triduum, add*: Alleluia.)

Leader: Oremus: Deus, qui nobis sub sacramento mirabili, passionis tuae memoriam reliquisti: tribue, quaesumus, ita nos corporis et sanguinis tui sacra mysteria venerari, ut redemptionis tuae fructum in nobis iugiter sentiamus. Qui vivis et regnas in saecula saeculorum.

All: Amen.

Down in adoration falling,
Lo, the sacred Host we hail,
Lo, o'er ancient forms departing
Newer rites of grace prevail:
Faith for all defects supplying,
When the feeble senses fail.

To the Everlasting Father
And the Son who comes on high
With the Holy Spirit proceeding
Forth from each eternally,
Be salvation, honor, blessing,
Might and endless majesty.
Amen. (*In other than Lent and the Triduum, add*: Alleluia.)

Leader: You have given them bread from heaven. (*In other than Lent and the Triduum, add*: Alleluia.)

All: Having all delight within it. (*In other than Lent and the Triduum, add*: Alleluia.)

Leader: Let us pray.
O God, who in this wonderful Sacrament
left us a memorial of your Passion:
grant, we implore you,
that we may so venerate
the sacred mysteries of your Body and Blood,
as always to be conscious of the fruit of your Redemption.
You who live and reign forever and ever.
All: Amen.

Holy Week: Good Friday

COLLECT PRAYER[2]

Remember your mercies, O Lord, and with your eternal protection
sanctify your servants for whom Christ your Son, by the shedding of
his Blood, established the Paschal Mystery. Who lives and reigns for
ever and ever. Amen.

A reading from the Holy Gospel according to Saint Mark.
(Mk 14:26—15:47)

And when they had sung a hymn, they went out to the Mount of
Olives. And Jesus said to them, "You will all fall away; for it is written,
'I will strike the shepherd, and the sheep will be scattered.' But after I
am raised up, I will go before you to Galilee." Peter said to him, "Even
though they all fall away, I will not." And Jesus said to him, "Truly, I
say to you, this very night, before the cock crows twice, you will deny
me three times." But he said vehemently, "If I must die with you, I
will not deny you." And they all said the same.

And they went to a place which was called Gethsemane; and he
said to his disciples, "Sit here, while I pray." And he took with him
Peter and James and John, and began to be greatly distressed and
troubled. And he said to them, "My soul is very sorrowful, even to

---

[2] According to the Church's ancient tradition, the sacraments are not celebrated on Good
Friday or Holy Saturday. This Collect prayer is from what is known as the "Celebration of
the Lord's Passion" for the afternoon of Good Friday.

death; remain here, and watch." And going a little farther, he fell on the ground and prayed that, if it were possible, the hour might pass from him. And he said, "Abba, Father, all things are possible to you; remove this chalice from me; yet not what I will, but what you will." And he came and found them sleeping, and he said to Peter, "Simon, are you asleep? Could you not watch one hour? Watch and pray that you may not enter into temptation; the spirit indeed is willing, but the flesh is weak." And again he went away and prayed, saying the same words. And again he came and found them sleeping, for their eyes were very heavy; and they did not know what to answer him. And he came the third time, and said to them, "Are you still sleeping and taking your rest? It is enough; the hour has come; the Son of man is betrayed into the hands of sinners. Rise, let us be going; see, my betrayer is at hand."

And immediately, while he was still speaking, Judas came, one of the Twelve, and with him a crowd with swords and clubs, from the chief priests and the scribes and the elders. Now the betrayer had given them a sign, saying, "The one I shall kiss is the man; seize him and lead him away safely." And when he came, he went up to him at once, and said, "Master!" And he kissed him. And they laid hands on him and seized him. But one of those who stood by drew his sword, and struck the slave of the high priest and cut off his ear. And Jesus said to them, "Have you come out as against a robber, with swords and clubs to capture me? Day after day I was with you in the temple teaching, and you did not seize me. But let the Scriptures be fulfilled." And they all deserted him and fled.

And a young man followed him, with nothing but a linen cloth about his body; and they seized him, but he left the linen cloth and ran away naked.[3]

And they led Jesus to the high priest; and all the chief priests and the elders and the scribes were assembled. And Peter had followed him at a distance, right into the courtyard of the high priest; and he was sitting with the guards, and warming himself at the fire. Now the chief priests and the whole council sought testimony against Jesus to put him to death; but they found none. For many bore false witness against him, and their witness did not agree. And some stood up and bore false

---

[3] This young man is usually supposed to have been St. Mark, author of this account.

witness against him, saying, "We heard him say, 'I will destroy this temple that is made with hands, and in three days I will build another, not made with hands.'" Yet not even so did their testimony agree. And the high priest stood up in their midst, and asked Jesus, "Have you no answer to make? What is it that these men testify against you?" But he was silent and made no answer. Again the high priest asked him, "Are you the Christ, the Son of the Blessed?" And Jesus said, "I am; and you will see the Son of man sitting at the right hand of Power, and coming with the clouds of heaven." And the high priest tore his clothes, and said, "Why do we still need witnesses? You have heard his blasphemy. What is your decision?" And they all condemned him as deserving death. And some began to spit on him, and to cover his face, and to strike him, saying to him, "Prophesy!" And the guards received him with blows.

And as Peter was below in the courtyard, one of the maids of the high priest came; and seeing Peter warming himself, she looked at him, and said, "You also were with the Nazarene, Jesus." But he denied it, saying, "I neither know nor understand what you mean." And he went out into the gateway. And the maid saw him, and began again to say to the bystanders, "This man is one of them." But again he denied it. And after a little while again the bystanders said to Peter, "Certainly you are one of them; for you are a Galilean." But he began to invoke a curse on himself and to swear, "I do not know this man of whom you speak." And immediately the cock crowed a second time. And Peter remembered how Jesus had said to him, "Before the cock crows twice, you will deny me three times." And he broke down and wept.

And as soon as it was morning the chief priests, with the elders and scribes, and the whole council held a consultation; and they bound Jesus and led him away and delivered him to Pilate. And Pilate asked him, "Are you the King of the Jews?" And he answered him, "You have said so." And the chief priests accused him of many things. And Pilate again asked him, "Have you no answer to make? See how many charges they bring against you." But Jesus made no further answer, so that Pilate wondered.

Now at the feast he used to release for them one prisoner for whom they asked. And among the rebels in prison, who had committed murder in the insurrection, there was a man called Barabbas. And the crowd came up and began to ask Pilate to do as he always did for them. And he answered them, "Do you want me to release for you the King of the Jews?" For he perceived that it was out of envy that the chief priests had delivered him up. But the chief priests stirred up the crowd to have him release for them Barabbas instead. And Pilate again said to them, "Then what shall I do with the man whom you call the King of the Jews?" And they cried out again, "Crucify him." And Pilate said to them, "Why, what evil has he done?" But they shouted all the more, "Crucify him." So Pilate, wishing to satisfy the crowd, released for them Barabbas; and having scourged Jesus, he delivered him to be crucified.

And the soldiers led him away inside the palace (that is, the praetorium); and they called together the whole battalion. And they clothed him in a purple cloak, and plaiting a crown of thorns they put it on him. And they began to salute him, "Hail, King of the Jews!" And they struck his head with a reed, and spat upon him, and they knelt down in homage to him. And when they had mocked him, they stripped him of the purple cloak, and put his own clothes on him. And they led him out to crucify him.

And they compelled a passer-by, Simon of Cyrene, who was coming in from the country, the father of Alexander and Rufus, to carry his cross. And they brought him to the place called Golgotha (which means the place of a skull). And they offered him wine mingled with myrrh; but he did not take it. And they crucified him, and divided his garments among them, casting lots for them, to decide what each should take. And it was the third hour, when they crucified him. And the inscription of the charge against him read, "The King of the Jews." And with him they crucified two robbers, one on his right and one on his left. And those who passed by derided him, shaking their heads, and saying, "Aha! You who would destroy the temple and build it in three days, save yourself, and come down from the cross!" So also the chief priests mocked him to one another with the scribes, saying, "He saved others; he cannot save himself. Let the Christ, the King of Israel, come down now from the cross, that we may see and believe." Those who were crucified with him also reviled him.

And when the sixth hour had come, there was darkness over the whole land until the ninth hour. And at the ninth hour Jesus cried with a loud voice, "Elo-i, Elo-i, lama sabach-thani?" which means, "My God, my God, why have you forsaken me?" And some of the bystanders hearing it said, "Behold, he is calling Elijah." And one ran and, filling a sponge full of vinegar, put it on a reed and gave it to him to drink, saying, "Wait, let us see whether Elijah will come to take him down." And Jesus uttered a loud cry, and breathed his last. And the curtain of the temple was torn in two, from top to bottom. And when the centurion, who stood facing him, saw that he thus breathed his last, he said, "Truly this man was the Son of God!" There were also women looking on from afar, among whom were Mary Magdalene, and Mary the mother of James the younger and of Joses, and Salome, who, when he was in Galilee, followed him, and ministered to him; and also many other women who came up with him to Jerusalem.

And when evening had come, since it was the day of Preparation, that is, the day before the sabbath, Joseph of Arimathea, a respected member of the council, who was also himself looking for the kingdom of God, took courage and went to Pilate, and asked for the body of Jesus. And Pilate wondered if he were already dead; and summoning the centurion, he asked him whether he was already dead. And when he learned from the centurion that he was dead, he granted the body to Joseph. And he bought a linen shroud, and taking him down, wrapped him in the linen shroud, and laid him in a tomb which had been hewn out of the rock; and he rolled a stone against the door of the tomb. Mary Magdalene and Mary the mother of Joses saw where he was laid.

The Gospel of the Lord.

All: Praise to you, Lord Jesus Christ.

Veneration of the Cross

Veneration of the Cross is an ancient tradition, powerful to do for grown-ups and kids alike but easy to manage. The Manual of Indulgences *states: "A plenary indulgence is granted to the faithful who devoutly assist at the adoration of the Cross in the solemn liturgical action of Good Friday."[4] The usual conditions for gaining indulgences apply.*

---

[4] *Manual of Indulgences*, grant 13.1. See the introduction of this book for the usual conditions for indulgences.

It is offered at many churches on Good Friday. It can be done as a family at a parish, using an accessible cross or crucifix, or at home using any relatively large crucifix or even just two pieces of wood nailed together into a homemade cross. The cross should be placed so that it is somewhat erect, perhaps resting on a bottom stair of a staircase, or propped up against a pile of books. If present, a priest or deacon leads the prayers; otherwise, the head of the household does so.

All make the sign of the cross, then recite this invocation of the Holy Cross by Saint Thomas Aquinas:[5]

Leader: The Cross is my sure salvation.

All: The Cross it is that I worship evermore.

Leader: The Cross of our Lord is with me.

All: The Cross is my refuge.

A reading from the First Letter of Saint Paul to the Corinthians. (1 Cor 1:23–25)

We preach Christ crucified, a stumbling block to Jews and folly to Gentiles, but to those who are called, both Jews and Greeks, Christ the power of God and the wisdom of God. For the foolishness of God is wiser than men, and the weakness of God is stronger than men.

The Word of the Lord.

All: Thanks be to God.

A reading from the Holy Gospel according to Saint Luke. (Lk 9:23–24)

He said to all, "If any man would come after me, let him deny himself and take up his cross daily and follow me. For whoever would save his life will lose it; and whoever loses his life for my sake, he will save it."

The Gospel of the Lord.

All: Praise to you, Lord Jesus Christ.

---

[5] *Raccolta*, no. 186.

Everyone in the family lines up behind the leader. He turns to the first person in line and says:

Leader: Behold the wood of the Cross.

The first person in line kneels down. Placing his forehead first, then his lips, on the wood or corpus, he kisses the cross.

Person 1: I adore you, O Christ, and I praise you, because by your Holy Cross, you have redeemed the world.

He stands and turns to the next person in line and says:

Person 1: Behold the wood of the Cross.

Person 2 kneels and kisses the cross as above.

Person 2: I adore you, O Christ, and I praise you, because by your Holy Cross, you have redeemed the world.

He stands and turns to the next person in line and says:

Person 2: Behold the wood of the Cross.

Person 3 kneels and kisses the cross as above, and so on, until the last person in line says, "Behold the wood of the Cross" to the head of the household, who kneels and kisses the cross.

After venerating the Cross, you may wish to recite Prayer to Our Lord Jesus Christ Crucified, p. 161.

Closing Prayer

Leader: Lord, I give you thanks,
All: That you died upon the Cross for my sins.

All make the sign of the cross.

SONG SUGGESTIONS: *Were You There When They Crucified My Lord; O Sacred Head Surrounded;* Stabat Mater

Divine Mercy Novena (Good Friday to the vigil of Divine Mercy Sunday)[6]

The feast of the Divine Mercy is based on apparitions received by the nun Saint Faustina Kowalska. Jesus asked that the feast of the Divine Mercy be preceded by a novena to the Divine Mercy that would begin on Good Friday. In her diary, Saint Faustina wrote that Jesus told her, "On each day of the novena you will bring to my heart a different group of souls and you will immerse them in this ocean of my mercy.... On each day you will beg my Father, on the strength of my passion, for the graces for these souls."[7]

After the prayers for each day, pray the Divine Mercy Chaplet, p. 369.

First Day (Good Friday)

"Today bring to me all mankind, especially all sinners, and immerse them in the ocean of my mercy. In this way you will console me in the bitter grief into which the loss of souls plunges me."

Most merciful Jesus, whose very nature it is to have compassion on us and to forgive us, do not look upon our sins but upon our trust which we place in your infinite goodness. Receive us all into the abode of your most compassionate heart, and never let us escape from it. We beg this of you by your love which unites you to the Father and the Holy Spirit.

Eternal Father, turn your merciful gaze upon all mankind and especially upon poor sinners, all enfolded in the most compassionate heart of Jesus. For the sake of his sorrowful Passion show us your mercy, that we may praise the omnipotence of your mercy for ever and ever. Amen.

Continue with the Divine Mercy Chaplet, p. 369.

---

[6] "The Divine Mercy Novena of Chaplets", The Divine Mercy, Marian Fathers of the Immaculate Conception of the B.V.M., https://www.thedivinemercy.org/message/devotions/novena. Prayers in the novena are from Faustina Kowalska, *Diary of Saint Maria Faustina Kowalska: Divine Mercy in My Soul* (Stockbridge, Mass.: Marian Press, 1987). Used with permission of the Marian Fathers of the Immaculate Conception of the B.V.M.
[7] Ibid., 271.

Second Day (Holy Saturday)

"Today bring to me the souls of priests and religious, and immerse them in my unfathomable mercy. It was they who gave me strength to endure my bitter Passion. Through them as through channels my mercy flows out upon mankind."

Most merciful Jesus, from whom comes all that is good, increase your grace in men and women consecrated to your service, that they may perform worthy works of mercy; and that all who see them may glorify the Father of Mercy who is in heaven.

Eternal Father, turn your merciful gaze upon the company of chosen ones in your vineyard—upon the souls of priests and religious; and endow them with the strength of your blessing. For the love of the heart of your Son in which they are enfolded, impart to them your power and light, that they may be able to guide others in the way of salvation and with one voice sing praise to your boundless mercy for ages without end. Amen.

Continue with the Divine Mercy Chaplet, p. 369.

Third Day (Easter Sunday)

"Today bring to me all devout and faithful souls, and immerse them in the ocean of my mercy. These souls brought me consolation on the Way of the Cross. They were a drop of consolation in the midst of an ocean of bitterness."

Most merciful Jesus, from the treasury of your mercy, you impart your graces in great abundance to each and all. Receive us into the abode of your most compassionate heart and never let us escape from it. We beg this grace of you by that most wondrous love for the heavenly Father with which your heart burns so fiercely.

Eternal Father, turn your merciful gaze upon faithful souls, as upon the inheritance of your Son. For the sake of his sorrowful Passion, grant them your blessing and surround them with your constant protection. Thus may they never fail in love or lose the treasure of the holy faith, but rather, with all the hosts of angels and saints, may they glorify your boundless mercy for endless ages. Amen.

Continue with the Divine Mercy Chaplet, p. 369.

Fourth Day (Easter Monday)

"Today bring to me those who do not believe in God and those who do not know me. I was thinking also of them during my bitter Passion, and their future zeal comforted my heart. Immerse them in the ocean of my mercy."

Most compassionate Jesus, you are the light of the whole world. Receive into the abode of your most compassionate heart the souls of those who do not believe in God and of those who as yet do not know you. Let the rays of your grace enlighten them that they, too, together with us, may extol your wonderful mercy; and do not let them escape from the abode which is your most compassionate heart.

Eternal Father, turn your merciful gaze upon the souls of those who do not believe in you, and of those who as yet do not know you, but who are enclosed in the most compassionate heart of Jesus. Draw them to the light of the Gospel. These souls do not know what great happiness it is to love you. Grant that they, too, may extol the generosity of your mercy for endless ages. Amen.

Continue with the Divine Mercy Chaplet, p. 369.

Fifth Day (Easter Tuesday)

"Today bring to me the souls of those who have separated themselves from my Church, and immerse them in the ocean of my mercy. During my bitter Passion they tore at my body and heart, that is, my Church. As they return to unity with the Church my wounds heal and in this way they alleviate my Passion."

Most merciful Jesus, goodness itself, you do not refuse light to those who seek it of you. Receive into the abode of your most compassionate heart the souls of those who have separated themselves from your Church. Draw them by your light into the unity of the Church, and do not let them escape from the abode of your most compassionate heart; but bring it about that they, too, come to glorify the generosity of your mercy.

Eternal Father, turn your merciful gaze upon the souls of those who have separated themselves from your Son's Church, who have squandered your blessings and misused your graces by obstinately persisting in their errors. Do not look upon their errors, but upon the love of your own Son and upon his bitter Passion, which he underwent for their sake, since they, too, are enclosed in his most compassionate heart. Bring it about that they also may glorify your great mercy for endless ages. Amen.

Continue with the Divine Mercy Chaplet, p. 369.

Sixth Day (Easter Wednesday)

"Today bring to me the meek and humble souls and the souls of little children, and immerse them in my mercy. These souls most closely resemble my heart. They strengthened me during my bitter agony. I saw them as earthly angels, who will keep vigil at my altars. I pour out upon them whole torrents of grace. I favor humble souls with my confidence."

Most merciful Jesus, you yourself have said, "Learn from me for I am meek and humble of heart." Receive into the abode of your most compassionate heart all meek and humble souls and the souls of little children. These souls send all heaven into ecstasy, and they are the heavenly Father's favorites. They are a sweet-smelling bouquet before the throne of God; God himself takes delight in their fragrance. These souls have a permanent abode in your most compassionate heart, O Jesus, and they unceasingly sing out a hymn of love and mercy.

Eternal Father, turn your merciful gaze upon meek souls, upon humble souls, and upon little children who are enfolded in the abode which is the most compassionate heart of Jesus. These souls bear the closest resemblance to your Son. Their fragrance rises from the earth and reaches your very throne. Father of mercy and of all goodness, I beg you by the love you bear these souls and by the delight you take in them: Bless the whole world, that all souls together may sing out the praises of your mercy for endless ages. Amen.

Continue with the Divine Mercy Chaplet, p. 369.

Seventh Day (Easter Thursday)

"Today bring to me the souls who especially venerate and glorify my mercy, and immerse them in my mercy. These souls sorrowed most over my Passion and entered most deeply into my spirit. They are living images of my compassionate heart. These souls will shine with a special brightness in the next life. Not one of them will go into the fire of hell. I shall particularly defend each one of them at the hour of death."

Most merciful Jesus, whose heart is love itself, receive into the abode of your most compassionate heart the souls of those who particularly extol and venerate the greatness of your mercy. These souls are mighty with the very power of God himself. In the midst of all afflictions and adversities they go forward, confident of your mercy; and united to you, O Jesus, they carry all mankind on their shoulders. These souls will not be judged severely, but your mercy will embrace them as they depart from this life.

Eternal Father, turn your merciful gaze upon the souls who glorify and venerate your greatest attribute, that of your fathomless mercy, and who are enclosed in your most compassionate heart. These souls are a living Gospel; their hands are full of deeds of mercy, and their hearts, overflowing with joy, sing a canticle of mercy to you, O Most High! I beg you, O God:

Show them your mercy according to the hope and trust they have placed in you. Let there be accomplished in them the promise of Jesus, who said to them that during their life, but especially at the hour of death, the souls who will venerate this fathomless mercy of his, he himself will defend as his glory. Amen.

Continue with the Divine Mercy Chaplet, p. 369.

Eighth Day (Easter Friday)

"Today bring to me the souls who are in the prison of purgatory, and immerse them in the abyss of my mercy. Let the torrents of my blood cool down their scorching flames. All these souls are greatly loved by me. They are making retribution to my justice. It is in your power to bring them relief. Draw all the indulgences from the treasury of my Church and offer them on their behalf. Oh, if you only knew the torments they suffer, you would continually offer for them the alms of the spirit and pay off their debt to my justice."

Most merciful Jesus, you yourself have said that you desire mercy; so I bring into the abode of your most compassionate heart the souls in purgatory, souls who are very dear to you, and yet, who must make retribution to your justice. May the streams of blood and water which gushed forth from your heart put out the flames of purgatory, that there, too, the power of your mercy may be celebrated.

Eternal Father, turn your merciful gaze upon the souls suffering in purgatory, who are enfolded in the most compassionate heart of Jesus. I beg you, by the sorrowful Passion of Jesus your Son, and by all the bitterness with which his most sacred soul was flooded: Manifest your mercy to the souls who are under your just scrutiny. Look upon them in no other way but only through the wounds of Jesus, your dearly beloved Son; for we firmly believe that there is no limit to your goodness and compassion. Amen.

Continue with the Divine Mercy Chaplet, p. 369.

Ninth Day (Easter Saturday)

"Today bring to me the souls who have become lukewarm, and immerse them in the abyss of my mercy. These souls wound my heart most painfully. My soul suffered the most dreadful loathing in the Garden of Olives because of lukewarm souls. They were the reason I cried out: 'Father, take this cup away from me, if it be your will.' For them, the last hope of salvation is to run to my mercy."

Most compassionate Jesus, you are compassion itself. I bring lukewarm souls into the abode of your most compassionate heart. In this fire of your pure love, let these tepid souls who, like corpses, filled you with such deep loathing, be once again set aflame. O most compassionate Jesus, exercise the omnipotence of your mercy and draw them into the very ardor of your love, and bestow upon them the gift of holy love, for nothing is beyond your power.

Eternal Father, turn your merciful gaze upon lukewarm souls who are nonetheless enfolded in the most compassionate heart of Jesus. Father of mercy, I beg you by the bitter Passion of your Son and by his three-hour agony on the cross: Let them, too, glorify the abyss of your mercy. Amen.

Continue with the Divine Mercy Chaplet, p. 369.

Holy Week: Holy Saturday

There is no Holy Saturday liturgy. The next liturgy, celebrated Saturday night, is the Easter Vigil. The Collect below is from the Easter Vigil Mass.

COLLECT PRAYER

O God, who make this most sacred night radiant with the glory of the Lord's Resurrection, stir up in your Church a spirit of adoption, so that, renewed in body and mind, we may render you undivided service. Through our Lord Jesus Christ, your Son, who lives and reigns with you in the unity of the Holy Spirit, one God, for ever and ever. Amen.

Holy Saturday Prayer

From the Liturgy of the Hours Lauds (Morning Prayer).

Almighty, ever-living God, whose Only-begotten Son descended to the realm of the dead, and rose from there to glory, grant that your faithful people, who were buried with him in baptism, may, by his resurrection, obtain eternal life. Through Christ our Lord. Amen.

The Lord's Descent into Hell[8]

From an ancient homily for Holy Saturday attributed to Saint Melito of Sardis (+180).

What is happening? Today there is a great silence over the earth, a great silence, and stillness, a great silence because the King sleeps; the

---

[8] "The Lord's Descent into Hell", prepared by Pontifical University of Saint Thomas Aquinas, http://www.vatican.va/spirit/documents/spirit_20010414_omelia-sabato-santo_en .html. Note: What we call the "limbo of the fathers" was understood by earlier Christians as a separate, nonpunishing section of hell in which the just waited for Jesus' redemption of mankind. We can see this use of the word *hell* in the Apostles' Creed when we say that Jesus "descended into hell".

earth was in terror and was still, because God slept in the flesh and raised up those who were sleeping from the ages. God has died in the flesh, and the underworld has trembled.

Truly he goes to seek out our first parent like a lost sheep; he wishes to visit those who sit in darkness and in the shadow of death. He goes to free the prisoner Adam and his fellow-prisoner Eve from their pains, he who is God, and Adam's son.

The Lord goes in to them holding his victorious weapon, his cross. When Adam, the first created man, sees him, he strikes his breast in terror and calls out to all: "My Lord be with you all." And Christ in reply says to Adam: "And with your spirit." And grasping his hand he raises him up, saying: "Awake, O sleeper, and arise from the dead, and Christ shall give you light.

"I am your God, who for your sake became your son, who for you and your descendants now speak and command with authority those in prison: Come forth, and those in darkness: Have light, and those who sleep: Rise.

"I command you: Awake, sleeper, I have not made you to be held a prisoner in the underworld. Arise from the dead; I am the life of the dead. Arise, O man, work of my hands, arise, you who were fashioned in my image. Rise, let us go hence; for you in me and I in you, together we are one undivided person.

"For you, I your God became your son; for you, I the Master took on your form, that of slave; for you, I who am above the heavens came on earth and under the earth; for you, man, I became as a man without help, free among the dead; for you, who left a garden, I was handed over to Jews from a garden and crucified in a garden.

"Look at the spittle on my face, which I received because of you, in order to restore you to that first divine inbreathing at creation. See the blows on my cheeks, which I accepted in order to refashion your distorted form to my own image.

"See the scourging of my back, which I accepted in order to disperse the load of your sins which was laid upon your back. See my hands nailed to the tree for a good purpose, for you, who stretched out your hand to the tree for an evil one.

"I slept on the cross and a sword pierced my side, for you, who slept in paradise and brought forth Eve from your side. My side healed the pain of your side; my sleep will release you from your sleep in Hades; my sword has checked the sword which was turned against you.

"But arise, let us go hence. The enemy brought you out of the land of paradise; I will reinstate you, no longer in paradise, but on the throne of heaven. I denied you the tree of life, which was a figure, but now I myself am united to you, I who am life. I posted the cherubim to guard you as they would slaves; now I make the cherubim worship you as they would God.

"The cherubim throne has been prepared, the bearers are ready and waiting, the bridal chamber is in order, the food is provided, the everlasting houses and rooms are in readiness; the treasures of good things have been opened; the kingdom of heaven has been prepared before the ages."

Prayer for the Lighting of the Paschal Candle[9]

May the light of Christ, rising in glory,
dispel the darkness of our hearts and minds. Amen.

Exsultet: The Easter Proclamation[10]

Exult, let them exult, the hosts of heaven,
exult, let Angel ministers of God exult,
let the trumpet of salvation
sound aloud our mighty King's triumph!

Be glad, let earth be glad, as glory floods her,
ablaze with light from her eternal King,
let all corners of the earth be glad,
knowing an end to gloom and darkness.

Rejoice, let Mother Church also rejoice,
arrayed with the lightning of his glory,
let this holy building shake with joy,
filled with the mighty voices of the peoples.

[9] *Roman Missal*, The Easter Vigil, no. 17.
[10] Ibid., no. 19.

Lift up your hearts.

All: We lift them up to the Lord.

Let us give thanks to the Lord our God.

All: It is right and just.

It is truly right and just, with ardent love of mind and heart
and with devoted service of our voice,
to acclaim our God invisible, the almighty Father,
and Jesus Christ, our Lord, his Son, his Only Begotten.
Who for our sake paid Adam's debt to the eternal Father,
and, pouring out his own dear Blood,
wiped clean the record of our ancient sinfulness.

These, then, are the feasts of Passover,
in which is slain the Lamb, the one true Lamb,
whose Blood anoints the doorposts of believers.

This is the night,
when once you led our forebears, Israel's children,
from slavery in Egypt
and made them pass dry-shod through the Red Sea.

This is the night
that with a pillar of fire
banished the darkness of sin.

This is the night
that even now, throughout the world,
sets Christian believers apart from worldly vices
and from the gloom of sin,
leading them to grace
and joining them to his holy ones.

This is the night,
when Christ broke the prison-bars of death
and rose victorious from the underworld.

Our birth would have been no gain,
had we not been redeemed.

O wonder of your humble care for us!
O love, O charity beyond all telling,

to ransom a slave you gave away your Son!
O truly necessary sin of Adam,
destroyed completely by the Death of Christ!
O happy fault
that earned so great, so glorious a Redeemer!

O truly blessed night,
worthy alone to know the time and hour
when Christ rose from the underworld!

This is the night
of which it is written:
The night shall be as bright as day,
dazzling is the night for me,
and full of gladness.

The sanctifying power of this night
dispels wickedness, washes faults away,
restores innocence to the fallen, and joy to mourners,
drives out hatred, fosters concord, and brings down the mighty.
On this, your night of grace, O holy Father,
accept this candle, a solemn offering,
the work of bees and of your servants' hands,
an evening sacrifice of praise,
this gift from your most holy Church.
But now we know the praises of this pillar,
which glowing fire ignites for God's honor,
a fire into many flames divided,
yet never dimmed by sharing of its light,
for it is fed by melting wax,
drawn out by mother bees
to build a torch so precious.

O truly blessed night,
when things of heaven are wed to those of earth,
and divine to the human.

Therefore, O Lord,
we pray you that this candle,
hallowed to the honor of your name,
may persevere undimmed,
to overcome the darkness of this night.

Receive it as a pleasing fragrance,
and let it mingle with the lights of heaven.

May this flame be found still burning
by the Morning Star:
the one Morning Star who never sets,
Christ your Son,
who, coming back from death's domain,
has shed his peaceful light on humanity,
and lives and reigns for ever and ever.

All: Amen.

9

Movable Feasts: Eastertide

See appendix B for the exact dates of these movable feasts in a particular year.

Prayer after Blessing before Meals: The Paschal Greeting

An Easter custom among Eastern Catholics is to replace the usual "Hello" with this paschal greeting throughout Eastertide. We use this as our prayer after Blessing before Meals from Easter to Pentecost.

Greeting: He is risen.

Response: He is risen, indeed!

Marian Antiphon III: Regina Caeli

One of the four seasonal liturgical Marian antiphons, the Regina Caeli is sung, chanted, or recited during Mass and at the end of the office of Compline, or Night Prayer, throughout Eastertide—that is, from the Easter Vigil through Pentecost Sunday. The Regina Caeli is also recited in place of the daily Angelus during Eastertide. The antiphon is often credited to Pope Gregory V (+998).

Regina caeli, laetare, alleluia; quia quem meruisti portare, alleluia; resurrexit sicut dixit, alleluia. Ora pro nobis Deum, alleluia.

Queen of Heaven, rejoice, alleluia; for he whom you did merit to bear, alleluia; has risen as he said, alleluia. Pray for us to God, alleluia.

For the same prayer in an expanded form (in English) with a leader and responses, see p. 362.

223

EASTER SUNDAY OF THE RESURRECTION OF THE LORD (Solemnity)

COLLECT PRAYER

O God, who on this day, through your Only Begotten Son, have conquered death and unlocked for us the path to eternity, grant, we pray, that we who keep the solemnity of the Lord's Resurrection may, through the renewal brought by your Spirit, rise up in the light of life. Through our Lord Jesus Christ, your Son, who lives and reigns with you in the unity of the Holy Spirit, one God, for ever and ever. Amen.

Urbi et Orbi Indugence

Watch the papal Urbi et Orbi blessing in person, on TV, or online for a plenary indulgence; see p. 93. See also Renewal of Baptismal Promises, p. 353.

A reading from the Holy Gospel according to Saint Mark.
(Mk 16:9–18)

Now when he rose early on the first day of the week, he appeared first to Mary Magdalene, from whom he had cast out seven demons. She went and told those who had been with him, as they mourned and wept. But when they heard that he was alive and had been seen by her, they would not believe it.

After this he appeared in another form to two of them, as they were walking into the country. And they went back and told the rest, but they did not believe them.

Afterward he appeared to the Eleven themselves as they sat at table; and he upbraided them for their unbelief and hardness of heart, because they had not believed those who saw him after he had risen. And he said to them, "Go into all the world and preach the gospel to the whole creation. He who believes and is baptized will be saved; but he who does not believe will be condemned. And these signs will accompany those who believe: in my name they will cast out demons; they will speak in new tongues; they will pick up serpents, and if they drink any deadly thing, it will not hurt them; they will lay their hands on the sick, and they will recover."

A reading from the Holy Gospel according to Saint Luke.
(Lk 24:1–49)

But on the first day of the week, at early dawn, they went to the tomb, taking the spices which they had prepared. And they found the stone rolled away from the tomb, but when they went in they did not find the body. While they were perplexed about this, behold, two men stood by them in dazzling apparel; and as they were frightened and bowed their faces to the ground, the men said to them, "Why do you seek the living among the dead? He is not here, but has risen. Remember how he told you, while he was still in Galilee, that the Son of man must be delivered into the hands of sinful men, and be crucified, and on the third day rise." And they remembered his words, and returning from the tomb they told all this to the Eleven and to all the rest. Now it was Mary Magdalene and Joanna and Mary the mother of James and the other women with them who told this to the apostles; but these words seemed to them an idle tale, and they did not believe them. But Peter rose and ran to the tomb; stooping and looking in, he saw the linen cloths by themselves; and he went home wondering at what had happened.

That very day two of them were going to a village named Emmaus, about seven miles from Jerusalem, and talking with each other about all these things that had happened. While they were talking and discussing together, Jesus himself drew near and went with them. But their eyes were kept from recognizing him. And he said to them, "What is this conversation which you are holding with each other as you walk?" And they stood still, looking sad. Then one of them, named Cleopas, answered him, "Are you the only visitor to Jerusalem who does not know the things that have happened there in these days?" And he said to them, "What things?" And they said to him, "Concerning Jesus of Nazareth, who was a prophet mighty in deed and word before God and all the people, and how our chief priests and rulers delivered him up to be condemned to death, and crucified him. But we had hoped that he was the one to redeem Israel. Yes, and besides all this, it is now the third day since this happened. Moreover, some women of our company amazed us. They were at the tomb early in the morning and did not find his body; and they came back saying that they had even seen a vision of angels, who said that he was alive. Some of those who were with us went to the tomb, and found it just as the women had said; but him they did not see." And he said to them, "O foolish men, and slow of heart to believe all that the prophets have spoken! Was it not necessary that the Christ should suffer these things and enter into his glory?" And beginning with Moses and all the prophets, he interpreted to them in all the Scriptures the things concerning himself.

So they drew near to the village to which they were going. He appeared to be going further, but they constrained him, saying, "Stay with us, for it is toward evening and the day is now far spent." So he went in to stay with them. When he was at table with them, he took the bread and blessed and broke it, and gave it to them. And their eyes were opened and they recognized him; and he vanished out of their sight. They said to each other, "Did not our hearts burn within us while he talked to us on the road, while he opened to us the Scriptures?" And they rose that same hour and returned to Jerusalem; and they found the Eleven gathered together and those who were with them, who said, "The Lord has risen indeed, and has appeared to Simon!" Then they told what had happened on the road, and how he was known to them in the breaking of the bread.

As they were saying this, Jesus himself stood among them, and said to them, "Peace to you." But they were startled and frightened, and supposed that they saw a spirit. And he said to them, "Why are you troubled, and why do questionings rise in your hearts? See my hands and my feet, that it is I myself; handle me, and see; for a spirit has not flesh and bones as you see that I have." And when he had said this he showed them his hands and his feet. And while they still disbelieved for joy, and wondered, he said to them, "Have you anything here to eat?" They gave him a piece of broiled fish, and he took it and ate before them. Then he said to them, "These are my words which I spoke to you, while I was still with you, that everything written about me in the law of Moses and the prophets and the psalms must be fulfilled." Then he opened their minds to understand the Scriptures, and said to them, "Thus it is written, that the Christ should suffer and on the third day rise from the dead, and that repentance and forgiveness of sins should be preached in his name to all nations, beginning from Jerusalem. You are witnesses of these things. And behold, I send the promise of my Father upon you; but stay in the city, until you are clothed with power from on high."

EASTER SONG SUGGESTIONS: Ye Sons and Daughters; Jesus Christ Is Risen Today; Alleluia! Sing to Jesus

Second Sunday of Easter— Sunday of Divine Mercy

COLLECT PRAYER

God of everlasting mercy, who in the very recurrence of the paschal feast kindle the faith of the people you have made your own, increase, we pray, the grace you have bestowed, that all may grasp and rightly understand in what font they have been washed, by whose Spirit they have been reborn, by whose Blood they have been redeemed. Through our Lord Jesus Christ, your Son, who lives and reigns with you in the unity of the Holy Spirit, one God, for ever and ever. Amen.

Divine Mercy Indulgence Prayer

According to a Church decree on the indulgences attached to Divine Mercy devotions, "a plenary indulgence [is] granted under the usual conditions (sacramental confession, Eucharistic Communion and prayer for the intentions of the Supreme Pontiff) to the faithful who, on the Second Sunday of Easter or Divine Mercy Sunday, in any church or chapel, in a spirit completely detached from the affection for a sin, even a venial sin, take part in the prayers and devotions held in honor of Divine Mercy, or who, in the presence of the Blessed Sacrament exposed or reserved in the tabernacle, recite the Our Father and the Creed, adding a devout prayer to the merciful Lord Jesus."[1]

Merciful Jesus, I trust in you!

Our Father, see p. 349; Hail Mary, see p. 350; Apostles' Creed, see p. 366. See also Divine Mercy Chaplet, p. 369.

---

[1] Apostolic Penitentiary, Decree on Indulgences Attached to Devotions in Honor of Divine Mercy (June 13, 2002), http://www.vatican.va/roman_curia/tribunals/apost_penit/documents/rc_trib_appen_doc_20020629_decree-ii_en.html. See the introduction of this book for the usual conditions for indulgences.

228 Thursday Forty Days after Easter (or Seventh Sunday of Easter): THE ASCENSION OF THE LORD

as he went, behold, two men stood by them in white robes, and said, "Men of Galilee, why do you stand looking into heaven? This Jesus, who was taken up from you into heaven, will come in the same way as you saw him go into heaven."

The Word of the Lord.

All: Thanks be to God.

Pentecost Novena[3]

Although the Pentecost Novena can be said at any time, it is traditionally begun on the Friday after Ascension Thursday (or before Ascension Sunday). The first of all novenas, it is based on the fact that after Jesus' Ascension into heaven, Mary and the disciples came together in the upper room to devote themselves to prayer (cf. Acts 1:14). After nine days, they received the Holy Spirit on Pentecost (cf. Acts 2:1–4).

On May 4, 1897, Pope Leo XIII proclaimed, "We decree and command that throughout the whole Catholic Church, this year and in every subsequent year, a novena shall take place before Whit-Sunday [Pentecost], in all parish churches."[4] It has been reported that Pope Leo XIII was inspired to mandate a Pentecost novena because of a letter from a housewife in Italy. Pope Saint John Paul II reiterated Pope Leo XIII's command for a worldwide Pentecost novena.[5] It is one of three novenas for which an indulgence is available (the other two being before Christmas and before the Immaculate Conception). No official prayers are set. Here is one option.

Holy Spirit Prayer

To be prayed each of the nine days.

Leader: Come, Holy Spirit, fill the hearts of your faithful, and kindle in them the fire of your love. Send forth your Spirit, and they shall be created,

---

[3] Charles J. Callan and John Ambrose McHugh, *Blessed Be God: A Complete Catholic Prayer Book* (New York: Kennedy, 1961).

[4] Leo XIII, encyclical *Divinum Illud Munus* (May 9, 1897), no. 13, http://www.vatican.va /content/leo-xiii/en/encyclicals/documents/hf_l-xiii_enc_09051897_divinum-illud-munus .html.

[5] John Paul II, General Audience (May 30, 1979), no. 2, https://www.vatican.va/content /john-paul-ii/en/audiences/1979/documents/hf_jp-ii_aud_19790530.html.

All: And you shall renew the face of the earth.

Leader: Let us pray. O God, who by the light of the Holy Spirit, did instruct the hearts of your faithful, grant that by that same Holy Spirit, we may be truly wise and ever rejoice in his consolation, through Christ our Lord.

All: Amen.

First Day (Friday)

Come, O Holy Spirit, the Lord and giver of life; take up your dwelling within my soul, and make of it your sacred temple. Make me live by grace as an adopted child of God. Pervade all the energies of my soul, and create in me a fountain of living water springing up into life everlasting.

All: Amen.

Our Father, Hail Mary, Glory Be.

Second Day (Saturday)

Come, O Spirit of Wisdom, and reveal to my soul the mysteries of heavenly things, their exceeding greatness and power and beauty. Teach me to love them above and beyond all the passing joys and satisfactions of earth. Show me the way by which I may be able to attain to them and possess them, and hold them hereafter, my own forever.

All: Amen.

Our Father, Hail Mary, Glory Be.

Third Day (Sunday)

Come, Spirit of Understanding, and enlighten our minds, that we may know and believe all the mysteries of salvation, and may merit at last to see the eternal light in your light; and in the light of glory to have the clear vision of you and the Father and the Son.

All: Amen.

Our Father, Hail Mary, Glory Be.

Fourth Day (Monday)

Come, O Spirit of Counsel, help and guide me in all my ways, that I may always do your holy will. Incline my heart to that which is good, turn it away from all that is evil, and direct me by the path of your commandments to the goal of eternal life for which I long.

All: Amen.

Our Father, Hail Mary, Glory Be.

Fifth Day (Tuesday)

Come, O Spirit of Fortitude, and give fortitude to our souls. Make our hearts strong in all trials and in all distress, pouring forth abundantly into them the gifts of strength, that we may be able to resist the attacks of the devil.

All: Amen.

Our Father, Hail Mary, Glory Be.

Sixth Day (Wednesday)

Come, O Spirit of Knowledge, and make us understand and avoid emptiness and nothingness in the world. Give us grace to use the world for your glory and the salvation of your creatures. May we always be very faithful in putting your rewards before every earthly gift.

All: Amen.

Our Father, Hail Mary, Glory Be.

Seventh Day (Thursday)

Come, O Spirit of Piety, possess my heart; incline it to a true faith in you, to a holy love of you, my God, that with my whole soul I may seek you, and find you my best, my truest joy.

All: Amen.

Our Father, Hail Mary, Glory Be.

Eighth Day (Friday)

Come, O Spirit of Holy Fear, penetrate my inmost heart, that I may set you, my Lord and God, before my face forever; and shun things that can offend you, so that I may be made worthy to appear before the pure eyes of your divine Majesty in the heaven of heavens, where you live and reign in the unity of the Blessed Trinity, God, world without end.

All: Amen.

Our Father, Hail Mary, Glory Be.

Ninth Day (Saturday)

Come, O Holy Comforter, and grant us a desire for heavenly things. Produce in our souls the flowers and fruits of virtue, so that, being filled with all sweetness and joy in the pursuit of good, we may attain unto eternal blessedness.

All: Amen.

Our Father, Hail Mary, Glory Be.

After the ending prayers on the ninth day:

O God, you have taught the hearts of your faithful people by sending them the light of your Holy Spirit. Grant us by the same Spirit to have a right judgment in all things and evermore to rejoice in his holy comfort. Through Christ our Lord.

All: Amen.

10

April

The month of the Blessed Sacrament

Prayer after Blessing before Meals: *O sacrum convivium*

O sacred banquet! in which Christ is received, the memory of his Passion is renewed, the mind is filled with grace, and a pledge of future glory to us is given. Alleluia.

Tantum ergo, *p. 203.*

For two Acts of Spiritual Communion, see p. 255.

April 23: Saint George, Martyr (Optional Memorial)

When Saint George's Day falls between Palm Sunday and the Second Sunday of Easter inclusive, it is transferred to the Monday after the Second Sunday of Easter.

COLLECT PRAYER

Extolling your might, O Lord, we humbly implore you, that, as Saint George imitated the Passion of the Lord, so he may lend us ready help in our weakness. Through our Lord Jesus Christ, your Son, who lives and reigns with you in the unity of the Holy Spirit, one God, for ever and ever. Amen.

Prayer to Saint George

Almighty God, who gave to your servant George boldness to confess the name of our Savior Jesus Christ before the rulers of this world, and courage to die for this faith, grant that we may always be ready to give a reason for the hope that is in us and to suffer gladly for the sake of our Lord Jesus Christ, who lives and reigns with you and the Holy Spirit, one God, for ever and ever. Amen.

April 25: Saint Mark, Evangelist (Feast)

When Saint George's Day or Saint Mark's Day falls between Palm Sunday and the Second Sunday of Easter inclusive, the saint's day is transferred to the Monday after the Second Sunday of Easter. If both fall in this period, Saint George's Day is transferred to the Monday, and Saint Mark's Day to the Tuesday.

The Major Rogation also falls on April 25. See below for how to celebrate it.

COLLECT PRAYER

O God, who raised up Saint Mark, your Evangelist, and endowed him with the grace to preach the Gospel, grant, we pray, that we may so profit from his teaching as to follow faithfully in the footsteps of Christ. Who lives and reigns with you in the unity of the Holy Spirit, one God, for ever and ever. Amen.

A reading from the Holy Gospel according to Saint Mark. (Mk 14:48–52)

And Jesus said to them, "Have you come out as against a robber, with swords and clubs to capture me? Day after day I was with you in the temple teaching, and you did not seize me. But let the Scriptures be fulfilled." And they all deserted him and fled. And a young man followed him, with nothing but a linen cloth about his body; and they seized him, but he left the linen cloth and ran away naked.[1]

The Gospel of the Lord.

All: Praise to you, Lord Jesus Christ.

---

[1] This young man is usually supposed to have been the evangelist himself.

April 25: Major Rogation Day

If April 25 falls on Easter Sunday or Monday, the Rogation Day procession is transferred to Easter Tuesday.

Rogation Days are set apart to bless the fields and invoke God's mercy on all creation. They are April 25, which is called the Major Rogation (and is only coincidentally the same day as the feast of Saint Mark), and the three days preceding Ascension Thursday, which are called the Minor Rogations. Traditionally, on these days, the congregation marches the boundaries of the parish, blessing every tree and stone, while chanting or reciting the Litany of All Saints. At home, a Rogation Day procession can cover the boundaries of the yard, the house, or the neighborhood. Find the Litany of All Saints on p. 336.

Prayer for a Sprouting Seed[2]

To you, O Lord, we cry and pray: Bless this sprouting seed, strengthen it in the gentle movement of soft winds, refresh it with the dew of heaven, and let it grow to full maturity for the good of body and soul. Amen.

It may be sprinkled with holy water.

Farmer's Prayer

O God, source and giver of all things, who manifest your infinite majesty, power, and goodness in the earth about us, we give you honor and glory. For the sun and rain, for the manifold fruits of the fields, for the increase of herds and flocks, we thank you. For the enrichment of our souls with divine grace, we are grateful. Supreme Lord of the harvest, graciously accept us and the fruits of toil, in union

---

[2]J. H. Schlarman, trans., *With the Blessing of the Church* (Des Moines, Iowa: National Catholic Rural Life Conference, 1946), Eternal Word Television Network, https://www.ewtn.com/catholicism/library/with-the-blessing-of-the-church-11899. This work contains translations of various blessings in the *Roman Ritual*.

with Christ your Son, as atonement for our sins, for the growth of your Church, for peace and charity in our homes, for salvation for all. Amen.

April 28: Saint Gianna Beretta Molla (Optional Memorial)

COLLECT PRAYER[3]

O God, who gladden us each year with the feast day of blessed Saint Gianna Molla, grant, we pray, that we, who are called to honor her, may also follow her example of holy living. Through our Lord Jesus Christ, your Son, who lives and reigns with you in the unity of the Holy Spirit, one God, for ever and ever. Amen.

Prayer of Saint Gianna Beretta Molla[4]

My most sweet Jesus, infinitely merciful God, most tender Father of souls, and in a particular way of the weakest, most miserable, most infirm that you carry with special tenderness in your divine arms, I come to you to ask you, through the love and merits of your Sacred Heart, the grace to comprehend and to do always your holy will, the grace to confide in you, the grace to rest securely through time and eternity in your loving divine arms. Amen.

Prayer during Physical and Spiritual Trials[5]

Saint Gianna, heroically Christlike wife, mother, and physician, I ask the help of your prayers as I strive to follow your holy example

---

[3] *Roman Missal*, Commons for Holy Women, no. V.1.

[4] "Prayer of Saint Gianna Beretta Molla", the Society of Saint Gianna Beretta Molla, https://saintgianna.org/main.htm.

[5] Raymond Leo Burke, "Prayer to St. Gianna", St. Gianna Physician's Guild, http://www.stgiannaphysicians.org/prayer_to_st_gianna.

in my physical and spiritual trials. Help me, by your prayers, to recognize the suffering of the Cross as the way to pure and selfless love of God and my neighbor. May your practice of medicine with priestly care of both body and soul inspire physicians to see the face of the suffering Christ in their patients. May your loving acceptance of illness and death help patients to know and do God's will in all things, uniting their sufferings to the Passion and death of Christ for the salvation of the world. Saint Gianna, pray for us always, that we may have a heart, meek and courageous, like the heart of Jesus, in whom we find our healing and strength. We ask this through Christ our Lord. Amen.

April 29: Saint Catherine of Siena, Virgin and Doctor of the Church (Memorial)

COLLECT PRAYER

O God, who set Saint Catherine of Siena on fire with divine love in her contemplation of the Lord's Passion and her service for your Church, grant, through her intercession, that your people, participating in the mystery of Christ, may ever exult in the revelation of his glory. Who lives and reigns with you in the unity of the Holy Spirit, one God, for ever and ever. Amen.

Saint Catherine Prayer[6]

O great Saint Catherine of Siena, glory of the Dominican order, who served the sick and suffering in time of plague and brought back the exiled popes from Avignon to Rome, pray for us, that we may have some measure of your courage and self-sacrifice. Blessed be the name of God! Amen.

---

[6]Blanche Jennings Thompson, *All Day with God* (Milwaukee: Bruce, 1939), Catholic Culture, https://www.catholicculture.org/culture/liturgicalyear/prayers/view.cfm?id=1222.

Closing of World Youth Day 2000 Homily of Pope Saint John Paul II[7]

Thank God for the World Youth Days! Thanks be to God for all the young people who have been involved in them in the past sixteen years! Many of them are now adults who continue to live their faith in their homes and workplaces. I am sure, dear friends, that you too will be as good as those who preceded you. You will carry the proclamation of Christ into the new millennium. When you return home, do not grow lax. Reinforce and deepen your bond with the Christian communities to which you belong. From Rome, from the City of Peter and Paul, the pope follows you with affection and, paraphrasing Saint Catherine of Siena's words, reminds you: "If you are what you should be, you will set the whole world ablaze!"

[7]John Paul II, Homily at the Closing of World Youth Day (Tor Vergata, August 20, 2000), no. 7, http://www.vatican.va/content/john-paul-ii/en/homilies/2000/documents/hf_jp-ii_hom_20000820_gmg.html.

11

May

The month of Mary

Prayer after Blessing before Meals: *Sub tuum praesidium*

The oldest known prayer to Mary, dating from the third century.

We fly to your protection, O holy Mother of God; despise not our petitions in our necessities, but deliver us always from all dangers, O glorious and blessed Virgin. Amen.

At-Home May Crowning

An at-home May Crowning can be as simple as parents and children saying a Hail Mary and taping a paper crown on a printed-out picture of Our Lady. It can also be done in a larger group with more pomp and circumstance.[1] We like to make a flower crown and place it on the three-foot-tall statue of Mary in our garden. Someone is selected to place the crown on the statue; priority is given to anyone who has made his First Communion that year. A May Crowning is a good excuse to wear those First Communion clothes again. If we have friends joining us, sometimes we end up with multiple May queens and kings who crown Mary together! Other participants can hold flowers, swords, or banners. The ceremony begins with a hymn in Mary's honor.

Hail, Holy Queen Enthroned Above

1. Hail, Holy Queen enthroned above, O Maria!
   Hail, Mother of mercy and of love, O Maria!
   Triumph, all ye cherubim!

[1] A May Crowning that takes place in a church should follow the instructions available in National Conference of Catholic Bishops, *Order of Crowning an Image of the Blessed Virgin Mary* (New Jersey: Catholic Book Publishing Corp., 2005).

Sing with us, ye seraphim!
Heaven and earth resound the hymn!
Salve, salve, salve, Regina!

2. Our life, our sweetness here below, O Maria!
Our hope in sorrow and in woe, O Maria!
Triumph, all ye cherubim!
Sing with us, ye seraphim!
Heaven and earth resound the hymn!
Salve, salve, salve, Regina!

Mense Maio (The month of May)[2]

From an encyclical of Pope Paul VI on prayers during May for preservation of peace, April 29, 1965.

This is the month during which Christians, in their churches and their homes, offer the Virgin Mother more fervent and loving acts of homage and veneration; and it is the month in which a greater abundance of God's merciful gifts comes down to us from our Mother's throne.

We are delighted and consoled by this pious custom associated with the month of May, which pays honor to the Blessed Virgin and brings such rich benefits to the Christian people. Since Mary is rightly to be regarded as the way by which we are led to Christ, the person who encounters Mary cannot help but encounter Christ likewise. For what other reason do we continually turn to Mary except to seek the Christ in her arms, to seek our Savior in her, through her, and with her? To him men are to turn amid the anxieties and perils of this world, urged on by duty and driven by the compelling needs of their heart, to find a haven of salvation, a transcendent fountain of life.

Reading

A reading from the Holy Gospel according to Saint Luke.
(Lk 1:26–28)

In the sixth month the angel Gabriel was sent from God to a city of Galilee named Nazareth, to a virgin betrothed to a man whose name was Joseph, of the house of David; and the virgin's name was Mary.

---

[2] Paul VI, encyclical *Mense Maio* (April 28, 1965), nos. 1–2, http://www.vatican.va/content/paul-vi/en/encyclicals/documents/hf_p-vi_enc_29041965_mense-maio.html.

And he came to her and said, "Hail, full of grace, the Lord is with you!"

The Gospel of the Lord.

All: Praise to you, Lord Jesus Christ.

All sing a Marian hymn (see below). Repeat as the group processes to the statue and the crown is placed on the image. Other participants may each place a flower in a vase at the feet of the statue.

Immaculate Mary

1. Immaculate Mary, your praises we sing;
   You reign now in splendor with Jesus our King.

Refrain: Ave, ave, ave, Maria! Ave, ave, Maria!

2. In heaven, the blessed your glory proclaim;
   On earth we your children invoke your sweet name. *Refrain*

3. We pray for the Church, our true Mother on earth,
   And beg you to watch o'er the land of our birth. *Refrain*

After the crowning, the Litany of Loreto is recited. See p. 52.

The celebration ends with a song.

Bring Flowers of the Rarest

Bring flow'rs of the fairest,
Bring flow'rs of the rarest,
From garden and woodland
And hillside and vale;
Our full hearts are swelling,
Our glad voices telling
The praise of the loveliest
Rose of the vale.

O Mary! We crown thee with
blossoms today,
Queen of the Angels, Queen of
the May,
O Mary! We crown thee with
blossoms today,
Queen of the Angels, Queen of
the May.

May 1: Saint Joseph the Worker (Optional Memorial)

COLLECT PRAYER

O God, Creator of all things, who laid down for the human race the law of work, graciously grant that by the example of Saint Joseph and under his patronage we may complete the works you set us to do and attain the rewards you promise. Through our Lord Jesus Christ, your Son, who lives and reigns with you in the unity of the Holy Spirit, one God, for ever and ever. Amen.

Prayer for Catholic Workers[3]

From Divini Redemptoris, *a 1937 encyclical of Pope Pius XI on atheistic Communism.*

[Catholic workers, young and old] have been given, perhaps as a reward for their often heroic fidelity in these trying days, a noble and an arduous mission. Under the guidance of their bishops and priests, they are to bring back to the Church and to God those immense multitudes of their fellow workers who, because they were not understood or treated with the respect to which they were entitled, in bitterness have strayed far from God. Let Catholic workers show these their wandering brethren by word and example that the Church is a tender Mother to all those who labor and suffer, and that she has never failed, and never will fail, in her sacred maternal duty of protecting her children. If this mission, which must be fulfilled in mines, in factories, in shops, wherever they may be laboring, should at times require great sacrifices, Catholic workers will remember that the Savior of the world has given them an example not only of toil but of self-immolation. Amen.

See also Litany of Saint Joseph, p. 187; To You O Blessed Joseph, p. 368.

May 13: Our Lady of Fatima (Optional Memorial)

COLLECT PRAYER

O God, who chose the Mother of your Son to be our Mother also, grant us that, persevering in penance and prayer for the salvation of

[3] Pius XI, encyclical *Divini Redemptoris* (March 19, 1937), no. 70, http://www.vatican.va/content/pius-xi/en/encyclicals/documents/hf_p-xi_enc_19370319_divini-redemptoris.html.

the world, we may further more effectively each day the reign of Christ. Who lives and reigns with you in the unity of the Holy Spirit, one God, for ever and ever. Amen.

Fatima Pardon Prayer

Delivered by the Angel of Peace during the first apparition of the angel to the three shepherd children of Fatima in spring 1916.

My God, I believe, I adore, I trust, and I love you! I beg pardon for those who do not believe, do not adore, do not trust, and do not love you. Amen.

Fatima Angel's Prayer

Delivered by the Angel of Peace during the third apparition of the angel in October 1916. The angel appeared to the three shepherd children holding a chalice in his hands, with a Host above it from which drops of blood were falling into the chalice.

O Most Holy Trinity, Father, Son, and Holy Spirit, I adore you profoundly. I offer you the most precious Body, Blood, Soul, and Divinity of Jesus Christ, present in all the tabernacles of the world, in reparation for the outrages, sacrileges, and indifference by which he is offended. By the infinite merits of the Sacred Heart of Jesus and the Immaculate Heart of Mary, I beg the conversion of poor sinners. Amen.

Fatima Rosary Decade Prayer

Delivered by Our Lady during the third apparition of Our Lady of Fatima to the three shepherd children on July 13, 1917. It is traditionally prayed after the Glory Be for each decade of the Rosary.

O my Jesus, forgive us our sins, save us from the fires of hell. Lead all souls to heaven, especially those most in need of thy mercy. Amen.

See also Litany of Loreto, p. 52. See prayers and instructions for the Rosary, p. 363.

May 21: Saint Christopher Magallanes, Priest, and Companions, Martyrs (Optional Memorial)

COLLECT PRAYER

Almighty and eternal God, who made the Priest Saint Christopher Magallanes and his companions faithful to Christ the King even to the point of martyrdom, grant us, through their intercession, that, persevering in confession of the true faith, we may always hold fast to the commandments of your love. Through our Lord Jesus Christ, your Son, who lives and reigns with you in the unity of the Holy Spirit, one God, for ever and ever. Amen.

Cristero Prayer

Composed by the martyr Blessed Anacleto Gonzalez Flores (+1927) and prayed by the Cristeros of Jalisco at the end of the Rosary.[4]

My sins are more numerous than the drops of blood that you shed for me. I do not deserve to belong to the army that defends the rights of your Church and fights for you. I would that I had never sinned so that my life were an offering pleasing to your eyes. Wash away my iniquity and cleanse me from my sins.

By your holy cross, by my most holy Mother of Guadalupe, forgive me; I have not known how to make penance for my sins, so I want to receive my death as a deserved punishment for them. I do not want to fight, or live, or die, but for you and your Church.

Holy Mother Guadalupe! Accompany in his agony this poor sinner. Grant that my last word on earth and my first song in heaven be: VIVA CRISTO REY [Long live Christ the King]!

[4] Translated by Fr. Jordi Rivero of Love Crucified Catholic Community (LoveCrucified .com). I spent months securing permissions to include various prayers in this book. The permission for this prayer was my favorite: "Dear Kendra, GOD BLESS YOU. I pray that your book is blessed and that many people are blessed by it. What you see in the link is the prayer of Blessed Anacleto and my translation into English. I do not believe anybody holds the rights to the original. The author is a blessed martyr now in heaven! He will be glad and pray for you! In regard to my translation, you are free to use it—all for the glory of GOD. Hope to meet you in heaven after both having persevered.—Fr. Jordi Rivero."

May 22: Saint Rita of Cascia, Religious (Optional Memorial)

COLLECT PRAYER

Bestow on us, we pray, O Lord, the wisdom and strength of the Cross, with which you were pleased to endow Saint Rita, so that, suffering in every tribulation with Christ, we may participate ever more deeply in his Paschal Mystery. Who lives and reigns with you in the unity of the Holy Spirit, one God, for ever and ever. Amen.

Prayer to Saint Rita

O holy protectress of those who are in greatest need, you who shine as a star of hope in the midst of darkness, blessed Saint Rita, bright mirror of God's grace, in patience and fortitude you are a model of all the states in life. I unite my will with the will of God through the merits of my Savior Jesus Christ, and in particular through his patient wearing of the crown of thorns, which with tender devotion you did daily contemplate. Through the merits of the holy Virgin Mary and your own graces and virtues, I ask you to obtain my earnest petition, provided it be for the greater glory of God and my own sanctification. Guide and purify my intention, O holy protectress and advocate, so that I may obtain the pardon of all my sins and the grace to persevere daily, as you did in walking with courage, generosity, and fidelity down the path of life. (*Here mention your request.*) Saint Rita, advocate of the impossible, pray for us. Saint Rita, advocate of the helpless, pray for us. Amen.

May 30: Saint Joan of Arc, Virgin and Martyr (Optional Memorial)

COLLECT PRAYER[5]

O God, by whose gifts strength is made perfect in weakness, grant to all who honor the glory of blessed Saint Joan of Arc that she, who

[5] *Roman Missal*, Common for a Holy Woman Martyr, no. V.

drew from you the strength to triumph, may likewise always obtain from you the grace of victory for us. Through our Lord Jesus Christ, your Son, who lives and reigns with you in the unity of the Holy Spirit, one God, for ever and ever. Amen.

Prayer to Saint Joan of Arc

Saint Joan of Arc, you are filled with compassion for those who invoke you, and filled with love for those who suffer; heavily laden with the weight of my troubles, I kneel at your feet and humbly beg you to take my present need under your special protection. (*Here mention your request.*) Grant to recommend it to the Blessed Virgin Mary, and lay it before the throne of Jesus. Cease not to intercede for me until my request is granted. Above all, obtain for me the grace one day to meet God face to face, and with you and Mary, and all the angels and saints, praise him through all eternity. O most powerful Saint Joan, do not let me lose my soul, but obtain for me the grace of winning my way to heaven, forever and ever. Amen.

Transcript of the Trial of Joan of Arc[6]

The trial of Saint Joan of Arc took place over fifteen sessions between February 21 and March 17, 1431. For a nineteen-year-old French peasant with no formal education, her witty retorts and well-crafted responses to questions that were calculated to entrap her are as impressive as her victories on the battlefield during the Hundred Years' War. The English were determined to regain face through a sham trial, and on March 25, she was convicted of a relapse into the "heresy" of having worn men's clothing.

She was martyred by burning at the stake on May 30. Four years later, the record of her trial was translated from the French daily notes into Latin by the trial's chief notary, Guillaume Manchon. Five copies were produced, three of which are still in existence. The trial verdict was later reversed on

---

[6] *The Trial of Jeanne d'Arc, Translated into English from the Original Latin and French Documents,* by *W. P. Barrett* (New York: Gotham House, 1932), retrieved from https://sourcebooks .fordham.edu/basis/joanofarc-trial.asp.

appeal by Jean Bréhal, the inquisitor general, in 1456, thereby completely
exonerating her. She was declared a saint in 1920.

This is a short excerpt from the official trial record for February 22, 1431,
which has been abridged and adapted by the author.

Joan declared that, on her departure from Vaucouleurs, she wore the
habit of a man, and carried a sword which Robert de Baudricourt
had given her, but no other arms; and accompanied by a knight,
a squire, and four servants, she reached the town of Saint Urbain,
where she slept in an abbey.

She said also that it was altogether necessary to change her wom-
en's clothes for men's. She believed that her counsel said well.

After this Joan said that she went without hindrance to him whom
she calls her king.[7] And when she had arrived at Ste. Catherine de
Fierbois, then she sent first to Chinon, where he who she calls her
king was. She reached Chinon towards noon and lodged at an inn;
and after dinner she went to him whom she calls king, who was at the
castle. She said that when she entered her king's room she recognized
him among many others by the counsel of her voice, which revealed
him to her. She told him she wanted to make war on the English.

Then Joan said that there is not a day when she does not hear this
voice; and she has much need of it. She said she never asked of it
any final reward but the salvation of her soul. The voice told her to
remain at Saint-Denis in France, and the said Joan wished to remain;
but against her will the lords took her away. However, if she had
not been wounded, she would not have left; she was wounded in
the trenches before Paris, after she left Saint-Denis; but recovered
in five days. Further she confessed that she caused an assault to be
made before Paris.

And she added, "I tell you, take good heed of what you say, that
you are my judge, for you assume a great responsibility, and over-
burden me."

Asked if she knows she is in God's grace, she answered: "If I am
not, may God put me there; and if I am, may God so keep me. I

---

[7] The convoluted wording here is a result of the long and complicated Hundred Years'
War. The English scribe would have been required to recognize Henry V of England as the
self-declared king of France, while St. Joan recognized the French Charles VII as the rightful
king.

should be the saddest creature in the world if I knew I were not in his grace."

May 31: The Visitation of the Blessed Virgin Mary (Feast)

COLLECT PRAYER

Almighty ever-living God, who, while the Blessed Virgin Mary was carrying your Son in her womb, inspired her to visit Elizabeth, grant us, we pray, that, faithful to the promptings of the Spirit, we may magnify your greatness with the Virgin Mary at all times. Through our Lord Jesus Christ, your Son, who lives and reigns with you in the unity of the Holy Spirit, one God, for ever and ever. Amen.

A reading from the Holy Gospel according to Saint Luke.
(Lk 1:39–45, 56)

In those days Mary arose and went with haste into the hill country, to a city of Judah, and she entered the house of Zechariah and greeted Elizabeth. And when Elizabeth heard the greeting of Mary, the child leaped in her womb; and Elizabeth was filled with the Holy Spirit and she exclaimed with a loud cry, "Blessed are you among women, and blessed is the fruit of your womb! And why is this granted me, that the mother of my Lord should come to me? For behold, when the voice of your greeting came to my ears, the child in my womb leaped for joy. And blessed is she who believed that there would be a fulfilment of what was spoken to her from the Lord."

And Mary remained with her about three months, and returned to her home.

The Gospel of the Lord.

All: Praise to you, Lord Jesus Christ.

The Magnificat prayer, also known as the Canticle of Mary, is the words of Mary to her cousin Elizabeth at the Visitation. It is based on Luke 1:46–55 and can be found on p. 80.

12

Movable Feasts: Pentecost and after Eastertide

Fifty Days after Easter: PENTECOST SUNDAY
(Solemnity)

The vigil of Pentecost is a day of recommended fasting and abstinence in preparation for the feast. The summer Ember Days fall on the Wednesday, Friday, and Saturday after Pentecost.[1] This season's days are offered for the wheat harvest in thanksgiving for the Holy Eucharist. Saturday is also offered as a day of prayer for priests and for vocations. See Ember Days Prayer, p. 57; Farmer's Prayer, p. 235; Blessing for the Products of Nature, p. 124; Prayer for Priests, p. 102; Prayer for Vocations, p. 357.

COLLECT PRAYER

Almighty ever-living God, who willed the Paschal Mystery to be encompassed as a sign in fifty days, grant that from out of the scattered nations the confusion of many tongues may be gathered by heavenly grace into one great confession of your name. Through our Lord Jesus Christ, your Son, who lives and reigns with you in the unity of the Holy Spirit, one God, for ever and ever. Amen.

A reading from the Acts of the Apostles. (Acts 2:1–4, 42–47)

When the day of Pentecost had come, they were all together in one place. And suddenly a sound came from heaven like the rush of a mighty wind, and it filled all the house where they were sitting. And there appeared to them tongues as of fire, distributed and resting on each one of them. And they were all filled with the Holy Spirit and began to speak in other tongues, as the Spirit gave them utterance.

---

[1] For more on Ember Days, vigils, and general fasting and abstinence requirements and recommendations, see appendix A of *The Catholic All Year Compendium*.

And they held steadfastly to the apostles' teaching and fellowship, to the breaking of the bread and to the prayers.

And fear came upon every soul; and many wonders and signs were done through the apostles. And all who believed were together and had all things in common; and they sold their possessions and goods and distributed them to all, as any had need. And day by day, attending the temple together and breaking bread in their homes, they partook of food with glad and generous hearts, praising God and having favor with all the people. And the Lord added to their number day by day those who were being saved.

The Word of the Lord.

All: Thanks be to God.

A plenary indulgence is available, subject to the usual conditions, for the recitation or singing of Veni Creator Spiritus *(Come, Holy Ghost) on Pentecost; see p. 109.*[2] *See also Holy Spirit Prayer, p. 229.*

Saint Augustine's Prayer to the Holy Spirit

Breathe in me, O Holy Spirit, that my thoughts may all be holy. Act in me, O Holy Spirit, that my work, too, may be holy. Draw my heart, O Holy Spirit, that I love but what is holy. Strengthen me, O Holy Spirit, to defend all that is holy. Guard me, then, O Holy Spirit, that I always may be holy. Amen.

ORDINARY TIME BEGINS

Marian Antiphon IV: Salve Regina

One of the four seasonal liturgical Marian antiphons, the Salve Regina is sung, chanted, or recited during Mass and at the end of the office of Compline, or Night Prayer, from the day after Pentecost Sunday until the First Sunday of Advent. It is attributed to Saint Bernard of Clairvaux (+1153). In its English translation it is known as the Hail Holy Queen and is recited at the conclusion of the Rosary.

[2] *Manual of Indulgences*, grant 26.1.2. See the introduction of this book for the usual conditions for indulgences.

Salve Regina, mater misericordiae, vita, dulcedo, et spes nostra, salve. Ad te clamamus, exules filii Evae. Ad te suspiramus, gementes et flentes, in hac lacrimarum valle. Eia ergo, advocata nostra, illos tuos misericordes oculos, ad nos converte. Et Jesum, benedictum fructum ventris tui, nobis post hoc exsilium ostende. O clemens, o pia, o dulcis virgo Maria.

Hail, holy Queen, mother of mercy, our life, our sweetness, and our hope. To thee we cry, poor banished children of Eve; to thee we send up our sighs, mourning and weeping in this valley of tears. Turn, then, most gracious advocate, thine eyes of mercy toward us; and after this, our exile, show unto us the blessed fruit of thy womb, Jesus. O clement, O loving, O sweet Virgin Mary.

Monday after Pentecost: Blessed Virgin Mary, Mother of the Church (Memorial)[3]

COLLECT PRAYER

O God, Father of mercies, whose Only Begotten Son, as he hung upon the Cross, chose the Blessed Virgin Mary, his Mother, to be our Mother also, grant, we pray, that with her loving help your Church may be more fruitful day by day and, exulting in the holiness of her children, may draw to her embrace all the families of the peoples. Through our Lord Jesus Christ, your Son, who lives and reigns with you in the unity of the Holy Spirit, one God, for ever and ever. Amen.

Prayer to Mary, Mother of the Church and Mother of Our Faith

By Pope Francis, at the conclusion of the encyclical Lumen Fidei.[4]

Mother, help our faith! Open our ears to hear God's word and to recognize his voice and call. Awaken in us a desire to follow in his footsteps, to go forth from our own land and to receive his promise. Help

---

[3] This feast day was added to the liturgical calendar in 2018.

[4] Francis, encyclical *Lumen Fidei* (June 28, 2013), no. 60, http://w2.vatican.va/content /francesco/en/encyclicals/documents/papa-francesco_20130629_enciclica-lumen-fidei.html.

us to be touched by his love, that we may touch him in faith. Help us to entrust ourselves fully to him and to believe in his love, especially at times of trial, beneath the shadow of the cross, when our faith is called to mature. Sow in our faith the joy of the Risen One. Remind us that those who believe are never alone. Teach us to see all things with the eyes of Jesus, that he may be light for our path. And may this light of faith always increase in us, until the dawn of that undying day which is Christ himself, your Son, our Lord! Amen.

Sunday after Pentecost: THE MOST HOLY TRINITY (Solemnity)

COLLECT PRAYER

God our Father, who by sending into the world the Word of truth and the Spirit of sanctification made known to the human race your wondrous mystery, grant us, we pray, that in professing true faith, we may acknowledge the Trinity of eternal glory and adore your Unity, powerful in majesty. Through our Lord Jesus Christ, your Son, who lives and reigns with you in the unity of the Holy Spirit, one God, for ever and ever. Amen.

A reading from the First Letter of Saint Peter.
(1 Pet 1:1–9, NABRE[5])

In the foreknowledge of God the Father, through sanctification by the Spirit, for obedience and sprinkling with the blood of Jesus Christ: may grace and peace be yours in abundance.

Blessed be the God and Father of our Lord Jesus Christ, who in his great mercy gave us a new birth to a living hope through the resurrection of Jesus Christ from the dead, to an inheritance that is imperishable, undefiled, and unfading, kept in heaven for you who by the power of God are safeguarded through faith, to a salvation that is ready to be revealed in the final time. In this you rejoice, although now for a little while you may have to suffer through various trials, so that the genuineness of your faith, more precious than gold that is perishable even though tested by fire, may prove to be for praise,

[5] New American Bible Revised Edition.

glory, and honor at the revelation of Jesus Christ. Although you have not seen him you love him; even though you do not see him now yet believe in him, you rejoice with an indescribable and glorious joy, as you attain the goal of your faith, the salvation of your souls.

The Word of the Lord.

All: Thanks be to God.

Glory Be

The Glory Be—in Latin, the Gloria Patri—is also known as the Lesser Doxology, as distinguished from the Great Doxology (Gloria in excelsis Deo). As well as praising God, it is regarded as a short declaration of faith in the equality of the three Persons of the Holy Trinity.

Gloria Patri, et Filio, et Spiritui Sancto; sicut erat in principio, et nunc, et semper, et in sæcula sæculorum. Amen.

Glory be to the Father, and to the Son, and to the Holy Spirit; as it was in the beginning, is now, and ever shall be, world without end. Amen.

See also The Doxology (hymn), p. 326; Gloria in excelsis Deo, p. 96.

Second Sunday after Pentecost: THE MOST HOLY BODY AND BLOOD OF CHRIST (CORPUS CHRISTI) (Solemnity, Holy Day of Obligation)[6]

The feast of Corpus Christi is traditionally associated with Mass, a Eucharistic procession through the streets, and Benediction of the Blessed Sacrament. None of these is a liturgical living tradition for which there is a true at-home substitute. If your parish does a Eucharistic procession, be sure to participate!

[6] The solemnity of Corpus Christi technically falls on the Thursday after Trinity Sunday (Trinity Sunday being one week after Pentecost Sunday), and eight weeks after Holy Thursday (when we celebrated the institution of the Eucharist). In most countries, however, including the United States, Canada, England and Wales, Ireland, Australia, Argentina, Italy, Uganda, Hong Kong, and the Philippines, the celebration of Corpus Christi (and thus the obligation to attend Mass) has been transferred to the following Sunday—that is, one week after Trinity Sunday. Countries maintaining the Thursday celebration of the solemnity include Mexico and Poland. Consult your local diocese for your local observance. See appendix B for the dates of Corpus Christi in upcoming years.

And if your parish lacks one, why not ask Father what you could do to help make it possible? Maybe you're just a processional canopy away from bringing Jesus into your neighborhood! Regardless of whether you have access to a Eucharistic procession at church, you can celebrate at home by having a procession using a crucifix, or an image of Jesus or of the Eucharist, and reciting the Litany of the Precious Blood.

COLLECT PRAYER

O God, who in this wonderful Sacrament have left us a memorial of your Passion, grant us, we pray, so to revere the sacred mysteries of your Body and Blood, that we may always experience in ourselves the fruits of your redemption. Who live and reign with God the Father in the unity of the Holy Spirit, one God, for ever and ever. Amen.

A reading from the Holy Gospel according to Saint John.
(Jn 6:52–59)

The Jews then disputed among themselves, saying, "How can this man give us his flesh to eat?" So Jesus said to them, "Truly, truly, I say to you, unless you eat the flesh of the Son of man and drink his blood, you have no life in you; he who eats my flesh and drinks my blood has eternal life, and I will raise him up at the last day. For my flesh is food indeed, and my blood is drink indeed. He who eats my flesh and drinks my blood abides in me, and I in him. As the living Father sent me, and I live because of the Father, so he who eats me will live because of me. This is the bread which came down from heaven, not such as the fathers ate and died; he who eats this bread will live for ever." This he said in the synagogue, as he taught at Capernaum.

The Gospel of the Lord.

All: Praise to you, Lord Jesus Christ.

Prayers in Honor of the Blessed Sacrament

An act of spiritual communion is useful when one is unable to attend Mass; when one is at Mass but not in a state of grace or is otherwise unable to receive Communion; when passing a Catholic church; or as an ending prayer for a visit to the Blessed Sacrament. A partial indulgence is available for the use of an approved prayer as an act of spiritual communion.

When one is able to receive the Blessed Sacrament, it is important to take time afterward to offer a prayer of thanksgiving. The Anima Christi, below; Prayer to Our Lord Jesus Christ Crucified *(En ego, o bone et dulcissime Iesu) on p. 159; and the* Tantum ergo *on p. 203 are recommended and qualify for the partial indulgence.*[7]

Act of Spiritual Communion I[8]

From a school catechism published in 1800 by the Piarist fathers in Saragossa, Spain. Saint Josemaría Escrivá copied out this prayer by hand as a student and recommended its use as a preparation for Holy Communion and as an act of spiritual communion.

I wish, my Lord, to receive you, with the purity, humility, and devotion with which your most holy Mother received you, with the spirit and fervor of the saints. Amen.

Act of Spiritual Communion II[9]

Composed by Saint Alphonsus Liguori (+1787).

My Jesus, I believe that you are present in the Most Holy Sacrament. I love you above all things, and I desire to receive you into my soul. Since I cannot at this moment receive you sacramentally, come at least spiritually into my heart. I embrace you as if you were already there and unite myself wholly to you. Never permit me to be separated from you. Amen.

Anima Christi

Often attributed to Saint Ignatius of Loyola (+1556), this prayer dates to the early fourteenth century and was possibly written by Pope John XXII (+1334).

---

[7] *Manual of Indulgences*, grant 8.2.1–2. See the introduction of this book for the usual conditions for indulgences.

[8] Jesus Sancho, "Spiritual Communion: A Prayer That Traveled Around the World", Opus Dei, January 8, 2019, https://opusdei.org/en-us/article/spiritual-communion-a-prayer-that-has-traveled-around-the-world/. Used by permission of Fundación Studium.

[9] Alphonsus Liguori, *Visits to the Most Holy Sacrament and the Blessed Virgin Mary*, trans. R. A. Coffin (London: Burns and Lambert, 1855), 17.

Soul of Christ, sanctify me. Body of Christ, save me. Blood of Christ, inebriate me. Water from the side of Christ, wash me. Passion of Christ, strengthen me. O good Jesus, hear me. Within your wounds hide me. Permit me not to be separated from you. From the wicked foe defend me. At the hour of my death, call me and bid me come to you, that with your saints I may praise you forever and ever. Amen.

Litany of the Most Precious Blood of Our Lord Jesus Christ[10]

The Litany of the Most Precious Blood was approved for public use in 1960 by Pope John XXIII. A partial indulgence is available to the faithful who devoutly recite this litany.

Leader: Lord, have mercy;

All: Lord, have mercy.

Leader: Christ, have mercy;

All: Christ, have mercy.

Leader: Lord, have mercy;

All: Lord, have mercy.

Leader: God, our Father in heaven,

All: Have mercy on us.

Leader: God the Son, Redeemer of the world,

All: Have mercy on us.

Leader: God the Holy Spirit,

All: Have mercy on us.

Leader: Holy Trinity, one God,

All: Have mercy on us.

The leader announces each description of the Precious Blood.

All reply: save us.

[10] *Manual of Indulgences*, grant 22. See the introduction of this book for the usual conditions for indulgences.

Blood of Christ, only Son of the Father, *save us.*
Blood of Christ, incarnate Word, *save us.*
Blood of Christ, of the new and eternal covenant, *save us.*
Blood of Christ, that spilled to the ground, *save us.*
Blood of Christ, that flowed at the scourging, *save us.*
Blood of Christ, dripping from the thorns, *save us.*
Blood of Christ, shed on the Cross, *save us.*
Blood of Christ, price of our redemption, *save us.*
Blood of Christ, our only claim to pardon, *save us.*
Blood of Christ, our blessing cup, *save us.*
Blood of Christ, in which we are washed, *save us.*
Blood of Christ, torrent of mercy, *save us.*
Blood of Christ, that overcomes evil, *save us.*
Blood of Christ, strength of the martyrs, *save us.*
Blood of Christ, endurance of the saints, *save us.*
Blood of Christ, that makes the barren fruitful, *save us.*
Blood of Christ, protection of the threatened, *save us.*
Blood of Christ, comfort of the weary, *save us.*
Blood of Christ, solace of the mourner, *save us.*
Blood of Christ, hope of the repentant, *save us.*
Blood of Christ, consolation of the dying, *save us.*
Blood of Christ, our peace and refreshment, *save us.*
Blood of Christ, our pledge of life, *save us.*
Blood of Christ, by which we pass to glory, *save us.*
Blood of Christ, most worthy of honor, *save us.*

Leader: Lamb of God, you take away the sins of the world;

All: Have mercy on us.

Leader: Lamb of God, you take away the sins of the world;

All: Have mercy on us.

Leader: Lamb of God, you take away the sins of the world;

All: Have mercy on us.

Leader: Lord, you redeemed us by your blood.

All: You have made us a kingdom to serve our God.

Leader: Let us pray. Father, by the blood of your Son you have set us free and saved us from death. Continue your work of love within us, that by constantly celebrating the mystery of our salvation we may reach the eternal life it promises. We ask this through Christ our Lord.

All: Amen.

See also Chaplet of Reparation, p. 370.

Friday after Corpus Christi: THE MOST SACRED HEART OF JESUS (Solemnity)

COLLECT PRAYER

Grant, we pray, almighty God, that we, who glory in the Heart of your beloved Son and recall the wonders of his love for us, may be made worthy to receive an overflowing measure of grace from that fount of heavenly gifts. Through our Lord Jesus Christ, your Son, who lives and reigns with you in the unity of the Holy Spirit, one God, for ever and ever. Amen.

Litany of the Sacred Heart of Jesus[11]

This version, based on litanies that date back to the seventeenth century, has thirty-three invocations, one for each year of Jesus' life, and was approved for public use by Pope Leo XIII in 1899. A partial indulgence is attached to this litany at any time.

Leader: Lord, have mercy;

All: Lord, have mercy.

Leader: Christ, have mercy;

All: Christ have mercy.

Leader: Lord, have mercy;

All: Lord, have mercy.

Leader: God our Father in heaven,

---

[11] *Manual of Indulgences*, grant 22. See the introduction of this book for the usual conditions for indulgences.

All: Have mercy on us.

Leader: God the Son, Redeemer of the world,

All: Have mercy on us.

Leader: God the Holy Spirit,

All: Have mercy on us.

Leader: Holy Trinity, one God,

All: Have mercy on us.

The leader announces each title of the Heart of Jesus.

All reply: have mercy on us.

Heart of Jesus, Son of the eternal Father, *have mercy on us.*

Heart of Jesus, formed by the Holy Spirit in the womb of the Virgin Mother, *have mercy on us.*

Heart of Jesus, one with the eternal Word, *have mercy on us.*

Heart of Jesus, infinite in majesty, *have mercy on us.*

Heart of Jesus, holy temple of God, *have mercy on us.*

Heart of Jesus, tabernacle of the Most High, *have mercy on us.*

Heart of Jesus, house of God and gate of heaven, *have mercy on us.*

Heart of Jesus, aflame with love for us, *have mercy on us.*

Heart of Jesus, source of justice and love, *have mercy on us.*

Heart of Jesus, full of goodness and love, *have mercy on us.*

Heart of Jesus, wellspring of all virtue, *have mercy on us.*

Heart of Jesus, worthy of all praise, *have mercy on us.*

Heart of Jesus, king and center of all hearts, *have mercy on us.*

Heart of Jesus, treasure-house of wisdom and knowledge, *have mercy on us.*

Heart of Jesus, in whom there dwells the fullness of God, *have mercy on us.*

Heart of Jesus, in whom the Father is well pleased, *have mercy on us.*

Heart of Jesus, from whose fullness we have all received, *have mercy on us.*

Heart of Jesus, desire of the eternal hills, *have mercy on us.*

Heart of Jesus, patient and full of mercy, *have mercy on us.*

Heart of Jesus, generous to all who turn to you, *have mercy on us.*

Heart of Jesus, fountain of life and holiness, *have mercy on us.*

Heart of Jesus, atonement for our sins, *have mercy on us.*

Heart of Jesus, overwhelmed with insults, *have mercy on us.*
Heart of Jesus, broken for our sins, *have mercy on us.*
Heart of Jesus, obedient even to death, *have mercy on us.*
Heart of Jesus, pierced by a lance, *have mercy on us.*
Heart of Jesus, source of all consolation, *have mercy on us.*
Heart of Jesus, our life and resurrection, *have mercy on us.*
Heart of Jesus, our peace and reconciliation, *have mercy on us.*
Heart of Jesus, victim of our sins, *have mercy on us.*
Heart of Jesus, salvation of all who trust in you, *have mercy on us.*
Heart of Jesus, hope of all who die in you, *have mercy on us.*
Heart of Jesus, delight of all the saints, *have mercy on us.*

Leader: Lamb of God, you take away the sins of the world;

All: Have mercy on us.

Leader: Lamb of God, you take away the sins of the world;

All: Have mercy on us.

Leader: Lamb of God, you take away the sins of the world;

All: Have mercy on us.

Leader: Jesus, gentle and humble of heart.

All: Touch our hearts and make them like your own.

Leader: Let us pray. Father, we rejoice in the gifts of love we have received from the heart of Jesus your Son. Open our hearts to share his life and continue to bless us with his love. We ask this in the name of Jesus the Lord.

All: Amen.

See Morning Offering, p. 350.

Saturday after Corpus Christi:
The Immaculate Heart of the Blessed Virgin Mary
(Memorial)

COLLECT PRAYER

Grant, Lord God, that we, your servants, may rejoice in unfailing health of mind and body, and, through the glorious intercession of

Blessed Mary ever-Virgin, may we be set free from present sorrow and come to enjoy eternal happiness. Amen.

Prayer to the Immaculate Heart of Mary

Immaculate Heart of Mary, full of love for God and mankind, and of compassion for sinners, I consecrate myself to you. I entrust to you the salvation of my soul. May my heart be ever united with yours, so that I may hate sin, love God and my neighbor, and reach eternal life with those whom I love. May I experience the kindness of your motherly heart and the power of your intercession with Jesus during my life and at the hour of my death. Amen.

See also Litany of Loreto, p. 52.

13

June

The month of the Sacred Heart of Jesus[1]

Prayer after Blessing before Meals: O Sacred Heart

O Sacred Heart of Jesus, most obedient to the will of the Father, incline our hearts to you, that we may always do what is most pleasing to him. Amen.

Act of Consecration of the Family to the Sacred Heart of Jesus[2]

A plenary indulgence, subject to the usual conditions, is granted to the members of the family on the day on which it is first consecrated, if at all possible by a priest or deacon, to the Most Sacred Heart of Jesus, if they devoutly recite the duly approved prayer before an image of the Sacred Heart. On the anniversary of the consecration, a partial indulgence is available.[3] The prayers are led by a priest, a deacon, or the head of the household.

All members of the family kneel and pray before an image of the Sacred Heart of Jesus.

Leader: Sacred Heart of Jesus, you made clear to Saint Margaret Mary your desire of being King in Christian families. We today

---

[1] The feast of the Sacred Heart is always in June but is movable, falling on the Friday after Corpus Christi. See p. 258.

[2] lban J. Dachauer, *The Rural Life Prayerbook* (Des Moines, Ia.: The National Catholic Rural Life Conference, 1956). Retrieved from https://www.ewtn.com/catholicism/library/rural-life-prayerbook-11881.

[3] *Manual of Indulgences*, grant 1. See the introduction of this book for the usual conditions for indulgences.

wish to proclaim your most complete kingly dominion over our own family. We want to live in the future with your life. We want to cause to flourish in our midst those virtues to which you have promised peace here below. We want to banish far from us the spirit of the world which you have cursed. You shall be King over our minds in the simplicity of our faith, and over our hearts by the wholehearted love with which they shall burn for you, the flame of which we will keep alive by the frequent reception of your divine Eucharist.

Be so kind, O divine Heart, as to preside over our assemblings, to bless our enterprises, both spiritual and temporal, to dispel our cares, to sanctify our joys, and to alleviate our sufferings. If ever one or other of us should have the misfortune to afflict you, remind him, O Heart of Jesus, that you are good and merciful to the penitent sinner. And when the hour of separation strikes, when death shall come to cast mourning into our midst, we will all, both those who go and those who stay, be submissive to your eternal decrees. We shall console ourselves with the thought that a day will come when the entire family, reunited in heaven, can sing forever your glories and your mercies.

May the Immaculate Heart of Mary and the glorious patriarch Saint Joseph present this consecration to you, and keep it in our minds all the days of our life. All glory to the Heart of Jesus, our King and our Father!

All: Amen.

June 13: Saint Anthony of Padua, Priest and Doctor of the Church (Memorial)

COLLECT PRAYER

Almighty ever-living God, who gave Saint Anthony of Padua to your people as an outstanding preacher and an intercessor in their need, grant that, with his assistance, as we follow the teachings of the Christian life, we may know your help in every trial. Through our Lord Jesus Christ, your Son, who lives and reigns with you in the unity of the Holy Spirit, one God, for ever and ever. Amen.

Si quaeris[4]

This prayer in honor of Saint Anthony was composed by the friar Julian of Speyer. It is part of the Officium rhythmicum S. Antonii, *which dates back to 1233, two years after Saint Anthony's death. It is sung at Saint Anthony's Basilica in Padua every Tuesday.*

If then you ask for miracles: death, error, all calamities, leprosy, and demons fly, and health succeeds infirmities. The sea obeys and fetters break, and lifeless limbs you do restore; while treasures lost are found again, men young and old your aid implore. All dangers vanish at your prayer, and direst need does quickly flee. Let those who know your power proclaim, let Paduans say: These are yours. To Father, Son may glory be, and Holy Spirit, eternally. Amen.

Help Me Find[5]

Saint Anthony is petitioned from all over the world to help find lost objects: keys, important documents, even the faith itself. This prayer from the Friars of Saint Anthony in Padua invokes the aid of Saint Anthony in search of what has been lost.

Glorious Saint Anthony, you have exercised the divine power to find what was lost. Help me to recover the grace of God, and make me zealous in the service of God and in the practice of living the virtues. Let me find what I have lost, thus showing me the presence of your goodness. *Our Father, Hail Mary, Glory Be.*

Let us pray. Anthony, glorious servant of God, famous for your merits and powerful miracles, help us to find what was lost. Give us your help in times of temptation, and enlighten our minds in searching the will of God. Help us to find again the life of grace, which our sin destroyed, and lead us to the possession of the glory promised us by the Savior. We ask this through Christ our Lord. Amen.

Or the express version:

Tony, Tony, look around. Something's lost that must be found!

[4] Julian of Speyer, "Si quaeris", Friars Minor Conventual at the Basilica of St. Anthony, Padua, https://www.santantonio.org/en/content/si-quaeris. Used with kind permission of *Messenger of Saint Anthony* magazine and www.saintanthonyofpadua.net.

[5] "Help Me Find", ibid., https://www.santantonio.org/en/content/help-me-find.

If you are praying the Three-Part Prayer to Saint John the Baptist (p. 305) as a novena for the Nativity of Saint John the Baptist (June 24), start it on June 15.

June 22: Saints John Fisher, Bishop, and Thomas More, Martyrs (Optional Memorial)

COLLECT PRAYER

O God, who in martyrdom have brought true faith to its highest expression, graciously grant that, strengthened through the intercession of Saints John Fisher and Thomas More, we may confirm by the witness of our life the faith we profess with our lips. Through our Lord Jesus Christ, your Son, who lives and reigns with you in the unity of the Holy Spirit, one God, for ever and ever. Amen.

Prayer to Saint Thomas More for Lawyers and Judges[6]

Dear Scholar and Martyr, it was not the king of England but you who were the true Defender of the Faith. Like Christ unjustly condemned, neither promises nor threats could make you accept a civil ruler as head of the Christian Church. Perfect in your honesty and love of truth, grant that lawyers and judges may imitate you and achieve true justice for all people. Amen.

Prayer for Good Humor by Saint Thomas More

Grant me, O Lord, good digestion, and also something to digest. Grant me a healthy body, and the necessary good humor to maintain it. Grant me a simple soul that knows to treasure all that is good and that doesn't frighten easily at the sight of evil but rather finds the means to put things back in their place. Give me a soul that knows not boredom, grumblings, sighs and laments, nor excess of stress, because of

---

[6]"Our Patron Saint", St. Thomas More Society, Dallas, https://www.stmsdallas.org/patron-saint. Used with permission.

that obstructing thing called "I". Grant me, O Lord, a sense of good humor. Allow me the grace to be able to take a joke, to discover in life a bit of joy, and to be able to share it with others. Amen.

Prayer for Holy Bishops by Saint John Fisher

This prayer was part of a sermon that Bishop Fisher preached in 1508, twenty-seven years before he was executed for treason because he refused to acknowledge Henry VIII as head of the Church in England.

Lord, according to your promise that the Gospel should be preached throughout the whole world, raise up men fit for such work. The apostles were but soft and yielding clay till they were baked hard by the fire of the Holy Spirit. So, good Lord, do now in like manner with your Church Militant; change and make the soft and slippery earth into hard stones. Set in your Church strong and mighty pillars that may suffer and endure great labors—watching, poverty, thirst, hunger, cold, and heat—which also shall not fear the threatenings of princes, persecution, neither death, but always persuade and think with themselves to suffer with a good will, slanders, shame, and all kinds of torments, for the glory and laud of your Holy Name. By this manner, good Lord, the truth of your Gospel shall be preached throughout the world. Therefore, merciful Lord, exercise your mercy, show it indeed upon your Church. Amen.

SONG SUGGESTION: Faith of Our Fathers

June 24: THE NATIVITY OF SAINT JOHN THE BAPTIST (Solemnity)

Blessing of a Bonfire on the Eve of the Nativity of Saint John the Baptist[7]

Perhaps the oldest liturgical living tradition of the Catholic Church, the building of bonfires in honor of Saint John the Baptist on June 23 (the eve of the

---

[7] *Roman Ritual*, ed. and trans. Philip T. Weller, complete edition (Milwaukee: Bruce, 1964), Catholic Culture, https://www.catholicculture.org/culture/liturgicalyear/prayers/view.cfm?id=1056.

feast of his nativity) has been practiced since ancient times, being found in records as early as the fourth century. This version of the blessing of a bonfire is from the 1964 Roman Ritual. It can be performed on or about the eve of the feast day by a priest or deacon. If you aren't able to invite an ordained person to join you, just light your fire, sprinkle some holy water on it, read Matthew 3:11, and skip ahead to the Canticle of Zechariah.

Priest: Our help is in the name of the Lord.

All: Who made heaven and earth.

Priest: The Lord be with you.

All: And with your spirit.

A reading from the Holy Gospel according to Saint Matthew. (Mt 3:11)

I baptize you with water for repentance, but he who is coming after me is mightier than I, whose sandals I am not worthy to carry; he will baptize you with the Holy Spirit and with fire.

The Gospel of the Lord.

All: Praise to you, Lord Jesus Christ.

Leader: Let us pray. Lord God, almighty Father, the light that never fails and the source of all light, sanctify (*the priest or deacon makes the sign of the cross over the fire*) this new fire, and grant that after the darkness of this life we may come unsullied to you who are light eternal; through Christ our Lord.

All: Amen.

The fire is sprinkled with holy water.

Priest: There was a man sent from God.

All: Whose name was John.

The hymn Ut queant laxis may be sung, if desired, or continue to the prayers.

Canticle of Zechariah

Also known as the Benedictus, the Canticle of Zechariah is based on Luke 1:68–79. The prayer can be recited individually or as a call and response by two groups (1 and 2).

1. Blessed be the Lord, the God of Israel;
   he has come to his people and set them free.

2. He has raised up for us a mighty Savior,
   born of the house of his servant David.

1. Through his holy prophets he promised of old
   that he would save us from our enemies,
   from the hands of all who hate us.

2. He promised to show mercy to our fathers
   and to remember his holy covenant.

1. This was the oath he swore to our father Abraham: to set us free
   from the hands of our enemies,
   free to worship him without fear,
   holy and righteous in his sight all the days of our life.

2. You, my child, shall be called the prophet of the Most High;
   for you will go before the Lord to prepare his way,
   to give his people knowledge of salvation
   by the forgiveness of their sins.

1. In the tender compassion of our God
   the dawn from on high shall break upon us,
   to shine on those who dwell in darkness and the shadow of death,

2. And to guide our feet into the way of peace.

All: Glory to the Father and to the Son and to the Holy Spirit, as it was in the beginning, is now, and will be forever. Amen.

Closing Prayer

Let us pray. God, who by reason of the birth of blessed John have made this day praiseworthy, give your people the grace of spiritual joy, and keep the hearts of your faithful fixed on the way that leads to everlasting salvation. Through Christ our Lord.

All: Amen.

COLLECT PRAYER

Grant, we pray, almighty God, that your family may walk in the way of salvation and, attentive to what Saint John the Precursor urged, may come safely to the One he foretold, our Lord Jesus Christ, who lives and reigns with you in the unity of the Holy Spirit, one God, for ever and ever. Amen.

A reading from the Holy Gospel according to Saint Luke.
(Lk 1:57–66, 80)

Now the time came for Elizabeth to be delivered, and she gave birth to a son. And her neighbors and kinsfolk heard that the Lord had shown great mercy to her, and they rejoiced with her. And on the eighth day they came to circumcise the child; and they would have named him Zechariah after his father, but his mother said, "Not so; he shall be called John." And they said to her, "None of your kindred is called by this name." And they made signs to his father, inquiring what he would have him called. And he asked for a writing tablet, and wrote, "His name is John." And they all marveled. And immediately his mouth was opened and his tongue loosed, and he spoke, blessing God. And fear came on all their neighbors. And all these things were talked about through all the hill country of Judea; and all who heard them laid them up in their hearts, saying, "What then will this child be?" For the hand of the Lord was with him.

And the child grew and became strong in spirit, and he was in the wilderness till the day of his manifestation to Israel.

The Gospel of the Lord.

All: Praise to you, Lord Jesus Christ.

See also Three-Part Prayer to Saint John the Baptist, p. 305.

June 26: Saint Josemaría Escrivá de Balaguer y Albás, Priest (Optional Memorial)

COLLECT PRAYER

Grant, O Lord, that we may always revere and love your holy name, for you never deprive of your guidance those you set firm on the foundation of your love. Through our Lord Jesus Christ, your Son, who lives and reigns with you in the unity of the Holy Spirit, one God, for ever and ever. Amen.

Prayer of Abandonment to God's Providence[8]

My Lord and my God, into your hands I abandon the past and the present and the future, what is small and what is great, what amounts to a little and what amounts to a lot, things temporal and things eternal. Amen.

See also Act of Spiritual Communion I, p. 255; On Guardian Angels, p. 323.

June 29: SAINTS PETER AND PAUL, APOSTLES (Solemnity)

COLLECT PRAYER

Grant, we pray, O Lord our God, that we may be sustained by the intercession of the blessed Apostles Peter and Paul, that, as through them you gave your Church the foundations of her heavenly office, so through them you may help her to eternal salvation. Through our Lord Jesus Christ, your Son, who lives and reigns with you in the unity of the Holy Spirit, one God, for ever and ever. Amen.

A reading from the Letter of Saint Paul to the Galatians.
(Gal 2:7–14)

On the contrary, when they saw that I had been entrusted with the gospel to the uncircumcised, just as Peter had been entrusted with the gospel to the circumcised (for he who worked through Peter for the mission to the circumcised worked through me also for the Gentiles), and when they perceived the grace that was given to me, James and Cephas and John, who were reputed to be pillars, gave to me and Barnabas the right hand of fellowship, that we should go to the Gentiles and they to the circumcised; only they would have us remember the poor, which very thing I was eager to do.

But when Cephas came to Antioch I opposed him to his face, because he stood condemned. For before certain men came from

[8]Josemaría Escrivá de Balaguer, *The Way of the Cross* (1981), no. 7, http://www.escrivaworks.org/book/the_way_of_the_cross-point-7.htm. Used by permission of Fundación Studium.

James, he ate with the Gentiles; but when they came he drew back and separated himself, fearing the circumcision party. And with him the rest of the Jews acted insincerely, so that even Barnabas was carried away by their insincerity. But when I saw that they were not straightforward about the truth of the gospel, I said to Cephas before them all, "If you, though a Jew, live like a Gentile and not like a Jew, how can you compel the Gentiles to live like Jews?"

The Word of the Lord.

All: Thanks be to God.

Holy Apostles Peter and Paul, Intercede for Us[9]

A partial indulgence is available for this prayer at any time.

Guard your people, who rely on the patronage of your apostles Peter and Paul, O Lord, and keep them under your continual protection. Through Christ our Lord. Amen.

Using Blessed Objects

When we ask God's blessing on an object, we are dedicating that item to God and reserving it for holy use. A priest's blessing on an object goes further and makes the item a sacramental. Sacramentals are sacred signs—things we can see—which bear a resemblance to the sacraments. The use of sacramentals helps prepare us to receive the graces available in the sacraments better and unites our prayers and devotions with the prayers and devotions of the whole Catholic Church.

Indulgence for the Solemnity of Saints Peter and Paul

The Manual of Indulgences *states: "A plenary indulgence is granted to the faithful who, on the Solemnity of the Holy Apostles Peter and Paul,*

---

[9] *Manual of Indulgences*, grant 20. See the introduction of this book for the usual conditions for indulgences.

make prayerful use of an article of devotion [a properly blessed crucifix or cross, rosary, scapular, or medal] ... that has been blessed by the Supreme Pontiff or by any bishop, provided the faithful also make a Profession of Faith using any legitimate formula. [See Nicene Creed, p. 46, or Apostles' Creed, p. 366.] A partial indulgence is granted to the faithful who devoutly use such articles of devotion properly blessed by either a priest or a deacon."[10] *The usual conditions for gaining indulgences apply.*

---

[10] *Manual of Indulgences*, grant 14. See the introduction of this book for the usual conditions for indulgences.

14

July

The month of the Precious Blood

Before the reorganization of the liturgical calendar in 1969, a feast day in honor of the Most Precious Blood was observed on the first Sunday of July. That feast day is now combined with the feast of Corpus Christi, on the eighth Sunday after Easter, but the monthly devotion remains.

Prayer after Blessing before Meals: O Most Precious Blood[1]

O Most Precious Blood of Jesus Christ, adoration and praise be yours forever. Amen.

A reading from the Holy Gospel according to Saint Luke. (Lk 22:17–20)

He took a chalice, and when he had given thanks he said, "Take this, and divide it among yourselves; for I tell you that from now on I shall not drink of the fruit of the vine until the kingdom of God comes." And he took bread, and when he had given thanks he broke it and gave it to them, saying, "This is my body which is given for you. Do this in remembrance of me." And likewise the chalice after supper, saying, "This chalice which is poured out for you is the new covenant in my blood."

The Gospel of the Lord.

All: Praise to you, Lord Jesus Christ.

---

[1] "Adoration Prayers", Association of the Precious Blood, https://www.preciousblood international.com/prayers_09.html. Used with permission of Precious Blood International.

See also Litany of the Precious Blood, p. 256; To You O Blessed Joseph, p. 368; Anima Christi, p. 255.

On Promoting Devotion to the Precious Blood of Our Lord Jesus Christ[2]

Excerpt from the apostolic letter Inde a Primis *from Pope Saint John XXIII, June 30, 1960.*

Nourished by his Body and Blood, sharing the divine strength that has sustained countless martyrs, they will stand up to the slings and arrows of each day's fortunes—even if need be to martyrdom itself for the sake of Christian virtue and the kingdom of God. Theirs will be the experience of that burning love which made Saint John Chrysostom cry out,

> Let us, then, come back from that table like lions breathing out fire, thus becoming terrifying to the Devil, and remaining mindful of our Head and of the love he has shown for us.... This Blood, when worthily received, drives away demons and puts them at a distance from us, and even summons to us angels and the Lord of angels.... This Blood, poured out in abundance, has washed the whole world clean.... This is the price of the world; by it Christ purchased the Church.... This thought will check in us unruly passions. How long, in truth, shall we be attached to present things? How long shall we remain asleep? How long shall we not take thought for our own salvation? Let us remember what privileges God has bestowed on us, let us give thanks, let us glorify him, not only by faith, but also by our very works.

July 14: Saint Kateri Tekakwitha, Virgin (Memorial)

COLLECT PRAYER

O God, who desired the Virgin Saint Kateri Tekakwitha to flower among Native Americans in a life of innocence, grant, through her intercession, that when all are gathered into your Church from every nation, tribe and tongue, they may magnify you in a single canticle

---

[2] John XXIII, apostolic letter *Inde a Primis* (June 30, 1960), http://www.vatican.va/content/john-xxiii/la/apost_letters/1960/documents/hf_j-xxiii_apl_19600630_indeaprimis.html. English translation at Papal Encyclicals Online, https://www.papalencyclicals.net/john23/j23pb.htm.

of praise. Through our Lord Jesus Christ, your Son, who lives and reigns with you in the unity of the Holy Spirit, one God, for ever and ever. Amen.

Saint Kateri, Protectress of Canada[3]

An excerpt from Pope Benedict XVI's homily at the canonization of Saint Kateri, delivered in Saint Peter's Square on October 21, 2012.

Kateri Tekakwitha was born in today's New York State in 1656 to a Mohawk father and a Christian Algonquin mother who gave to her a sense of the living God. She was baptized at twenty years of age and, to escape persecution, she took refuge in Saint Francis Xavier Mission near Montreal. There she worked, faithful to the traditions of her people, although renouncing their religious convictions until her death at the age of twenty-four. Leading a simple life, Kateri remained faithful to her love for Jesus, to prayer and to daily Mass. Her greatest wish was to know and to do what pleased God. She lived a life radiant with faith and purity.

Kateri impresses us by the action of grace in her life in spite of the absence of external help and by the courage of her vocation, so unusual in her culture. In her, faith and culture enrich each other! May her example help us to live where we are, loving Jesus without denying who we are. Saint Kateri, Protectress of Canada and the first Native American saint, we entrust to you the renewal of the faith in the first nations and in all of North America! May God bless the first nations!

July 16: Our Lady of Mount Carmel (Optional Memorial)

COLLECT PRAYER

May the venerable intercession of the glorious Virgin Mary come to our aid, we pray, O Lord, so that, fortified by her protection, we may

[3] Benedict XVI, Homily at the Holy Mass and Canonization of St. Kateri (St. Peter's Square, October 21, 2012), http://www.vatican.va/content/benedict-xvi/en/homilies/2012/documents/hf_ben-xvi_hom_20121021_canonizzazioni.html.

reach the mountain which is Christ. Who lives and reigns with you in the unity of the Holy Spirit, one God, for ever and ever. Amen.

Prayer of Accord with the Carmelites

O Blessed Lady of Mount Carmel, grant that we may share in all the prayers and penances of your holy cloistered daughters of the Carmelite order. Bless their labors and pray that they may be a source of spiritual strength to all of us who struggle in the world outside their peaceful walls.

O Mary, who entered the world free from stain, obtain for me from God that I may pass out of it free from sin. Amen.

The Brown Scapular

Tradition tells us that in the year 1251, in the town of Aylesford in England, Our Lady appeared to Saint Simon Stock. She handed him a brown woolen apron-type outer garment to wear over his brown Carmelite habit and said, "This shall be a privilege for you and all Carmelites, that anyone dying in this habit shall not suffer eternal fire."[4] In time, the Church extended this privilege to all the laity who are willing to be invested in the Brown Scapular of the Carmelites and who perpetually wear the small, lay version of the scapular.

It's important to note that the scapular is a sacramental, not a talisman. It is not to be regarded as a guarantee of salvation. Our Lady's message to Saint Simon Stock was one of faithfulness. If he were to die in his habit, it would indicate that he had lived his life true to his vows and his vocation. This is what she asks of laypersons as well.

The scapular should be made of brown wool and worn under the clothes. A person must be enrolled in the Brown Scapular by a priest; after enrollment, the person can replace the scapular as needed. A Carmelite priest would be especially happy to perform the rite of blessing and enrollment for you, but any priest may do it.[5]

---

[4] "Statue of Our Lady of Mt. Carmel (of the Holy Scapular)", Discalced Carmelite Fathers, Munster, Ind., https://carmelitefathers.com/our-lady-of-mt-carmel/.

[5] The Rite for the Blessing of and Enrollment in the Scapular of the Blessed Virgin Mary of Mount Carmel to be used by priests can be found on the web page of the Eternal Word Television Network (EWTN), https://www.ewtn.com/catholicism/library/rite-of-blessing-and-enrollment-with-the-brown-scapular-of-our-lady-of-mount-carmel-11829.

Flos Carmeli

This prayer is attributed to Saint Simon Stock and is used by the Carmelite order during Masses honoring that saint and Our Lady of Mount Carmel.

O beautiful flower of Carmel, most fruitful vine, splendor of heaven, holy and singular, who brought forth the Son of God, still ever remaining a pure virgin, assist me in this necessity.

O star of the sea, help and protect me! Show me that you are my Mother.

O Mary, conceived without sin, pray for us who have recourse to you!

Mother and beauty of Carmel, pray for us!

Virgin, flower of Carmel, pray for us!

Patroness of all who wear the scapular, pray for us!

Hope of all who die wearing the scapular, pray for us!

Saint Joseph, friend of the Sacred Heart, pray for us!

Saint Joseph, chaste spouse of Mary, pray for us!

Saint Joseph, our patron, pray for us!

O sweet heart of Mary, be our salvation! Amen.

See also Litany of Loreto, p. 52.

 The Saint Anne Novena traditionally begins on July 17; see p. 282.

July 22: Saint Mary Magdalene (Feast)

COLLECT PRAYER

O God, whose Only Begotten Son entrusted Mary Magdalene before all others with announcing the great joy of the Resurrection, grant, we pray, that through her intercession and example we may proclaim the living Christ and come to see him reigning in your glory. Who lives and reigns with you in the unity of the Holy Spirit, one God, for ever and ever. Amen.

A reading from the Holy Gospel according to Saint John.
(Jn 20:11–18)

But Mary stood weeping outside the tomb, and as she wept she stooped to look into the tomb; and she saw two angels in white, sitting where the body of Jesus had lain, one at the head and one at the feet. They said to her, "Woman, why are you weeping?" She said to them, "Because they have taken away my Lord, and I do not know where they have laid him." Saying this, she turned round and saw Jesus standing, but she did not know that it was Jesus. Jesus said to her, "Woman, why are you weeping? Whom do you seek?" Supposing him to be the gardener, she said to him, "Sir, if you have carried him away, tell me where you have laid him, and I will take him away." Jesus said to her, "Mary." She turned and said to him in Hebrew, "Rab-boni!" (which means Teacher). Jesus said to her, "Do not hold me, for I have not yet ascended to the Father; but go to my brethren and say to them, I am ascending to my Father and your Father, to my God and your God." Mary Magdalene went and said to the disciples, "I have seen the Lord"; and she told them that he had said these things to her.

The Gospel of the Lord.

All: Praise to you, Lord Jesus Christ.

Prayer to Saint Mary Magdalene[6]

An excerpt from a series of meditative poetic prayers written by Saint Anselm between 1070 and 1080.

Saint Mary Magdalene, you came with springing tears to the spring of mercy, Christ; from him your burning thirst was abundantly refreshed, through him your sins were forgiven; by him your bitter sorrow was consoled.... It is enough for us to understand, dear friend of God, to whom were many sins forgiven, because she loved much.... And, more than all this, what can I say, how can I find words to tell, about the burning love with which you sought him, weeping at the sepulcher, and wept for him in your seeking?

How he came, who can say how or with what kindness, to comfort you, and made you burn with love still more; how he hid from

---

[6] Anselm, "Prayer to St. Mary Magdalene and Our Lord", Catholic Tradition, http://www.catholictradition.org/Magdalen/magdalen2.htm.

you when you wanted to see him, and showed himself when you did not think to see him; how he was there all the time you sought him, and how he sought you when, seeking him, you wept....

Shake my heart out of its indolence, Lord, and in the ardor of your love bring me to the everlasting sight of your glory where with the Father and the Holy Spirit you live and reign, God, forever. Amen.

Apostle of the Apostles[7]

In 2016 Pope Francis, through the Congregation for Divine Worship, elevated the memorial of Saint Mary Magdalene to the rank of feast, a distinction reserved for important events in Christian history and for saints of particular significance, such as the twelve apostles. In this press release from the Holy See, Archbishop Arthur Roche, secretary of the Congregation for Divine Worship, explains the importance of this saint.

She has the honor of being the "prima testis" to the Resurrection of the Lord, the first to see the empty tomb and the first to hear the truth of his Resurrection. Christ has a special consideration and mercy for this woman, who shows her love for him, looking for him in the garden with anguish and suffering, with "lacrimas humilitatis", as Saint Anselm says.... In this sense, I would like to show the difference between the two women present in the garden of Paradise and in the garden of the Resurrection. The first disseminates death where there was life, and the second proclaims Life from a tomb, the place of death.... Likewise, it is in the garden of the Resurrection that the Lord says to Mary Magdalene, "Noli me tangere." It is an invitation not only to Mary but also to all the Church, to enter into an experience of faith that overcomes any materialistic appropriation or human understanding of the divine mystery. It has ecclesial importance! It is a good lesson for every disciple of Jesus: do not seek human securities and worldly honors, but faith in the Living and Risen Christ.

Precisely since she was an eyewitness to the Risen Christ, she was also the first to testify before the apostles. She fulfills the mandate the

[7] Vatican Press Office, "Mary Magdalene, Apostle of the Apostles" (June 10, 2016), https://press.vatican.va/content/salastampa/en/bollettino/pubblico/2016/06/10/160610c.html.

Risen Christ gives her: "'Go to my brothers and say to them....' Mary Magdalene went and announced to the disciples, 'I have seen the Lord'—and that he had said these things to her." In this way she becomes, as is already known, an evangelist, or rather a messenger who announces the good news of the Resurrection of the Lord; or, as Rabano Mauro and Saint Thomas Aquinas said, "apostolorum apostola" [apostle of the apostles], as she announces to the apostles what they in turn will announce to all the world. The Angelic Doctor is right to apply this term to Mary Magdalene: she is the witness to the Risen Christ and announces the message of the Resurrection of the Lord, like the other apostles. Therefore it is right that the liturgical celebration of this woman should have the same level of festivity given to the apostles in the general Roman calendar, and that the special mission of this woman be highlighted as an example and model to every woman in the Church.

July 23: Saint Bridget, Religious (Optional Memorial)

COLLECT PRAYER

O God, who guided Saint Bridget of Sweden along different paths of life and wondrously taught her the wisdom of the Cross as she contemplated the Passion of your Son, grant us, we pray, that, walking worthily in our vocation, we may seek you in all things. Through our Lord Jesus Christ, your Son, who lives and reigns with you in the unity of the Holy Spirit, one God, for ever and ever. Amen.

Prayer of Saint Bridget of Sweden

O sweet Jesus! Pierce my heart so that my tears of penitence and love will be my bread day and night. May I be converted entirely to you; may my heart be your perpetual dwelling; may my conversation be pleasing to you; and may the end of my life be so praiseworthy that I may merit heaven and, there with your saints, praise you forever. Amen.

July 26: Saints Joachim and Anne, Parents of the Blessed Virgin Mary (Memorial)

COLLECT PRAYER

O Lord, God of our Fathers, who bestowed on Saints Joachim and Anne this grace, that of them should be born the Mother of your incarnate Son, grant, through the prayers of both, that we may attain the salvation you have promised to your people. Through our Lord Jesus Christ, your Son, who lives and reigns with you in the unity of the Holy Spirit, one God, for ever and ever. Amen.

The Kiss at the Golden Gate[8]

This lovely reflection from the Secretariat for Pro-Life Activities of the United States Conference of Catholic Bishops is based on a very early legend about Saints Anne and Joachim. Their kiss at Jerusalem's Golden Gate was a popular subject in medieval art.

Each year the Church venerates the memory of Saints Anne and Joachim on July 26. An ancient story dating to the first centuries of the Church's life recalls how Saints Anne and Joachim, like Abraham and Sarah, were scorned by their neighbors because they had no children.

Years of longing did not weaken their trust in God, but grief eventually drove Saint Joachim into the wilderness to fast and pray. Saint Anne, remaining at home, dressed in mourning clothes and wept because she had no child of her own. Seeing her mistress distressed, a servant girl reminded Anne to put her trust in God. Saint Anne washed her face, put on her bridal clothes, and went to a garden to plead with God for a child.

Angels appeared to Saint Anne in her garden and Saint Joachim in the desert, promising that, despite their old age, they would give

---

[8] Diocesan Development Program for Natural Family Planning, Secretariat for Pro-Life Activities, United States Conference of Catholic Bishops, "Faith and Perseverance: Saints Anne and Joachim; Novena", publication no. 0422, http://www.usccb.org/issues-and-action/marriage-and-family/natural-family-planning/upload/nfp-sts-anne-joachim-novena.pdf.

birth to a child who would be known throughout the world. The new parents ran to meet one another at Jerusalem's Golden Gate, and with a kiss rejoiced in the new life which God had promised would be theirs.

Saints Anne and Joachim are powerful intercessors for all married couples, expectant mothers, and married couples who are having difficulty conceiving, as well as all who have grown old.

Saint Anne Novena[9]

A novena to Saint Anne can be prayed for any intention, but her intercession is frequently invoked by those seeking a spouse or hoping for a child. It can be prayed anytime but is often begun on July 17, to end on July 25, the eve of her feast day.

Begin and end each day's prayers with the sign of the cross.

First Day

Great Saint Anne, engrave indelibly on my heart and in my mind the words that have reclaimed and sanctified so many sinners: "What shall it profit a man to gain the whole world if he lose his own soul?" May this be the principal fruit of these prayers by which I will strive to honor you during this novena. I cast myself at your feet; renew my resolution to invoke you daily, not only for the success of my temporal affairs and to be preserved from sickness and suffering, but above all, that I may be preserved from all sin, that I may gain eternal salvation, and that I will receive the special grace of (*state your intention here*). O most powerful Saint Anne, do not let me lose my soul, but obtain for me the grace of heaven, there with you, your blessed spouse, and your glorious daughter, to sing the praise of the Most Holy and Adorable Trinity forever and ever. Amen.

Pray for us, Saint Anne, that we may be made worthy of the promises of Christ. Amen.

---

[9] This traditional and popular form of the novena can be found in many places as it is in public domain.

Second Day

Glorious Saint Anne, how can you be anything other than over-flowing with tenderness toward sinners like me, since you are the grandmother of him who shed his blood for us, and the mother of her whom the saints call advocate of sinners? To you, therefore, I address my prayers with confidence. Vouchsafe to commend me to Jesus and Mary so that, at your request, I may be granted remission of my sins, perseverance, the love of God, charity for all mankind, and the special grace of (*state your intention here*), for which I stand in need at the present time. O most powerful protectress, let me not lose my soul, but pray for me, that through the merits of Jesus Christ and the intercession of Mary, I may have the great happiness of seeing them, of loving and praising them with you through all eternity. Amen.

Pray for us, Saint Anne, that we may be made worthy of the prom-ises of Christ. Amen.

Third Day

Beloved of Jesus, Mary, and Joseph, mother of the Queen of Heaven, take us and all who are dear to us under your special care. Obtain for us the virtues you instilled in the heart of her who was destined to become Mother of God, and the graces with which you were endowed. O model of Christian womanhood, pray that we may imi-tate your example in our homes and families. Please listen to our peti-tions (*state your intention here*). Guardian of the infancy and childhood of the Most Blessed Virgin Mary, obtain the graces necessary for all who enter the marriage state, that by imitating your virtues, they may sanctify their homes and lead the souls entrusted to their care to eternal glory. Amen.

Pray for us, Saint Anne, that we may be made worthy of the prom-ises of Christ. Amen.

Fourth Day

Glorious Saint Anne, I kneel in confidence at your feet, for you also have tasted the bitterness and sorrow of life. My need, the cause of my request, is (*state your intention here*). Good Saint Anne, you who did suffer much during the twenty years that preceded your glorious maternity, I beseech you, by all your sufferings and humiliations, to grant my prayer. I pray to you, through your love for your glorious spouse Saint Joachim, through your love for your immaculate child, through the joy you felt at the moment of her happy birth, not to refuse me. Bless me, bless my family and all who are dear to me, so that someday we may all be with you in the glory of heaven, for all eternity. Amen.

Pray for us, Saint Anne, that we may be made worthy of the promises of Christ. Amen.

Fifth Day

Great Saint Anne, how far I am from resembling you. I so easily give way to impatience and discouragement and so easily give up praying when God does not at once answer my request. Prayer is the key to all heavenly treasures, and I cannot pray, because my weak faith and lack of confidence fail me at the slightest delay. O my powerful protectress, come to my aid, listen to my petition (*state your intention here*). Make my confidence and fervor, supported by the promise of Jesus Christ, increase as the trial to which God, in his goodness, subjects me is prolonged, that I may obtain, like you, more than I can venture to ask for. In the future I will remember that I am made for heaven and not for earth; for eternity and not for time; that consequently I must ask, above all, for the salvation of my soul. Amen.

Pray for us, Saint Anne, that we may be made worthy of the promises of Christ. Amen.

Sixth Day

Glorious Saint Anne, mother of the Mother of God, I beg for your powerful intercession for the freedom from my sins and the assistance I need in my troubles (*state your intention here*). What can I not hope for if you deign to take me under your protection? The Most High has been pleased to grant the prayers of sinners whenever you have been charitable enough to be their advocate. Therefore, I beg you to help me in all spiritual and temporal dangers, to guide me in the true path of Christian perfection, and finally to obtain for me the grace of a happy death, so that I may contemplate your beloved Jesus and daughter, Mary, in your loving companionship throughout all eternity. Amen.

Pray for us, Saint Anne, that we may be made worthy of the promises of Christ. Amen.

Seventh Day

O good Saint Anne, so justly called the mother of the infirm, the cure for those who suffer from disease, look kindly upon the sick for whom I pray. Alleviate their sufferings; cause them to sanctify their sufferings by patience and complete submission to the Divine Will; and finally, deign to obtain health for them and with it, the firm resolution to honor Jesus, Mary, and you by the faithful performance of duties. But, merciful Saint Anne, I ask you above all for the salvation of my soul, rather than bodily health, for I am convinced that this fleeting life is given to us solely to assure us a better one. I cannot obtain that better life without the help of God's graces. I earnestly beg for them from you for the sick and for myself, and especially for the petition for which I am making in this novena (*state your intention here*). Through the merits of our Lord Jesus Christ, through the intercession of his Immaculate Mother, and through your efficacious and powerful mediation, I pray. Amen.

Pray for us, Saint Anne, that we may be made worthy of the promises of Christ. Amen.

Eighth Day

Remember, O Saint Anne, you whose name signifies grace and mercy, that never was it known that anyone who fled to your protection, implored your help, and sought your intercession was left unaided. Inspired with this confidence, I fly unto you, good and kind mother; I take refuge at your feet, burdened with the weight of my sins. O holy mother of the Immaculate Virgin Mary, despise not my petition (*state your intention here*) but hear me and grant my prayer. Amen.

Pray for us, Saint Anne, that we may be made worthy of the promises of Christ.

Ninth Day

Most holy mother of the Virgin Mary, glorious Saint Anne, I, a miserable sinner, confiding in your kindness, choose you today as my special advocate. I offer all my interests to your care and maternal solicitude. O my very good mother and advocate, deign to accept me and to adopt me as your child. O glorious Saint Anne, I beg you, by the Passion of my most loving Jesus, the Son of Mary your most holy daughter, to assist me in all the necessities of both my body and my soul. Venerable Mother, I beg you to obtain for me the favor I seek in this novena (*state your intention here*) and the grace of leading a life perfectly conformed to all things of the Divine Will. I place my soul in your hands and in those of your kind daughter. I ask for your favor in order that, appearing under your patronage before the Supreme Judge, he may find me worthy of enjoying his divine presence in your holy companionship in heaven. Amen.

Pray for us, Saint Anne and Saint Joachim, that we may be made worthy of the promises of Christ.

Kissing the Wedding Ring[10]

This prayer was recommended in the 1957 Manual of Indulgences *(also known as the* Raccolta*) and was enriched at that time with a partial indulgence. The instructions were for the bride and groom to kiss the wife's wedding ring, whether individually or together, and recite this prayer with a contrite heart. It seems a pity to limit its use to just one's wedding day!*

Grant unto us, O Lord, that loving you we may love one another and live in accordance with your holy law. Amen.

---

[10] *Raccolta*, supplement, p. 25.

15

August

The month of the Immaculate Heart

Prayer after Blessing before Meals: O Heart Most Pure[1]

O heart most pure of the Blessed Virgin Mary, obtain for me from Jesus a pure and humble heart. Sweet heart of Mary, be my salvation. Amen.

Act of Consecration to the Immaculate Heart of Mary[2]

In 1917 Our Lady appeared to three children in Fatima, Portugal. They were given prophetic visions, including one of suffering souls in hell. One of the children, Lucia, who became a religious sister, reported that Our Lady of Fatima told them, "To save [the suffering souls of sinners], God wishes to establish in the world devotion to my Immaculate Heart." Mary asked that Russia be consecrated to her Immaculate Heart. She told them, "My Immaculate Heart will triumph." In 1941 this message was made public. Popes, including Pius XII in 1942 and Paul VI in 1967, proclaimed personal and world consecration to the Immaculate Heart, but it wasn't until 1984, during the pontificate of Pope John Paul II, that Sister Lucia believed that the consecration of Russia to the Immaculate Heart was accomplished. This is the prayer of consecration of the world to the Immaculate Heart of Mary by Pope Saint John Paul II.

O Mother of all men and women, and of all peoples, you who know all their sufferings and their hopes, you who have a mother's awareness

---

[1] *Raccolta*, no. 387.

[2] Congregation for the Doctrine of the Faith, "The Message of Fatima" (June 26, 2000), https://www.vatican.va/roman_curia/congregations/cfaith/documents/rc_con_cfaith_doc_20000626_message-fatima_en.html.

of all the struggles between good and evil, between light and darkness, which afflict the modern world, accept the cry which we, moved by the Holy Spirit, address directly to your Heart. Embrace with the love of the Mother and Handmaid of the Lord, this human world of ours, which we entrust and consecrate to you, for we are full of concern for the earthly and eternal destiny of individuals and peoples.

In a special way we entrust and consecrate to you those individuals and nations which particularly need to be thus entrusted and consecrated. We have recourse to your protection, holy Mother of God! Despise not our petitions in our necessities.

Behold, as we stand before you, Mother of Christ, before your Immaculate Heart, we desire, together with the whole Church, to unite ourselves with the consecration which, for love of us, your Son made of himself to the Father: "For their sake, I consecrate myself that they also may be consecrated in the truth" (Jn 17:19). We wish to unite ourselves with our Redeemer in this his consecration for the world and for the human race, which, in his divine Heart, has the power to obtain pardon and to secure reparation.

The power of this consecration lasts for all time and embraces all individuals, peoples, and nations. It overcomes every evil that the spirit of darkness is able to awaken, and has in fact awakened in our times, in the heart of man and in his history.

How deeply we feel the need for the consecration of humanity and the world—our modern world—in union with Christ himself! For the redeeming work of Christ must be shared in the world through the Church.

The present Year of the Redemption shows this: the special Jubilee of the whole Church. Above all creatures, may you be blessed, you, the Handmaid of the Lord, who in the fullest way obeyed the divine call!

Hail to you, who are wholly united to the redeeming consecration of your Son!

Mother of the Church! Enlighten the People of God along the paths of faith, hope, and love! Enlighten especially the peoples whose consecration and entrustment by us you are awaiting. Help us to live in the truth of the consecration of Christ for the entire human family of the modern world.

In entrusting to you, O Mother, the world, all individuals and peoples, we also entrust to you this very consecration of the world, placing it in your motherly Heart.

Immaculate Heart! Help us to conquer the menace of evil, which so easily takes root in the hearts of the people of today, and whose immeasurable effects already weigh down upon our modern world and seem to block the paths toward the future!

From famine and war, deliver us.

From nuclear war, from incalculable self-destruction, from every kind of war, deliver us.

From sins against the life of man from its very beginning, deliver us.

From hatred and from the demeaning of the dignity of the children of God, deliver us.

From every kind of injustice in the life of society, both national and international, deliver us.

From readiness to trample on the commandments of God, deliver us.

From attempts to stifle in human hearts the very truth of God, deliver us.

From the loss of awareness of good and evil, deliver us.

From sins against the Holy Spirit, deliver us, deliver us.

Accept, O Mother of Christ, this cry laden with the sufferings of all individual human beings, laden with the sufferings of whole societies.

Help us with the power of the Holy Spirit to conquer all sin: individual sin and the "sin of the world", sin in all its manifestations.

Let there be revealed, once more, in the history of the world the infinite saving power of the Redemption: the power of merciful love! May it put a stop to evil! May it transform consciences! May your Immaculate Heart reveal for all the light of hope! Amen.

A reading from the Holy Gospel according to Saint Luke.
(Lk 2:15–19)

When the angels went away from them into heaven, the shepherds said to one another, "Let us go over to Bethlehem and see this thing that has happened, which the Lord has made known to us." And they went with haste, and found Mary and Joseph, and the baby lying in a manger. And when they saw it they made known the saying which had been told them concerning this child; and all who heard it wondered at what the shepherds told them. But Mary kept all these things, pondering them in her heart.

The Gospel of the Lord.

All: Praise to you, Lord Jesus Christ.

See also Morning Offering, p. 350.

August 2: Feast of Our Lady Queen of Angels (Historical)

COLLECT PRAYER[3]

O God, who willed that at the message of an Angel your Word should take flesh in the womb of the Blessed Virgin Mary, grant that we, who pray to you and believe her to be truly the Mother of God, may be helped by her interceding before you. Through our Lord Jesus Christ, your Son, who lives and reigns with you in the unity of the Holy Spirit, one God, for ever and ever. Amen.

Our Lady Queen of Angels Prayer

August Queen of Heaven, sovereign queen of angels, you who at the beginning received from God the power and the mission to crush the head of Satan, we beseech you humbly, send your holy legions so that, on your orders and by your power, they will track down demons, fight them everywhere, curb their audacity, and plunge them into the abyss.

Who can be compared to God? O good and tender Mother, you will always be our love and our hope. O divine Mother, send the holy angels and archangels to defend me and to keep the cruel enemy far from me. Holy angels and archangels, defend us, protect us. Amen.

---

[3] *Roman Missal*, Common of the Blessed Virgin Mary in Advent.

The Portiuncula Indulgence of Saint Francis of Assisi[4]

The first broadly applicable plenary indulgence was suggested in an apparition of Jesus to Saint Francis and granted by Pope Honorius III. It was placed on this feast day in honor of the location of Saint Francis' Portiuncula Chapel inside the larger Basilica of Saint Mary of the Angels in Assisi. Subject to the usual conditions, the indulgence is available to the faithful who visit any basilica, cathedral, or parish church on August 2 and there devoutly recite an Our Father and a Creed. (See Our Father, p. 349; Nicene Creed, p. 46; and Apostles' Creed, p. 366.)

August 6: The Transfiguration of the Lord (Feast)

The feast of the Transfiguration remembers humanity's first look at Jesus in his glorified body: the ultimate flowering and fruitfulness of all creation. It is an ancient tradition to observe a blessing of the first fruits of the harvest, especially grapes or apples, on this day. See p. 124 for the Blessing for the Products of Nature or p. 294 for the Assumption Day Blessing of Produce.

COLLECT PRAYER

O God, who in the glorious Transfiguration of your Only Begotten Son confirmed the mysteries of faith by the witness of the Fathers and wonderfully prefigured our full adoption to sonship, grant, we pray, to your servants, that, listening to the voice of your beloved Son, we may merit to become co-heirs with him. Who lives and reigns with you in the unity of the Holy Spirit, one God, for ever and ever. Amen.

A reading from the Holy Gospel according to Saint Mark.
(Mk 9:2–8)

And after six days Jesus took with him Peter and James and John, and led them up a high mountain apart by themselves; and he was trans-figured before them, and his garments became glistening, intensely white, as no fuller on earth could bleach them. And there appeared

---

[4] *Manual of Indulgences*, norm 15. See the introduction of this book for the usual conditions for indulgences.

THE CATHOLIC ALL YEAR PRAYER COMPANION

to them Elijah with Moses; and they were talking to Jesus. And Peter said to Jesus, "Master, it is well that we are here; let us make three booths, one for you and one for Moses and one for Elijah." For he did not know what to say, for they were exceedingly afraid. And a cloud overshadowed them, and a voice came out of the cloud, "This is my beloved Son; listen to him." And suddenly looking around they no longer saw any one with them but Jesus only.

The Gospel of the Lord.

All: Praise to you, Lord Jesus Christ.

August 10: Saint Lawrence, Deacon and Martyr (Feast)

COLLECT PRAYER

O God, giver of that ardor of love for you by which Saint Lawrence was outstandingly faithful in service and glorious in martyrdom, grant that we may love what he loved and put into practice what he taught. Through our Lord Jesus Christ, your Son, who lives and reigns with you in the unity of the Holy Spirit, one God, for ever and ever. Amen.

Prayer to Saint Lawrence

Lord Jesus, we pray that the flames of your divine love may burn away all traces of vice within us, and that we may be practical and zealous in the service of the poor.

O generous patron of the Church's poor, Saint Lawrence, pray to the one God, Father, Son, and Holy Spirit, that all the poor of the Church in need in every corner of the world may feel the effect of the love of their brothers and sisters who seek to help them. Amen.

August 11: Saint Clare of Assisi, Virgin (Memorial)

COLLECT PRAYER

O God, who in your mercy led Saint Clare to a love of poverty, grant, through her intercession, that, following Christ in poverty of spirit, we may merit to contemplate you one day in the heavenly Kingdom. Through our Lord Jesus Christ, your Son, who lives and reigns with you in the unity of the Holy Spirit, one God, for ever and ever. Amen.

Letter of Saint Clare to Saint Agnes of Bohemia[5]

Saint Agnes of Bohemia wanted more than her life as a princess. She wished to give up her wealth and power for the simple life of a Franciscan, so she wrote a letter to Saint Clare of Assisi. Saint Clare encouraged her in her vocation, and the two wrote letters to one another for the next nineteen years. This excerpt is from the final letter from Clare to Agnes.

Happy, indeed, is she to whom it is given to share this sacred banquet, to cling with all her heart to him whose beauty all the heavenly hosts admire unceasingly, whose love inflames our love, whose contemplation is our refreshment, whose graciousness is our joy, whose gentleness fills us to overflowing, whose remembrance brings a gentle light, whose fragrance will revive the dead, whose glorious vision will be the happiness of all the citizens of the heavenly Jerusalem. Amen.

August 15: THE ASSUMPTION OF THE BLESSED VIRGIN MARY (Solemnity, Holy Day of Obligation)

COLLECT PRAYER

Almighty ever-living God, who assumed the Immaculate Virgin Mary, the Mother of your Son, body and soul into heavenly glory, grant, we pray, that, always attentive to the things that are above, we may merit to be sharers of her glory. Through our Lord Jesus Christ, your Son, who lives and reigns with you in the unity of the Holy Spirit, one God, for ever and ever. Amen.

[5] Laura Chun, "The Letters of St. Clare to St. Agnes", Secular Franciscans, San Luis Rey Fraternity, http://www.slr-ofs.org/st-clares-letters-to-st-agnes-of-prague.html.

Maronite Catholic Assumption Hymn[6]

Alleluia! O Mother who gave life to us, petition on our behalf the Son who appeared from you: may he remove from us the blows of punishment, and keep away divisions and disputes. May he lead us in the path of life in which we journey at all times. On your memorial day, we sing praise to your only Son.

Alleluia! Blessed are you, O Mary, for God, who feeds all creatures, was nourished by you and rested on your breast. O wonder! The Son of God was nourished by a human creature! He assumed what is ours and gave us what is his. On his Mother's memorial let us proclaim: Glory to you, O Lord.

Alleluia! As dew was falling gently over the city of Ephesus, Saint John wrote to its people. He instructed them to celebrate the memory of the Blessed Mary, three times each year: in January, during the time of planting of the seeds; in May, during the time of harvest; and in August, during the time of the grapes. For the mysteries of life are prefigured in these months.

Alleluia! On your memorial day, O Blessed Mary, angels and mortals are overwhelmed with joy. The dead rejoice in their tombs because of the glory in creation. God will bless those who celebrate your memory with faith and pour his mercy upon them.

Alleluia! Who is to see a new ship sustaining the One who is mighty; the One who sustains and rules all creation. Mary bore him, yet he bears all creation. He nourishes all living creatures, yet she nourished him with her milk. He is the Maker of all infants, yet he dwelt, as an infant, in her womb. The fiery beings in the heights sing hymns of praise to him! Alleluia!

Assumption Day Blessing of Produce[7]

The blessing of herbs is traditionally associated with the feast of the Assumption. According to the Congregation for Divine Worship, Our Lady's association with plants—especially herbs, which have traditionally been used

---

[6] "Maronite Catholic Hymn for the Feast of the Assumption of the Blessed Virgin Mary", taken from the *Book of Offering* of the Maronite Catholic Church. Used with permission of Chorbishop John D. Faris.
[7] *Book of Blessings*, nos. 1012, 1015, 1020, 1021.

*as natural healing remedies—came about in part "because of the biblical
images applied to her such as vine, lavender, cypress, and lily, partly from
seeing her in terms of a sweet-smelling flower because of her virtue, and most
of all because of Isaiah 11:1, and his reference to the 'shoot springing from
the side of Jesse', which would bear the blessed fruit of Jesus."*[8] *The following blessing for produce is appropriate for use in the home (or the fields!)
on this feast day or any time. But since the Assumption is a holy day of
obligation, it's also appropriate to bring herbs or other produce to Mass and
ask for Father's blessing.*

All make the sign of the cross.

Leader: Let us ever praise and extol God's all-embracing providence,
who gives us food from the fruits of the earth. Blessed be God for ever.

All: Blessed be God for ever.

A reading from the prophet Joel.   (Joel 2:21–24, 26, NAB)

Fear not, O land!
exult and rejoice!
for the LORD has done great things.
Fear not, beasts of the field!
for the pastures of the plain are green;
The tree bears its fruit,
the fig tree and the vine give their yield.
And do you, O children of Zion,
exult and rejoice in the LORD, your God!
He has given you the teacher of justice:
He has made the rain come down for you,
the early and the late rain as before.
The threshing floors shall be full of grain
and the vats shall overflow with wine and oil.
You shall eat and be filled,
and shall praise the name of the LORD, your God,
Because he has dealt wondrously with you.

The Word of the Lord.

---

[8] Congregation for Divine Worship, "Directory on Popular Piety and the Liturgy: Principles and Guidelines" (December 2001), no. 181, http://www.vatican.va/roman_curia
/congregations/ccdds/documents/rc_con_ccdds_doc_20020513_vers-direttorio_en.html.

All: Thanks be to God.

A minister who is a priest or deacon says the prayer of blessing with hands outstretched; a lay minister says the prayer with hands joined.

Leader: All-powerful God,
we appeal to your tender care
that even as you temper the winds and rains
to nurture the fruits of the earth
you will also send upon them
the gentle shower of your blessing.
Fill the hearts of your people with gratitude,
that from the earth's fertility
the hungry may be filled with good things
and the poor and needy proclaim the glory of your name.
We ask this through Christ our Lord.
All: Amen.

The produce may be sprinkled with holy water.

All make the sign of the cross.

The blessing may conclude with a suitable song. See Hail, Holy Queen Enthroned Above, p. 239, or Immaculate Mary, p. 241.

See also Regina Caeli, p. 223; Litany of Loreto, p. 52.

 If you are praying the Three-Part Prayer to Saint John the Baptist (p. 305) as a novena for the Passion of Saint John the Baptist (August 29), start it on August 20.

August 22: The Queenship of the Blessed Virgin Mary (Memorial)

COLLECT PRAYER

O God, who made the Mother of your Son to be our Mother and our Queen, graciously grant that, sustained by her intercession, we may attain in the heavenly Kingdom the glory promised to your children. Through our Lord Jesus Christ, your Son, who lives and reigns with you in the unity of the Holy Spirit, one God, for ever and ever. Amen.

A reading from the book of Revelation. (Rev 12:1)

And a great sign appeared in heaven, a woman clothed with the sun, with the moon under her feet, and on her head a crown of twelve stars.[9]

The Word of the Lord.

All: Thanks be to God.

Majestic Queen of Heaven[10]

Majestic Queen of Heaven and Mistress of the Angels, you received from God the power and commission to crush the head of Satan; wherefore we humbly beseech you, send forth the legions of heaven, that under your command, they may seek out all evil spirits, engage them everywhere in battle, curb their insolence, and hurl them back into the pit of hell.

O good and tender Mother, you will ever be our hope and the object of our love.

O Mother of God, send forth the holy angels to defend me and drive far from me the cruel foe.

Holy angels and archangels, defend us and keep us. Amen.

Ad Caeli Reginam[11]

From the encyclical of Pope Venerable Pius XII proclaiming the new feast day of the Queenship of Mary, delivered in Saint Peter's Square on October 11, 1954.

In this matter we do not wish to propose a new truth to be believed by Christians, since the title and the arguments on which Mary's queenly dignity is based have already been clearly set forth, and are

---

[9] The woman of Revelation 12:1, sometimes called "The Woman of the Apocalypse", is understood to represent both Mary, the Mother of God, and a symbolic figure of the Church, giving birth to the Christian faith and the New Covenant.

[10] *Raccolta*, no. 345.

[11] Pius XII, encyclical *Ad Caeli Reginam* (October 11, 1954), nos. 5–7, 39, 43, 48–50, http://www.vatican.va/content/pius-xii/en/encyclicals/documents/hf_p-xii_enc_11101954_ad-caeli-reginam.html.

to be found in ancient documents of the Church and in the books of the sacred liturgy....

Certainly, in the full and strict meaning of the term, only Jesus Christ, the God-Man, is King; but Mary, too, as Mother of the divine Christ, as his associate in the redemption, in his struggle with his enemies and his final victory over them, has a share, though in a limited and analogous way, in his royal dignity. For from her union with Christ she attains a radiant eminence transcending that of any other creature; from her union with Christ she receives the royal right to dispose of the treasures of the Divine Redeemer's Kingdom; from her union with Christ finally is derived the inexhaustible efficacy of her maternal intercession before the Son and his Father....

Let all Christians, therefore, glory in being subjects of the Virgin Mother of God, who, while wielding royal power, is on fire with a mother's love.

Let all, therefore, try to approach with greater trust the throne of grace and mercy of our Queen and Mother, and beg for strength in adversity, light in darkness, consolation in sorrow; above all, let them strive to free themselves from the slavery of sin and offer an unceasing homage, filled with filial loyalty, to their Queenly Mother. Let her churches be thronged by the faithful, her feast days honored; may the beads of the Rosary be in the hands of all; may Christians gather, in small numbers and large, to sing her praises in churches, in homes, in hospitals, in prisons. May Mary's name be held in highest reverence, a name sweeter than honey and more precious than jewels; may none utter blasphemous words, the sign of a defiled soul, against that name graced with such dignity and revered for its motherly goodness; let no one be so bold as to speak a syllable which lacks the respect due to her name.

See also Hail, Holy Queen Enthroned Above (hymn), p. 239; Immaculate Mary (hymn), p. 241; Regina Caeli, p. 223; Litany of Loreto, p. 52.

August 24: Saint Bartholomew, Apostle (Feast)

COLLECT PRAYER

Strengthen in us, O Lord, the faith, by which the blessed Apostle Bartholomew clung wholeheartedly to your Son, and grant that through the help of his prayers your Church may become for all the nations the sacrament of salvation. Through our Lord Jesus Christ, your Son, who lives and reigns with you in the unity of the Holy Spirit, one God, for ever and ever. Amen.

A reading from the Holy Gospel according to Saint John. (Jn 1:43–51)

Bartholomew—also known as Nathanael—meets Jesus.

The next day Jesus decided to go to Galilee. And he found Philip and said to him, "Follow me." Now Philip was from Bethsaida, the city of Andrew and Peter. Philip found Nathanael, and said to him, "We have found him of whom Moses in the law and also the prophets wrote, Jesus of Nazareth, the son of Joseph." Nathanael said to him, "Can anything good come out of Nazareth?" Philip said to him, "Come and see." Jesus saw Nathanael coming to him, and said of him, "Behold, an Israelite indeed, in whom is no guile!" Nathanael said to him, "How do you know me?" Jesus answered him, "Before Philip called you, when you were under the fig tree, I saw you." Nathanael answered him, "Rabbi, you are the Son of God! You are the King of Israel!" Jesus answered him, "Because I said to you, I saw you under the fig tree, do you believe? You shall see greater things than these." And he said to him, "Truly, truly, I say to you, you will see heaven opened, and the angels of God ascending and descending upon the Son of man."

The Gospel of the Lord.

All: Praise to you, Lord Jesus Christ.

Prayer to Saint Bartholomew

O glorious Saint Bartholomew, Jesus called you a person without guile, and you saw in this word a sign that he was the Son of God and King of Israel. Obtain for us the grace to be ever guileless and innocent as doves. At the same time, help us to have your gift of faith to see the divine hand in the events of daily life. May we discern the signs of the times that lead to Jesus on earth and will eventually unite us to him forever in heaven. Amen.

August 27: Saint Monica (Memorial)

COLLECT PRAYER

O God, who console the sorrowful and who mercifully accepted the motherly tears of Saint Monica for the conversion of her son Augustine, grant us, through the intercession of them both, that we may bitterly regret our sins and find the grace of your pardon. Through our Lord Jesus Christ, your Son, who lives and reigns with you in the unity of the Holy Spirit, one God, for ever and ever. Amen.

A reading from the Holy Gospel according to Saint Luke. (Lk 18:1–8)

And he told them a parable, to the effect that they ought always to pray and not lose heart. He said, "In a certain city there was a judge who neither feared God nor regarded man; and there was a widow in that city who kept coming to him and saying, 'Vindicate me against my adversary.' For a while he refused; but afterward he said to himself, 'Though I neither fear God nor regard man, yet because this widow bothers me, I will vindicate her, or she will wear me out by her continual coming.'" And the Lord said, "Hear what the unrighteous judge says. And will not God vindicate his elect, who cry to him day and night? Will he delay long over them? I tell you, he will vindicate them speedily. Nevertheless, when the Son of man comes, will he find faith on earth?"

The Gospel of the Lord.

All: Praise to you, Lord Jesus Christ.

Speak Less to Augustine about God and More to God about Augustine[12]

An excerpt from Saint Augustine's Confessions, *in which the saint discusses his mother Monica's role in his conversion, and the advice she received from Saint Ambrose.*

[12] *Confessions* 3.11–12. Translated by J. G. Pilkington. In *Nicene and Post-Nicene Fathers*, series 1, vol. 1, ed. Philip Schaff (Buffalo, N.Y.: Christian Literature, 1887). Revised and edited for New Advent by Kevin Knight, http://www.newadvent.org/fathers/110103.htm. Used with permission.

And you sent your hand from above, and drew my soul out of that profound darkness, when my mother, your faithful one, wept to you on my behalf more than mothers are wont to weep the bodily death of their children. For she saw that I was dead by that faith and spirit which she had from you, and you heard her, O Lord. You heard her, and despised not her tears, when, pouring down, they watered the earth under her eyes in every place where she prayed; yea, you heard her. . . .

For nearly nine years passed in which I wallowed in the slime of that deep pit and the darkness of falsehood, striving often to rise, but being all the more heavily dashed down. But yet that chaste, pious, and sober widow (such as you love), now more buoyed up with hope, though no whit less zealous in her weeping and mourning, desisted not, at all the hours of her supplications, to bewail my case unto you. And her prayers entered into your presence, and yet you still allowed me to be involved and re-involved in that darkness.

And meanwhile you granted her another answer, which I recall; for much I pass over, hastening on to those things which the more strongly impel me to confess unto you, and much I do not remember. You granted her then another answer, by a priest of yours, a certain bishop [Saint Ambrose], reared in your Church and well versed in your books. He, when this woman had entreated that he would vouchsafe to have some talk with me, refute my errors, unteach me evil things, and teach me good (for this he was in the habit of doing when he found people fitted to receive it), refused, very prudently, as I afterwards came to see. For he answered that I was still unteachable, being inflated with the novelty of that heresy, and that I had already perplexed various inexperienced persons with vexatious questions, as she had informed him. *But leave him alone for a time,* says he, *only pray God for him; he will of himself, by reading, discover what that error is, and how great its impiety.* . . . Which when he had said, and she would not be satisfied, but repeated more earnestly her entreaties, shedding copious tears, that he would see and discourse with me, he, a little vexed at her importunity, exclaimed, *Go your way, and God bless you, for it is not possible that the son of these tears should perish.* Which answer (as she often mentioned in her conversations with me) she accepted as though it were a voice from heaven.

Prayer to Saint Monica for the Conversion of Loved Ones

Dear Saint Monica, troubled wife and mother, many sorrows pierced your heart during your lifetime. Yet you never despaired or lost faith. With confidence, persistence, and profound faith, you prayed daily for the conversion of your beloved husband, Patricius, and your beloved son, Augustine; your prayers were answered. Grant me that same fortitude, patience, and trust in the Lord. Intercede for me, dear Saint Monica, that God may favorably hear my plea. Intercede for my loved ones (*here mention their names*). Grant me the grace to accept his will in all things, through Jesus Christ, our Lord, in the unity of the Holy Spirit, one God, forever and ever. Amen.

August 28: Saint Augustine, Bishop and Doctor of the Church (Memorial)

COLLECT PRAYER

Renew in your Church, we pray, O Lord, that spirit with which you endowed your Bishop Saint Augustine, that, filled with the same spirit, we may thirst for you, the sole fount of true wisdom, and seek you, the author of heavenly love. Through our Lord Jesus Christ, your Son, who lives and reigns with you in the unity of the Holy Spirit, one God, for ever and ever. Amen.

Saint Augustine and the Hole at the Beach[13]

One day, Augustine was walking along the beach in North Africa, pondering the mystery of the Holy Trinity and trying earnestly to understand once and for all how there could be three Persons in one God. He was distracted from his thoughts by the sight of a boy, who had dug a hole in the sand, and was running back and forth,

---

[13] Adapted from *The Golden Legend* by Jacobus de Voragine (1275), translated by William Caxton (1483).

from the ocean to the hole, dumping in bucketful after bucketful of water. Finally, Augustine's curiosity got the best of him and he asked the boy, "What are you doing?" The boy replied, "I'm emptying the ocean into this hole." The man, amused, said, "Why, you can't empty the ocean into a hole!" The boy looked into his eyes and said, "Neither can you understand the mystery of the Holy Trinity." And then the boy was gone.

Late Have I Loved You[14]

An excerpt from the Confessions *of Saint Augustine.*

Late have I loved you, Beauty so ancient and so new, late have I loved you! Lo, you were within, but I outside, seeking there for you, and upon the shapely things you have made I rushed headlong, I, misshapen.

You were with me, but I was not with you. They held me back far from you, those things which would have no being were they not in you.

You called, shouted, broke through my deafness; you flared, blazed, banished my blindness; you lavished your fragrance, I gasped, and now I pant for you; I tasted you, and I hunger and thirst; you touched me, and I burned for your peace.

See also Saint Augustine's Prayer to the Holy Spirit, p. 250; On Saint Peter and Saint John, p. 100; Saint Augustine on the Holy Innocents, p. 104; Night Prayer of Saint Augustine, p. 373.

August 29: The Passion of Saint John the Baptist (Memorial)

COLLECT PRAYER

O God, who willed that Saint John the Baptist should go ahead of your Son both in his birth and in his death, grant that, as he died a

[14] Augustine, *The Confessions, with an Introduction and Contemporary Criticism*, trans. Maria Boulding, ed. David Vincent Meconi, Ignatius Critical Editions, ed. Joseph Pearce (San Francisco: Ignatius Press, 2012), 10.27–28.

martyr for truth and justice, we, too, may fight hard for the confession of what you teach. Through our Lord Jesus Christ, your Son, who lives and reigns with you in the unity of the Holy Spirit, one God, for ever and ever. Amen.

A reading from the Holy Gospel according to Saint Mark. (Mk 6:14–29)

King Herod heard of it [Jesus' preaching and miracles]; for Jesus' name had become known. Some said, "John the Baptist has been raised from the dead; that is why these powers are at work in him." But others said, "It is Elijah." And others said, "It is a prophet, like one of the prophets of old." But when Herod heard of it he said, "John, whom I beheaded, has been raised." For Herod had sent and seized John, and bound him in prison for the sake of Herodias, his brother Philip's wife; because he had married her. For John said to Herod, "It is not lawful for you to have your brother's wife." And Herodias had a grudge against him, and wanted to kill him. But she could not, for Herod feared John, knowing that he was a righteous and holy man, and kept him safe. When he heard him, he was much perplexed; and yet he heard him gladly. But an opportunity came when Herod on his birthday gave a banquet for his courtiers and officers and the leading men of Galilee. For when Herodias' daughter came in and danced, she pleased Herod and his guests; and the king said to the girl, "Ask me for whatever you wish, and I will grant it." And he vowed to her, "Whatever you ask me, I will give you, even half of my kingdom." And she went out, and said to her mother, "What shall I ask?" And she said, "The head of John the Baptist." And she came in immediately with haste to the king, and asked, saying, "I want you to give me at once the head of John the Baptist on a platter." And the king was exceedingly sorry; but because of his oaths and his guests he did not want to break his word to her. And immediately the king sent a soldier of the guard and gave orders to bring his head. He went and beheaded him in the prison, and brought his head on a platter, and gave it to the girl; and the girl gave it to her mother. When his disciples heard of it, they came and took his body, and laid it in a tomb.

The Gospel of the Lord.

All: Praise to you, Lord Jesus Christ.

Three-Part Prayer to Saint John the Baptist

This prayer to Saint John the Baptist has three parts to reflect the three phases of his life: (1) the time of preparation in the wilderness, (2) his time preaching and leading his followers to Christ, and (3) his martyrdom. It can be used on this feast day or on the solemnity of his nativity on June 24. Used as a novena prayer, it would usually begin on June 15 or August 20.

1. O glorious Saint John the Baptist, greatest prophet among those born of woman, although you were sanctified in your mother's womb and led a most innocent life, nevertheless it was your will to retire into the wilderness, there to devote yourself to the practice of austerity and penance; obtain for us of your Lord the grace to be wholly detached, at least in our hearts, from earthly goods, and to practice Christian mortification with interior recollection and with the spirit of holy prayer. *Our Father, Hail Mary, Glory Be.*

2. O most zealous apostle, who, without working any miracle on others, but solely by the example of your life of penance and the power of your word, drew after you the multitudes, in order to dispose them to receive the Messiah worthily and to listen to his heavenly doctrine; grant that it may be given unto us, by means of your example of a holy life and the exercise of every good work, to bring many souls to God, but above all those souls that are enveloped in the darkness of error and ignorance and are led astray by vice. *Our Father, Hail Mary, Glory Be.*

3. O martyr invincible, who, for the honor of God and the salvation of souls did with firmness and constancy withstand the impiety of Herod even at the cost of your own life, and rebuked him openly for his wicked and dissolute life; by your prayers obtain for us a heart, brave and generous, in order that we may overcome all human respect and openly profess our faith in loyal obedience to the teachings of Jesus Christ, our divine Master. *Our Father, Hail Mary, Glory Be.*

Leader: Pray for us, Saint John the Baptist.

All: That we may be made worthy of the promises of Christ.

Leader: Let us pray. O God, who has made this day to be honorable in our eyes by the commemoration of blessed John the Baptist, grant unto your people the grace of spiritual joy, and direct the minds of all your faithful into the way of everlasting salvation. Through Christ our Lord.

All: Amen.

16

September

The month of the Seven Sorrows of Mary

Prayer after Blessing before Meals:
Mother of Love and Sorrow

Mother of love, of sorrow, and of mercy, look with favor upon me and obtain for me from your Son all the graces I need to endure the sufferings God allows me to face. Amen.

September 5: Saint Teresa of Calcutta
(Optional Memorial)

COLLECT PRAYER

God, who called blessed Teresa, virgin, to respond to the love of your Son thirsting on the cross with outstanding charity to the poorest of the poor, grant us, we beseech you, by her intercession, to minister to Christ in his suffering brothers. Through our Lord Jesus Christ, your Son, who lives and reigns with you and the Holy Spirit, one God, for ever and ever. Amen.

Fearless Messenger of Love[1]

This prayer was part of Pope Saint John Paul II's homily for the beatification of Mother Teresa of Calcutta on October 19, 2003. She was canonized by Pope Francis on September 4, 2016.

[1] John Paul II, Homily at the Beatification of Mother Teresa of Calcutta (October 19, 2003), no. 6, http://www.vatican.va/content/john-paul-ii/en/homilies/2003/documents/hf_jp-ii_hom_20031019_mother-theresa.html.

Virgin Mary, Queen of all the saints, help us to be gentle and humble of heart like this fearless messenger of Love. Help us to serve every person we meet with joy and a smile. Help us to be missionaries of Christ, our peace and our hope. Amen!

The Simple Path[2]

This reminder was printed on Mother Teresa's calling card.

The fruit of silence is prayer. The fruit of prayer is faith. The fruit of faith is love. The fruit of love is service. The fruit of service is peace.

Mother Teresa's Nobel Peace Prize Acceptance Speech[3]

Saint Teresa of Calcutta was awarded the Nobel Peace Prize on December 10, 1979, at the University of Oslo in Norway. She used her acceptance speech—given before dignitaries and presidents and royalty, broadcast on international television—to lead the world in prayer, decry the scourge of abortion, encourage personal holiness, and advocate for the poor. This is an excerpt.

Love begins at home. And love to be true has to hurt. I never forget a little child who taught me a very beautiful lesson. They heard in Calcutta, the children, that Mother Teresa had no sugar for her children, and this little one, Hindu boy four years old, he went home and he told his parents: I will not eat sugar for three days, I will give my sugar to Mother Teresa. How much a little child can give. After three days they brought [him] into our house, and there was this little one who could scarcely pronounce my name, he loved with great love, he loved until it hurt. And this is what I bring before you, to love one another until it hurts, but don't forget that there are many

---

[2] Pontifical Society of Holy Childhood, "Mother Teresa of Calcutta", http://www.vatican.va/roman_curia/congregations/cevang/p_missionary_works/infantia/documents/rc_ic_infantia_doc_20090324_boletin13p14_en.html.

[3] Teresa of Calcutta, Nobel Peace Prize acceptance speech, December 10, 1979, https://www.nobelprize.org/prizes/peace/1979/teresa/26200-mother-teresa-acceptance-speech-1979/. A video of Mother Teresa giving the speech is available on the Nobel Prize website.

children, many children, many men and women who haven't got what you have. And remember to love them until it hurts.

See also Memorare "flying novena", p. 363.

September 8: The Nativity of the Blessed Virgin Mary (Feast)

COLLECT PRAYER

Impart to your servants, we pray, O Lord, the gift of heavenly grace, that the feast of the Nativity of the Blessed Virgin may bring deeper peace to those for whom the birth of her Son was the dawning of salvation. Through our Lord Jesus Christ, your Son, who lives and reigns with you in the unity of the Holy Spirit, one God, for ever and ever. Amen.

Prayer to Maria Bambina (the Child Mary)

All: Hail, Infant Mary, full of grace, the Lord is with you; blessed are you forever, and blessed are your holy parents Joachim and Anne, of whom you were miraculously born. Mother of God, intercede for us. We fly to your patronage, holy and amiable Child Mary; despise not our prayers in our necessities, but deliver us from all dangers, glorious and blessed Virgin.

Leader: Pray for us, holy Child Mary.

All: That we may be made worthy of the promises of Christ.

Leader: Let us pray.

All: O almighty and merciful God, who through the cooperation of the Holy Spirit prepared the body and soul of the Immaculate Infant Mary that she might be the worthy mother of your Son, and preserved her from all stain, grant that we who venerate with all our hearts her most holy childhood may be freed, through her merits and intercession, from all uncleanness of mind and body, and be able to imitate her perfect humility, obedience, and charity. Through Christ our Lord. Amen.

See also Litany of Loreto, p. 52.

September 14: The Exaltation of the Holy Cross (Feast)

The autumn Ember Days fall on the Wednesday, Friday, and Saturday after the feast of the Holy Cross.[4] This season's days are offered for the grape harvest in thanksgiving for the Precious Blood. Saturday is also offered as a day of prayer for priests and for vocations. See Ember Days Prayer, p. 57; Farmer's Prayer, p. 235; Blessing for the Products of Nature, p. 124; Prayer for Priests, p. 102; Prayer for Vocations, p. 357.

COLLECT PRAYER

O God, who willed that your Only Begotten Son should undergo the Cross to save the human race, grant, we pray, that we, who have known his mystery on earth, may merit the grace of his redemption in heaven. Through our Lord Jesus Christ, your Son, who lives and reigns with you in the unity of the Holy Spirit, one God, for ever and ever. Amen.

Holy Cross Prayer[5]

O God, who willed to hallow the standard of the life-giving cross by the Precious Blood of your only-begotten Son, grant, we beseech you, that they who rejoice in honoring the same holy cross may rejoice also in your ever-present protection. Through the same Christ our Lord. Amen.

For instructions for Veneration of the Cross, see p. 208.

September 15: Our Lady of Sorrows (Memorial)

COLLECT PRAYER

O God, who willed that, when your Son was lifted high on the Cross, his Mother should stand close by and share his suffering, grant that your

---

[4] For more on Ember Days, vigils, and general fasting and abstinence requirements and recommendations, see appendix A of *The Catholic All Year Compendium.*

[5] *Raccolta*, no. 212.

Church, participating with the Virgin Mary in the Passion of Christ, may merit a share in his Resurrection. Who lives and reigns with you in the unity of the Holy Spirit, one God, for ever and ever. Amen.

To Mary in Honor of Her Seven Sorrows

O Mary, Mother of Sorrows, I beseech you, by the bitter agony you endured at the foot of the cross, offer to the eternal Father, in my name, your beloved Son, Jesus, all covered with blood and wounds, in satisfaction for my sins, for the needs of Holy Church, the conversion of sinners, the relief of the souls in purgatory, and the special grace I now implore *(here mention your request)*. Amen.

Seven Sorrows of Mary Scripture Activity

Devotion to the Seven Sorrows of Mary was spread by Saint Bridget of Sweden. Our family activity for the day is to read the Bible account of each sorrow, then eat a sour candy or slice of sour fruit and try not to make a sour face!

First Sorrow: The Prophecy of Simeon

A reading from the Holy Gospel according to Saint Luke. (Lk 2:25–35)

Now there was a man in Jerusalem, whose name was Simeon, and this man was righteous and devout, looking for the consolation of Israel, and the Holy Spirit was upon him. And it had been revealed to him by the Holy Spirit that he should not see death before he had seen the Lord's Christ. And inspired by the Spirit he came into the temple; and when the parents brought in the child Jesus, to do for him according to the custom of the law, he took him up in his arms and blessed God and said,

> "Lord, now let your servant depart in peace,
> according to your word;
> for my eyes have seen your salvation
> which you have prepared in the presence of all peoples,
> a light for revelation to the Gentiles,
> and for glory to your people Israel."

And his father and his mother marveled at what was said about him; and Simeon blessed them and said to Mary his mother,

"Behold, this child is set for the fall and rising of many in Israel,
and for a sign that is spoken against
(and a sword will pierce through your own soul also),
that thoughts out of many hearts may be revealed."

The Gospel of the Lord.

All: Praise to you, Lord Jesus Christ.

Second Sorrow: The Flight into Egypt

A reading from the Holy Gospel according to Saint Matthew. (Mt 2:13–15)

Now when they had departed, behold, an angel of the Lord appeared to Joseph in a dream and said, "Rise, take the child and his mother, and flee to Egypt, and remain there till I tell you; for Herod is about to search for the child, to destroy him." And he rose and took the child and his mother by night, and departed to Egypt, and remained there until the death of Herod. This was to fulfil what the Lord had spoken by the prophet, "Out of Egypt have I called my son."

The Gospel of the Lord.

All: Praise to you, Lord Jesus Christ.

Third Sorrow: The Loss of the Child Jesus in the Temple of Jerusalem

A reading from the Holy Gospel according to Saint Luke. (Lk 2:41–51)

Now his parents went to Jerusalem every year at the feast of the Passover. And when he was twelve years old, they went up according to custom; and when the feast was ended, as they were returning, the boy Jesus stayed behind in Jerusalem. His parents did not know it, but supposing him to be in the company they went a day's journey, and they sought him among their kinsfolk and acquaintances; and when they did not find him, they returned to Jerusalem, seeking him. After three days they found him in the temple, sitting among the teachers, listening to them and asking them questions; and all who heard him were amazed at his understanding and his answers. And when they saw him they were astonished; and his mother said to him, "Son, why have you treated us so? Behold, your father and I have been looking for you anxiously." And he said to them, "How is it that you sought me? Did you not know that I must be in my Father's house?" And they did not understand the saying which he spoke to them. And he went down with them and came to Nazareth, and was obedient to them; and his mother kept all these things in her heart.

The Gospel of the Lord.

All: Praise to you, Lord Jesus Christ.

Fourth Sorrow: The Meeting of Jesus and Mary on the Via Dolorosa[6]

A reading from the Holy Gospel according to Saint Luke.
Lk 23:26–31)

And as they led him away, they seized one Simon of Cyrene, who was coming in from the country, and laid on him the cross, to carry it behind Jesus. And there followed him a great multitude of the people, and of women who bewailed and lamented him. But Jesus turning to them said, "Daughters of Jerusalem, do not weep for me, but weep for yourselves and for your children. For behold, the days are coming when they will say, 'Blessed are the barren, and the wombs that never bore, and the breasts that never nursed!' Then they will begin to say to the mountains, 'Fall on us'; and to the hills, 'Cover us.' For if they do this when the wood is green, what will happen when it is dry?"

The Gospel of the Lord.

All: Praise to you, Lord Jesus Christ.

[6] The sorrow of the meeting of Jesus and Mary on the Via Dolorosa comes to us from long tradition but is not specifically mentioned in scripture. The verses included here recount the meeting of Jesus with the women of Jerusalem. It's possible that Mary was among them.

Fifth Sorrow: The Crucifixion

A reading from the Holy Gospel according to Saint John.
(Jn 19:17–18, 25–30)

So they took Jesus, and he went out, bearing his own cross, to the place called the place of a skull, which is called in Hebrew Golgotha. There they crucified him, and with him two others, one on either side, and Jesus between them. . . . But standing by the cross of Jesus were his mother, and his mother's sister, Mary the wife of Clopas, and Mary Magdalene. When Jesus saw his mother, and the disciple whom he loved standing near, he said to his mother, "Woman, behold, your son!" Then he said to the disciple, "Behold, your mother!" And from that hour the disciple took her to his own home.

After this Jesus, knowing that all was now finished, said (to fulfil the Scripture), "I thirst."

A bowl full of vinegar stood there; so they put a sponge full of the vinegar on hyssop and held it to his mouth. When Jesus had received the vinegar, he said, "It is finished"; and he bowed his head and gave up his spirit.

The Gospel of the Lord.

All: Praise to you, Lord Jesus Christ.

Sixth Sorrow: The Body of Jesus Is Removed from the Cross

A reading from the Holy Gospel according to Saint Mark.
(Mk 15:43–47)

Joseph of Arimathea, a respected member of the council, who was also himself looking for the kingdom of God, took courage and went to Pilate, and asked for the body of Jesus. And Pilate wondered if he were already dead; and summoning the centurion, he asked him whether he was already dead. And when he learned from the centurion that he was dead, he granted the body to Joseph. And he bought a linen shroud, and taking him down, wrapped him in the linen shroud, and laid him in a tomb which had been hewn out of the rock; and he rolled a stone against the door of the tomb. Mary Magdalene and Mary the mother of Joses saw where he was laid.

The Gospel of the Lord.

All: Praise to you, Lord Jesus Christ.

Seventh Sorrow: The Burial of Jesus

A reading from the Holy Gospel according to Saint John.
(Jn 19:39–42)

Nicodemus also, who had at first come to him by night, came bringing a mixture of myrrh and aloes, about a hundred pounds' weight.
They took the body of Jesus, and bound it in linen cloths with the
spices, as is the burial custom of the Jews. Now in the place where
he was crucified there was a garden, and in the garden a new tomb
where no one had ever been laid. So because of the Jewish day of
Preparation, as the tomb was close at hand, they laid Jesus there.

The Gospel of the Lord.

All: Praise to you, Lord Jesus Christ.

See also Litany of Loreto, p. 52.

September 21: Saint Matthew, Apostle and Evangelist (Feast)

COLLECT PRAYER

O God, who with untold mercy were pleased to choose as an Apostle
Saint Matthew, the tax collector, grant that, sustained by his example and intercession, we may merit to hold firm in following you.
Through our Lord Jesus Christ, your Son, who lives and reigns with
you in the unity of the Holy Spirit, one God, for ever and ever. Amen.

A reading from the Holy Gospel according to Saint Matthew.
(Mt 9:9–13)

As Jesus passed on from there, he saw a man called Matthew sitting
at the tax office; and he said to him, "Follow me." And he rose and
followed him. And as he sat at table in the house, behold, many tax
collectors and sinners came and sat down with Jesus and his disciples.
And when the Pharisees saw this, they said to his disciples, "Why

does your teacher eat with tax collectors and sinners?" But when he heard it, he said, "Those who are well have no need of a physician, but those who are sick. Go and learn what this means, 'I desire mercy, and not sacrifice.' For I came not to call the righteous, but sinners."

The Gospel of the Lord.

All: Praise to you, Lord Jesus Christ.

Prayer in Honor of Saint Matthew

Through the intercession of Saint Matthew, evangelist, may we always put aside worldly distractions and follow you, O Lord, as quietly as Saint Matthew left his work and immediately became one of your disciples. By his example and prayers help us to follow you without counting the cost and remain faithful in your service. Amen.

 The Novena Rose Prayer, prayed to Saint Thérèse, is often begun on September 22; see p. 321.

September 29: Saints Michael, Gabriel, and Raphael, Archangels / Michaelmas (Feast)

COLLECT PRAYER

O God, who dispose in marvelous order ministries both angelic and human, graciously grant that our life on earth may be defended by those who watch over us as they minister perpetually to you in heaven. Through our Lord Jesus Christ, your Son, who lives and reigns with you in the unity of the Holy Spirit, one God, for ever and ever. Amen.

An Invocation of Angels[7]

The tradition of an angelic hierarchy dates back to before Christ. In the Middle Ages angels were organized by Catholic scholars into nine "choirs". Beginning at the highest, they are:

[7] *Raccolta*, nos. 440, 441.

1. Seraphim: *fiery six-winged beings who attend the throne of God (cf. Is 6:1–7). Saint Michael is usually considered to be the highest of the seraphim, an "arch-archangel".*

2. Cherubim: *winged angels with four faces, who are accompanied by the thrones. They guard the Garden of Eden and the throne of God (cf. Gen 3:24; Ezek 10). (Although many people use the name "cherubs" for the baby angels popular in Renaissance artwork, those are actually called* putti *rather than cherubim.)*

3. Thrones: *described as double wheels covered with eyes that move along at the side of the cherubim (cf. Ezek 10; Eph 1:21; Col 1:16). Given this description, one understands why angels always greet humans by saying, "Do not be afraid" (cf. Tob 12:16; Mt 28:5; Lk 1:13, 30; 2:10).*

4. Dominions: *considered to be divinely beautiful human-looking angels with feathered wings, who regulate the actions of other angels.*

5. Principalities (or Rulers): *said to be the angels through which signs and miracles are made in the world.*

6. Powers: *God's warriors, who oppose evil spirits. They are usually represented in full armor.*

7. Virtues: *angels who are said to guide and protect the Church. They are depicted with crowns and scepters.*

8. Archangels: *said to be the guardians of nations, countries, and the world, who will announce the Second Coming (cf. Ex 32:34; 1 Thess 4:16).*

9. Angels: *beings sent as messengers to humanity and who serve as individual guardian angels (cf. Ps 91:11; Mt 18:10).*

You Angels and Archangels, you Thrones and Dominions, you Principalities and Powers, you Virtues of the heavens, Cherubim and Seraphim, bless the Lord forever. Bless the Lord, all you his Angels: you that are mighty in strength, and execute his word. Bless the Lord, all you his hosts: you ministers of his that do his will. Amen.

Saint Michael Prayer

Saint Michael the archangel, defend us in battle. Be our protection against the wickedness and snares of the devil. May God rebuke him, we humbly pray; and do thou, O prince of the heavenly host, by the power of God, cast into hell Satan and all the evil spirits, who prowl about the world, seeking the ruin of souls. Amen.

A reading from the book of Revelation.   (Rev 12:7–12)

Now war arose in heaven, Michael and his angels fighting against the dragon; and the dragon and his angels fought, but they were defeated and there was no longer any place for them in heaven. And the great dragon was thrown down, that ancient serpent, who is called the Devil and Satan, the deceiver of the whole world—he was thrown down to the earth, and his angels were thrown down with him. And I heard a loud voice in heaven, saying, "Now the salvation and the power and the kingdom of our God and the authority of his Christ have come, for the accuser of our brethren has been thrown down, who accuses them day and night before our God. And they have conquered him by the blood of the Lamb and by the word of their testimony, for they loved not their lives even unto death. Rejoice then, O heaven and you that dwell therein! But woe to you, O earth and sea, for the devil has come down to you in great wrath, because he knows that his time is short!"

The Word of the Lord.

All: Thanks be to God.

Saint Gabriel Prayer[8]

O God, who among all the angels chose the archangel Gabriel to announce the mystery of your Incarnation, mercifully grant that we who solemnly keep his feast on earth may feel the benefit of his patronage in heaven: who lives and reigns forever and ever. Amen.

A reading from the Holy Gospel according to Saint Luke.
(Lk 1:18–20, 26–38)

Zechariah said to the angel, "How shall I know this? For I am an old man, and my wife is advanced in years." And the angel answered him, "I am Gabriel, who stand in the presence of God; and I was sent to speak to you, and to bring you this good news. And behold, you will be silent and unable to speak until the day that these things come

---

[8] Ibid., no. 449.

to pass, because you did not believe my words, which will be fulfilled in their time." ...

In the sixth month the angel Gabriel was sent from God to a city of Galilee named Nazareth, to a virgin betrothed to a man whose name was Joseph, of the house of David; and the virgin's name was Mary. And he came to her and said, "Hail, full of grace, the Lord is with you!" But she was greatly troubled at the saying, and considered in her mind what sort of greeting this might be. And the angel said to her, "Do not be afraid, Mary, for you have found favor with God. And behold, you will conceive in your womb and bear a son, and you shall call his name Jesus.

> He will be great, and will be called the Son of the Most High;
> and the Lord God will give to him the throne of his father David,
> and he will reign over the house of Jacob for ever;
> and of his kingdom there will be no end."

And Mary said to the angel, "How can this be, since I have no husband?" And the angel said to her,

> "The Holy Spirit will come upon you,
> and the power of the Most High will overshadow you;
> therefore the child to be born will be called holy,
> the Son of God.

And behold, your kinswoman Elizabeth in her old age has also conceived a son; and this is the sixth month with her who was called barren. For with God nothing will be impossible." And Mary said, "Behold, I am the handmaid of the Lord; let it be to me according to your word." And the angel departed from her.

The Gospel of the Lord.

All: Praise to you, Lord Jesus Christ.

Saint Raphael Prayer[9]

Vouchsafe, O Lord God, to send unto our assistance Saint Raphael the archangel, and may he, who, we believe, evermore stands before

---

[9] Ibid., no. 451.

the throne of your majesty, offer unto you our humble petitions to be blessed by you. Through Christ our Lord. Amen.

A reading from the book of Tobit.   (Tob 12:15–22)

"I am Raphael, one of the seven holy angels who present the prayers of the saints and enter into the presence of the glory of the Lord."

They were both alarmed; and they fell upon their faces, for they were afraid. But he said to them, "Do not be afraid; you will be safe. But praise God for ever. For I did not come as a favor on my part, but by the will of our God. Therefore praise him for ever. All these days I merely appeared to you and did not eat or drink, but you were seeing a vision. And now bless the Lord upon the earth and give thanks to God, for I am ascending to him who sent me. Write in a book everything that has happened to you." Then they stood up; but they saw him no more. So they confessed the great and wonderful works of God, and acknowledged that the angel of the Lord had appeared to them.

The Word of the Lord.

All: Thanks be to God.

SONG SUGGESTIONS: Let All Mortal Flesh Keep Silence; Angels We Have Heard On High; Holy, Holy, Holy, Lord God Almighty

17

October[1]

The month of the Holy Rosary

Prayer after Blessing before Meals:
Fatima Rosary Decade Prayer

O my Jesus, forgive us our sins, save us from the fires of hell. Lead all souls to heaven, especially those most in need of thy mercy. Amen.

October 1: Saint Thérèse of the Child Jesus, Virgin and Doctor of the Church (Memorial)

COLLECT PRAYER

O God, who open your Kingdom to those who are humble and to little ones, lead us to follow trustingly in the little way of Saint Thérèse, so that through her intercession we may see your eternal glory revealed. Through our Lord Jesus Christ, your Son, who lives and reigns with you in the unity of the Holy Spirit, one God, for ever and ever. Amen.

Novena Rose Prayer

This prayer is usually said as a nine-day novena to Saint Thérèse. It can be said anytime but is prayed especially beginning on September 22, to end on the vigil of her feast day. Those who pray the novena often report being

[1] Note for Canadians, who celebrate their Thanksgiving Day in October: prayers for this holiday can be found in November, on p. 343.

"presented" in some way with a rose at the completion of the novena. This is understood to be a sign from heaven that the Little Flower is praying for our requests alongside us.

O little Thérèse of the Child Jesus, please pick for me a rose from the heavenly gardens and send it to me as a message of love. O Little Flower of Jesus, ask God to grant the favors I now place with confidence in your hands (*here mention your request*). Saint Thérèse, help me to always believe as you did in God's great love for me, so that I might imitate your "little way" each day. Amen.

October 2: The Holy Guardian Angels (Memorial)

COLLECT PRAYER

O God, who in your unfathomable providence are pleased to send your holy Angels to guard us, hear our supplication as we cry to you, that we may always be defended by their protection and rejoice eternally in their company. Through our Lord Jesus Christ, your Son, who lives and reigns with you in the unity of the Holy Spirit, one God, for ever and ever. Amen.

A reading from the Holy Gospel according to Saint Matthew. (Mt 18:10)

See that you do not despise one of these little ones; for I tell you that in heaven their angels always behold the face of my Father who is in heaven.

Guardian Angel Prayer[2]

A partial indulgence is available for this prayer anytime.

Angel of God, my guardian dear,
To whom God's love commits me here,

[2] *Raccolta*, no. 452. See an explanation of the choirs of angels on p. 316.

Ever this day be at my side,
To light and guard, to rule and guide. Amen.

On Guardian Angels[3]

Like many other saints, Saint Josemaría Escrivá had a great devotion to his guardian angel and encouraged the same in others. These notes are from The Way, *a book of maxims by the saint.*

Have confidence in your guardian angel. Treat him as a lifelong friend—that is what he is—and he will render you a thousand services in the ordinary affairs of each day.

Win over the guardian angel of that person whom you wish to draw to your apostolate. He is always a great "accomplice".

If you remembered the presence of your own angel and the angels of your neighbors, you would avoid many of the foolish things which slip into your conversations.

You are amazed that your guardian angel has done you such obvious favors. And you should not be amazed: that's why our Lord has placed him beside you.

You say that in such surroundings there are many occasions of going astray? That's true, but is there not also the presence of the guardian angels?

If you call upon your guardian angel at the moment of trial, he will protect you from the devil and will bring you holy inspirations.

How joyfully the holy guardian angels must have obeyed that soul who said to them: "Holy angels, I call on you, like the Spouse of the Song of Songs, *ut nuntietis ei quia amore langueo*, to tell him that I languish with love."

I know you will be glad to have this prayer to the holy guardian angels of our tabernacles: Angelic spirits that guard our tabernacles, wherein lies the adorable treasure of the Holy Eucharist, defend it from profanation and preserve it for our love.

---

[3] Josemaría Escrivá de Balaguer, *The Way*, nos. 562–69, https://www.escrivaworks.org/book/the_way.htm. Used by permission of Fundación Studium.

SONG SUGGESTIONS: Guardian Angel from Heaven So Bright; All Night, All Day (Angels Watching over Me)

October 4: Saint Francis of Assisi (Memorial)

COLLECT PRAYER

O God, by whose gift Saint Francis was conformed to Christ in poverty and humility, grant that, by walking in Francis' footsteps, we may follow your Son, and, through joyful charity, come to be united with you. Through our Lord Jesus Christ, your Son, who lives and reigns with you in the unity of the Holy Spirit, one God, for ever and ever. Amen.

Saint Francis' Prayer before the Crucifix

Most High, glorious God, enlighten the darkness of our minds. Give us a right faith, a firm hope, and a perfect charity, so that we may always and in all things act according to your holy will. Amen.

Canticle of the Sun[4]

This hymn in praise of God for creation was composed by Saint Francis of Assisi in 1224. It is believed to be the first piece of literature written down in the Italian language. According to tradition, the first time it was sung in its entirety was by Francis and Brothers Angelo and Leo, two of his original companions, on Francis' deathbed, the final verse praising "Sister Death" having been added only a few minutes before.

Most High, all-powerful, good Lord, yours are the praises, the glory, and the honor and all blessing. To you alone, Most High, do they belong, and no human is worthy to mention your name. Praised be

---

[4] Pontifical Theological Faculty "Saint Bonaventure" (Seraphicum), trans., " 'Letter to the Faithful' of Saint Francis of Assisi" (1224), http://www.vatican.va/spirit/documents/spirit_20020210_lettera-fedeli-3_en.html.

you, my Lord, with all your creatures, especially Sir Brother Sun, who is the day and through whom you give us light. And he is beautiful and radiant with great splendor and bears a likeness of you, Most High One.

Praised be you, my Lord, through Sister Moon and the stars in heaven. You formed them clear and precious and beautiful. Praised be you, my Lord, through Brother Wind, and through the air, cloudy and serene, and every kind of weather, through whom you give sustenance to your creatures. Praised be you, my Lord, through Sister Water, who is very useful and humble and precious and chaste. Praised be you, my Lord, through Brother Fire, through whom you light the night, and he is beautiful and playful and robust and strong. Praised be you, my Lord, through our Sister Mother Earth, who sustains and governs us, and who produces various fruits with colored flowers and herbs.

Praised be you, my Lord, through those who give pardon for your love and bear infirmity and tribulation. Blessed are those who endure in peace, for by you, Most High, shall they be crowned. Praised be you, my Lord, through our Sister Bodily Death, from whom no one living can escape. Woe to those who die in mortal sin. Blessed are those whom death will find in your most holy will, for the second death shall do them no harm. Praise and bless my Lord and give him thanks and serve him with great humility. Amen.

SONG SUGGESTIONS: All Creatures of Our God and King (an adaptation of the Canticle of the Sun); All Things Bright and Beautiful

Blessing of Animals[5]

According to the providence of the Creator, many animals have a certain role to play in human existence by helping with work or providing food and clothing. Thus, when the occasion arises, such as the feast of some saint, the custom of invoking God's blessing on animals may be continued.

The blessing below may be used by a priest or deacon. It may also be used by a layperson, who follows the rites and prayers designated for a lay minister.

[5] *Book of Blessings*, nos. 942–943, 962–965, 961.

Leader: Our help is in the name of the Lord.

All: Who made heaven and earth.

A reading from the book of Genesis.   (Gen 2:20a, NAB)

The man gave names to all the cattle, all the birds of the air, and all the wild animals.

A reading from the book of Psalms.   (Ps 8:7–9a, NAB)

You have given him rule over the works of your hands, putting all things under his feet: All sheep and oxen, yes, and the beasts of the field, the birds of the air, the fishes of the sea.

A minister who is a priest or deacon says the prayer of blessing with hands outstretched; a lay minister says the prayer with hands joined.

Leader: O God, you have done all things wisely; in your goodness you have made us in your image and given us care over other living things. Reach out with your right hand and grant that these animals may serve our needs and that your bounty in the resources of this life may move us to seek more confidently the goal of eternal life. We ask this through Christ our Lord.

All: Amen.

After the prayer of blessing, as circumstances suggest, the minister may sprinkle those present and the animals with holy water.

It is preferable to end the celebration with a suitable song.

The Doxology

This hymn is sung to the tune Old Hundredth, which was written in 1551 and is attributed to the French composer Louis Bourgeois. The tune gets its name from an association with Psalm 100. The text here is known as "The Doxology", an expression of praise sung to the Holy Trinity. The hymn text was written in 1674 by Thomas Ken.

> Praise God, from whom all blessings flow;
> Praise him, all creatures here below;
> Praise him above, ye heav'nly host;
> Praise Father, Son, and Holy Ghost.

All make the sign of the cross.

October 7: Our Lady of the Rosary (Memorial)

COLLECT PRAYER

Pour forth, we beseech you, O Lord, your grace into our hearts, that we, to whom the Incarnation of Christ your Son was made known by the message of an Angel, may, through the intercession of the Blessed Virgin Mary, by his Passion and Cross be brought to the glory of his Resurrection. Who lives and reigns with you in the unity of the Holy Spirit, one God, for ever and ever. Amen.

Rosarium Virginis Mariae[6]

This apostolic letter of Pope Saint John Paul II, issued on October 16, 2002, encourages the use of the Rosary by all the faithful, but especially families, and describes the history and theology behind the practice. In it, John Paul II also introduces the Luminous Mysteries. The following are a few excerpts from the letter.

The Rosary, though clearly Marian in character, is at heart a Christocentric prayer. In the sobriety of its elements, it has all the depth of the Gospel message in its entirety, of which it can be said to be a compendium. It is an echo of the prayer of Mary, her perennial Magnificat for the work of the redemptive Incarnation which began in her virginal womb. With the Rosary, the Christian people sits at the school of Mary and is led to contemplate the beauty of the face of Christ and to experience the depths of his love. Through the Rosary the faithful receive abundant grace, as though from the very hands of the Mother of the Redeemer....

Mary lived with her eyes fixed on Christ, treasuring his every word: "[Mary] kept all these things, pondering them in her heart" (Lk 2:19). The memories of Jesus, impressed upon her heart, were always with her, leading her to reflect on the various moments of her life at her Son's side. In a way those memories were to be the "Rosary" which she recited uninterruptedly throughout her earthly life.

---

[6]John Paul II, apostolic letter *Rosarium Virginis Mariae* (October 16, 2002), nos. 1, 11, 26, 39, 41, 42, http://w2.vatican.va/content/john-paul-ii/en/apost_letters/2002/documents/hf_jp-ii_apl_20021016_rosarium-virginis-mariae.html.

Even now, amid the joyful songs of the heavenly Jerusalem, the reasons for her thanksgiving and praise remain unchanged. They inspire her maternal concern for the pilgrim Church, in which she continues to relate her personal account of the Gospel. Mary constantly sets before the faithful the "mysteries" of her Son, with the desire that the contemplation of those mysteries will release all their saving power. In the recitation of the Rosary, the Christian community enters into contact with the memories and the contemplative gaze of Mary....

Meditation on the mysteries of Christ is proposed in the Rosary by means of a method designed to assist in their assimilation. It is a method based on repetition. This applies above all to the Hail Mary, repeated ten times in each mystery. If this repetition is considered superficially, there could be a temptation to see the Rosary as a dry and boring exercise. It is quite another thing, however, when the Rosary is thought of as an outpouring of that love which tirelessly returns to the person loved with expressions similar in their content but ever fresh in terms of the feeling pervading them....

One thing is clear: although the repeated Hail Mary is addressed directly to Mary, it is to Jesus that the act of love is ultimately directed, with her and through her. The repetition is nourished by the desire to be conformed ever more completely to Christ, the true program of the Christian life....

The Church has always attributed particular efficacy to this prayer, entrusting to the Rosary, to its choral recitation and to its constant practice, the most difficult problems. At times when Christianity itself seemed under threat, its deliverance was attributed to the power of this prayer, and Our Lady of the Rosary was acclaimed as the one whose intercession brought salvation....

As a prayer for peace, the Rosary is also, and always has been, a prayer of and for the family. At one time this prayer was particularly dear to Christian families, and it certainly brought them closer together. It is important not to lose this precious inheritance. We need to return to the practice of family prayer and prayer for families, continuing to use the Rosary....

To pray the Rosary for children, and even more, with children, training them from their earliest years to experience this daily "pause for prayer" with the family, is admittedly not the solution to every problem, but it is a spiritual aid which should not be underestimated. It could be objected that the Rosary seems hardly suited to the taste of children and young people of today. But perhaps the objection is directed to an impoverished method of praying it. Furthermore, without prejudice to the Rosary's basic structure, there is nothing to stop children and young people from praying it—either within the family or in groups—with appropriate symbolic and practical aids to understanding and appreciation. Why not try it?

For Rosary prayers and instructions, see p. 363. See also Litany of Loreto, p. 52.

October 18: Saint Luke, Evangelist (Feast)

COLLECT PRAYER

Lord God, who chose Saint Luke to reveal by his preaching and writings the mystery of your love for the poor, grant that those who already glory in your name may persevere as one heart and one soul and that all nations may merit to see your salvation. Through our Lord Jesus Christ, your Son, who lives and reigns with you in the unity of the Holy Spirit, one God, for ever and ever. Amen.

A reading from the Holy Gospel according to Saint Luke. (Lk 1:1–4)

Inasmuch as many have undertaken to compile a narrative of the things which have been accomplished among us, just as they were delivered to us by those who from the beginning were eyewitnesses and ministers of the word, it seemed good to me also, having followed all things closely for some time past, to write an orderly account for you, most excellent Theophilus, that you may know the truth concerning the things of which you have been informed.

The Gospel of the Lord.

All: Praise to you, Lord Jesus Christ.

Prayer to Saint Luke for Physicians

Saint Luke is the patron saint of physicians, among other patronages, because he was a physician. In Saint Paul's Letter to the Colossians, he relays, "Luke the beloved physician ... greet[s] you" (Col 4:14).

Most charming and saintly physician, you were animated by the heavenly Spirit of love. In faithfully detailing the humanity of Christ, you also showed his divinity and his genuine compassion for all human beings. Inspire our physicians with your professionalism and with the divine compassion for their patients. Enable them to cure the ills of both body and spirit that afflict so many in our day. Amen.

Nunc Dimittis (Canticle of Simeon)

The Nunc Dimittis, also known as the Canticle of Simeon, quotes holy Simeon when he encounters the infant Jesus at the Presentation in the Temple. It is recorded in Luke 2:29–32.

Nunc dimittis servum tuum, Domine, secundum verbum tuum in pace; quia viderunt oculi mei salutare tuum, quod parasti ante faciem omnium populorum, lumen ad revelationem gentium, et gloriam plebis tuae Israel. Amen.

Lord, now let your servant depart in peace, according to your word; for my eyes have seen your salvation, which you have prepared in the presence of all peoples, a light for revelation to the Gentiles, and for glory to your people Israel. Amen.

The Magnificat, also known as the Canticle of Mary, is taken from Luke 1:46–55 and can be found on p. 80. The Benedictus, also known as the Canticle of Zechariah, is taken from Luke 1:68–79 and can be found on p. 267.

October 22: Saint John Paul II, Pope (Optional Memorial)

COLLECT PRAYER

O God, who are rich in mercy and who willed that the blessed John Paul the Second should preside as Pope over your universal Church, grant, we pray, that instructed by his teaching, we may open our hearts to the saving grace of Christ, the sole Redeemer of mankind. Who lives and reigns with you in the unity of the Holy Spirit, one God, for ever and ever. Amen.

Prayer to Our Lady of Divine Love[7]

This prayer was delivered by Pope Saint John Paul II on a visit to the Marian Shrine of Our Lady of Divine Love, outside Rome, on May 1, 1979.

Hail, O Mother, Queen of the world. You are the Mother of fair Love, you are the Mother of Jesus, the source of all grace, the perfume of every virtue, the mirror of all purity. You are joy in weeping, victory in battle, hope in death. How sweet your name tastes in our mouth, how harmoniously it rings in our ears, what rapture it brings to our hearts! You are the happiness of the suffering, the crown of martyrs, the beauty of virgins. We beg you, guide us after this exile to possession of your Son, Jesus. Amen.

Offer Forgiveness and Receive Peace[8]

Pope Saint John Paul II's life and pontificate were marked by forgiveness. As pope, he recognized and accepted responsibility for failings of the Church throughout the ages. He publicly asked for forgiveness and sought reconciliation with groups who had been wronged by Christians.[9] He also offered forgiveness when he had been wronged. After surviving four gunshot wounds received at close range in 1981, he visited the man who had been hired to kill him, talking with him privately, and publicly forgiving him. The assassin converted to Christianity in prison. After his release, he visited the tomb of Pope John Paul II in 2014 and laid roses on his grave. This short excerpt from JPII's message for the celebration of the World Day of Peace in 1997 is focused on personal forgiveness.

Certainly there are many factors which can help restore peace while safeguarding the demands of justice and human dignity. But no process of peace can ever begin unless an attitude of sincere forgiveness takes root in human hearts. When such forgiveness is lacking,

[7] John Paul II, Prayer to Our Lady of the Divine Love (May 1, 1979), http://www.vatican.va/content/john-paul-ii/en/prayers/documents/hf_jp-ii_19790501_prayer-divino-amore.html

[8] John Paul II, Message for the World Day of Peace, "Offer Forgiveness and Receive Peace" (January 1, 1997), http://www.vatican.va/content/john-paul-ii/en/messages/peace/documents/hf_jp-ii_mes_08121996_xxx-world-day-for-peace.html.

[9] See the papal bull *Incarnationis Mysterium* and the homily "Day of Pardon", among other examples.

wounds continue to fester, fueling in the younger generation endless resentment, producing a desire for revenge and causing fresh destruction. Offering and accepting forgiveness is the essential condition for making the journey toward authentic and lasting peace.

With deep conviction therefore I wish to appeal to everyone to seek peace along the paths of forgiveness. I am fully aware that forgiveness can seem contrary to human logic, which often yields to the dynamics of conflict and revenge. But forgiveness is inspired by the logic of love, that love which God has for every man and woman, for every people and nation, and for the whole human family. If the Church dares to proclaim what, from a human standpoint, might appear to be sheer folly, it is precisely because of her unshakable confidence in the infinite love of God. As scripture bears witness, God is rich in mercy and full of forgiveness for those who come back to him (cf. Ezek 18:23; Ps 32:5; Ps 103:8–14; Eph 2:4–5; 2 Cor 1:3). God's forgiveness becomes in our hearts an inexhaustible source of forgiveness in our relationships with one another, helping us to live together in true brotherhood.

See also Act of Consecration to the Immaculate Heart of Mary, p. 287; Homily at the Canonization of Juan Diego Cuauhtlatoatzin, p. 50; Closing of World Youth Day 2000 Homily of Pope Saint John Paul II, p. 238; apostolic letter Rosarium Virginis Mariae, p. 327; Fearless Messenger of Love, p. 307.

October 31: All Hallows' Eve

Fasting and abstinence are recommended for the vigil of All Saints.[10]

All Hallows' Eve (or Halloween, October 31), All Saints' Day (November 1), and All Souls' Day (November 2) make up what is traditionally called Hallowtide. The spooky skeletons and ghosts and death imagery of Halloween celebrations are part of the Catholic tradition of memento mori— "Remember, you must die"—dating back to at least the medieval era. The

[10] United States Conference of Catholic Bishops, "Pastoral Statement on Penance and Abstinence" (November 18, 1966), https://www.usccb.org/prayer-and-worship/liturgical -year-and-calendar/lent/us-bishops-pastoral-statement-on-penance-and-abstinence. In our home, people who are able to fast do so during the day, and we all abstain from meat. After sunset, we indulge in Halloween candy!

idea is that we should remember our own mortality, and that of those we love, so that we can live each day preparing our souls to meet God and face our particular judgment, and helping those around us to be ready to face theirs.

In our home, alongside the fun of costumes and candy, we use Halloween and the other days of Hallowtide to focus on the three different parts of the Church. On Halloween we think of the Church Militant: all of us here on earth, struggling against temptation and our fallen natures, loving God and our neighbor, and hoping, through God's grace, to one day die a happy death and be welcomed into heaven. On All Saints' Day we focus on the Church Triumphant: all the saints who have died and are in heaven, beholding the face of our Lord and inspiring us and interceding for us. On All Souls' Day (and for the whole month of November) we focus on the Church Suffering: the Holy Souls in purgatory, who are guaranteed one day to be in heaven but are now suffering and need our prayers.

COLLECT PRAYER

Almighty ever-living God, increase our faith, hope and charity, and make us love what you command, so that we may merit what you promise. Through our Lord Jesus Christ, your Son, who lives and reigns with you in the unity of the Holy Spirit, one God, for ever and ever. Amen.

A reading from the book of Sirach.   (Sir 7:36)

> In all you do, remember the end of your life,
> and then you will never sin.

The Word of the Lord.

All: Thanks be to God.

The Skeleton[11]

G. K. Chesterton was an English Catholic writer, philosopher, theologian, and debate team champ. In this poem from the late 1890s, he uses the grinning

[11] G. K. Chesterton, *Collected Works of G. K. Chesterton*, vol. 10, *Collected Poetry*, pt. 1, ed. Aidan Mackey (San Francisco: Ignatius Press, 1994), 251.

aspect of a skeleton to make a hopeful statement about death. For someone in a state of grace, worries about death are as a joke to the eternal eyes of God, our "good King".

Chattering finch and water–fly
Are not merrier than I;
Here among the flowers I lie
Laughing everlastingly.
No; I may not tell the best;
Surely, friends, I might have guessed
Death was but the good King's jest,
It was hid so carefully.

18

November

Prayer after Blessing before Meals: Eternal Rest Prayer

Eternal rest grant unto them, O Lord, and let perpetual light shine upon them. May the souls of the faithful departed, through the mercy of God, rest in peace. Amen.

November 1: ALL SAINTS
(Solemnity, Holy Day of Obligation)

COLLECT PRAYER

Almighty ever-living God, by whose gift we venerate in one celebration the merits of all the Saints, bestow on us, we pray, through the prayers of so many intercessors, an abundance of the reconciliation with you for which we earnestly long. Through our Lord Jesus Christ, your Son, who lives and reigns with you in the unity of the Holy Spirit, one God, for ever and ever. Amen.

A reading from the Holy Gospel according to Saint Matthew. (Mt 5:3–12)

Blessed are the poor in spirit, for theirs is the kingdom of heaven.
Blessed are those who mourn, for they shall be comforted.
Blessed are the meek, for they shall inherit the earth.
Blessed are those who hunger and thirst for righteousness, for they shall be satisfied.
Blessed are the merciful, for they shall obtain mercy.
Blessed are the pure in heart, for they shall see God.

Blessed are the peacemakers, for they shall be called sons of God.

Blessed are those who are persecuted for righteousness' sake, for theirs is the kingdom of heaven.

Blessed are you when men revile you and persecute you and utter all kinds of evil against you falsely on my account. Rejoice and be glad, for your reward is great in heaven, for so men persecuted the prophets who were before you.

 The eight-day All Souls' Indulgence begins today (see p. 338).

Litany of All Saints[1]

Leader: Lord, have mercy;

All: Christ, have mercy.

Leader: Christ, have mercy;

All: Christ, have mercy.

All: Lord, have mercy;

All: Lord have mercy.

The leader announces each saint.

All reply: pray for us.

Holy Mary, Mother of God, *pray for us.*

Saint Michael, *pray for us.*

Holy angels of God, *pray for us.*

Saint John the Baptist, *pray for us.*

Saint Joseph, *pray for us.*

Saint Peter and Saint Paul, *pray for us.*

Saint Andrew, *pray for us.*

Saint John, *pray for us.*

Saint Mary Magdalene, *pray for us.*

Saint Stephen, *pray for us.*

Saint Ignatius of Antioch, *pray for us.*

Saint Lawrence, *pray for us.*

Saint Perpetua and Saint Felicity, *pray for us.*

Saint Agnes, *pray for us.*

Saint Gregory, *pray for us.*

Saint Augustine, *pray for us.*

Saint Athanasius, *pray for us.*

Saint Martin, *pray for us.*

Saint Nicholas, *pray for us.*

Saint Benedict, *pray for us.*

Saint Francis and Saint Dominic, *pray for us.*

Saint Francis Xavier, *pray for us.*

Saint John Vianney, *pray for us.*

Saint Catherine, *pray for us.*

Saint Teresa of Jesus, *pray for us.*

[1] *Manual of Indulgences*, grant 22. See the introduction of this book for the usual conditions for indulgences.

The names of other saints may be added, especially the patron saints of your parish, town, and family members.[2]

The leader announces each petition to the Lord. All reply: Lord, deliver us, we pray.

Lord, be merciful; *Lord, deliver us, we pray.*
From all evil, *Lord, deliver us, we pray.*
From every sin, *Lord, deliver us, we pray.*
From everlasting death, *Lord, deliver us, we pray.*
By your coming as a man, *Lord, deliver us, we pray.*
By your death and rising to new life, *Lord, deliver us, we pray.*
By your gift of the Holy Spirit, *Lord, deliver us, we pray.*

The leader announces each petition to the Lord.

All reply: Lord, we ask you, hear our prayer.

Be merciful to us sinners; *Lord, we ask you, hear our prayer.*
Guide and protect your holy Church; *Lord, we ask you, hear our prayer.*
Keep the pope and all the clergy in faithful service to your Church;
    Lord, we ask you, hear our prayer.
Bring all peoples together in trust and peace; *Lord, we ask you, hear our prayer.*
Strengthen us in your service; *Lord, we ask you, hear our prayer.*
Jesus, Son of the living God; *Lord, we ask you, hear our prayer.*

Leader: Christ, hear us;

All: Christ, hear us.

Leader: Christ, graciously hear us;

All: Christ, graciously hear us.

Leader: Let us pray. God of our ancestors who set their hearts on you, of those who fell asleep in peace, and of those who won the martyrs' violent crown: we are surrounded by these witnesses as by clouds of fragrant incense. In this age we would be counted in this communion of all the saints; keep us always in their good and blessed company. In their midst we make every prayer through Christ, who is our Lord for ever and ever.

All: Amen.

---

[2] *Roman Missal*, The Easter Vigil, no. 43.

SONG SUGGESTION: Oh, When the Saints Go Marching In; For All the Saints

November 2: The Commemoration of All the Faithful Departed (All Souls' Day) (Memorial)

COLLECT PRAYER

Listen kindly to our prayers, O Lord, and, as our faith in your Son, raised from the dead, is deepened, so may our hope of resurrection for your departed servants also find new strength. Through our Lord Jesus Christ, your Son, who lives and reigns with you in the unity of the Holy Spirit, one God, for ever and ever. Amen.

All Souls' Indulgence

During the first eight days of November, pray for the Holy Souls in a cemetery each day to gain a plenary indulgence (subject to the usual conditions)[3] applicable only to the poor souls. You can use any prayer. See the Eternal Rest Prayer, p. 335, and Prayer for the Souls in Purgatory, p. 339.

On November 2 only, the plenary indulgence for the Holy Souls can also be gained by praying an Our Father and a Creed for the dead in a church. See Our Father, p. 349; Apostles' Creed, p. 366; Nicene Creed, p. 46.

De profundis (Psalm 130—Prayer for the Dead)

According to the Rule of Saint Benedict established around 530, Psalm 130 was sung at the beginning of Vespers each Tuesday. Atop a mountain on June 7, 1925, Blessed Pier Giorgio Frassati asked his companions to join him in this prayer in memory of a friend who had died in a climbing accident. Less than a month later, Pier Giorgio himself died of polio.

Out of the depths I cry to you, O Lord!
   Lord, hear my voice!
Let your ears be attentive
   to the voice of my supplications!

---

[3] See the introduction of this book for the usual conditions for indulgences.

If you, O LORD, should mark iniquities,
  Lord, who could stand?
But there is forgiveness with you,
  that you may be feared.
I wait for the LORD, my soul waits,
  and in his word I hope;
my soul waits for the LORD
  more than watchmen for the morning,
  more than watchmen for the morning.
O Israel, hope in the LORD!
  For with the LORD there is mercy,
  and with him is plenteous redemption.
And he will redeem Israel
  from all his iniquities.

Prayer for the Souls in Purgatory

O Lord, who are ever merciful and bounteous with your gifts, look down upon the suffering souls in purgatory. Remember not their offenses and negligences but be mindful of your loving mercy, which is from all eternity. Cleanse them of their sins and fulfill their ardent desires that they may be made worthy to behold you face to face in your glory. May they soon be united with you and hear those blessed words that will call them to their heavenly home: "Come, O blessed of my Father, inherit the kingdom prepared for you from the foundation of the world" (Mt 25:34). Amen.

A reading from the second book of Maccabees.
(2 Mac 12:44–45)

For if he [Judas Maccabeus] were not expecting that those who had fallen would rise again, it would have been superfluous and foolish to pray for the dead. But if he was looking to the splendid reward that is laid up for those who fall asleep in godliness, it was a holy and pious thought. Therefore he made atonement for the dead, that they might be delivered from their sin.

The Word of the Lord.

All: Thanks be to God.

A reading from the First Letter of Saint Paul
to the Corinthians.   (1 Cor 3:11–15)

For no other foundation can any one lay than that which is laid, which is Jesus Christ. Now if any one builds on the foundation with gold, silver, precious stones, wood, hay, straw—each man's work will become manifest; for the Day will disclose it, because it will be revealed with fire, and the fire will test what sort of work each one has done. If the work which any man has built on the foundation survives, he will receive a reward. If any man's work is burned up, he will suffer loss, though he himself will be saved, but only as through fire.

The Word of the Lord.

All: Thanks be to God.

November 11: Saint Martin of Tours, Bishop (Martinmas) (Memorial)

COLLECT PRAYER

O God, who are glorified in the Bishop Saint Martin both by his life and death, make new, we pray, the wonders of your grace in our hearts, that neither death nor life may separate us from your love. Through our Lord Jesus Christ, your Son, who lives and reigns with you in the unity of the Holy Spirit, one God, for ever and ever. Amen.

Prayer of Saint Martin of Tours

Lord, if your people still have need of my services, I will not avoid the toil. Your will be done. I have fought the good fight long enough. Yet if you bid me continue to hold the battle line in defense of your camp, I will never beg to be excused from failing strength. I will do the work you entrust to me. While you command, I will fight beneath your banner. Amen.

May God Give Peace[4]

November 11 is Veterans Day in the United States and Remembrance Day in the Commonwealth and many other countries throughout the world. This date was chosen because the formal end of hostilities in the First World War occurred on the eleventh hour of the eleventh day of the eleventh month. It seems fitting that the armistice and this day to remember the armed forces falls on the feast day of Saint Martin, a soldier saint. This prayer is from an Anglican service for Remembrance Sunday.

Leader: Let us pray for all who suffer as a result of conflict, and ask that God may give us peace: for the servicemen and servicewomen who have died in the violence of war, each one remembered by and known to God; may God give peace.

All: God, give peace.

Leader: For those who love them in death as in life, offering the distress of our grief and the sadness of our loss; may God give peace.

All: God, give peace.

Leader: For all members of the armed forces who are in danger this day, remembering family, friends, and all who pray for their safe return; may God give peace.

All: God, give peace.

Leader: For civilian women, children, and men whose lives are disfigured by war or terror, calling to mind in penitence the anger and hatreds of humanity; may God give peace.

All: God, give peace.

Leader: For peacemakers and peacekeepers, who seek to keep this world secure and free; may God give peace.

All: God, give peace.

Leader: For all who bear the burden and privilege of leadership—political, military, and religious; asking for gifts of wisdom and resolve in the search for reconciliation and peace; may God give peace.

All: God, give peace.

[4] "An Order of Service for Remembrance Sunday", Churches Together in Britain and Ireland (London, 2005).

Leader: O God of truth and justice, we hold before you those whose memory we cherish and those whose names we will never know. Help us to lift our eyes above the torment of this broken world and grant us the grace to pray for those who wish us harm. As we honor the past, may we put our faith in your future; for you are the source of life and hope, now and forever.

All: Amen.

November 25: Saint Catherine of Alexandria, Virgin and Martyr (Optional Memorial)

COLLECT PRAYER

Almighty ever-living God, who gave Saint Catherine of Alexandria to your people as a Virgin and an invincible Martyr, grant that through her intercession we may be strengthened in faith and constancy and spend ourselves without reserve for the unity of the Church. Through our Lord Jesus Christ, your Son, who lives and reigns with you in the unity of the Holy Spirit, one God, for ever and ever. Amen.

Invocation of Saint Catherine[5]

Saint Catherine, glorious virgin and martyr, resplendent in the luster of wisdom and purity, your wisdom refuted the adversaries of divine truth and covered them with confusion; your immaculate purity made you a spouse of Christ, so that after your glorious martyrdom, angels carried your body to Mount Sinai. Implore for me progress in the science of the saints and the virtue of holy purity, that vanquishing the enemies of my soul, I may be victorious in my last combat and after death be conducted by the angels into the eternal beatitude of heaven. Amen.

 The Immaculate Conception Novena is usually begun on November 29, in order to finish on the vigil of the feast day. For the novena prayers, see p. 38.

see p. 38.

[5] *Raccolta*, no. 761.

Fourth Thursday of November (U.S.) and Second Monday of October (Canada): Thanksgiving Day (Public Holiday)

COLLECT PRAYER

Father all-powerful, your gifts of love are countless and your goodness infinite; as we come before you on Thanksgiving Day with gratitude for your kindness, open our hearts to have concern for every man, woman, and child, so that we may share your gifts in loving service. Through our Lord Jesus Christ, your Son, who lives and reigns with you in the unity of the Holy Spirit, one God, for ever and ever. Amen.

A reading from the First Letter of Saint Paul to the Corinthians. (1 Cor 1:3–9)

Grace to you and peace from God our Father and the Lord Jesus Christ.

I give thanks to God always for you because of the grace of God which was given you in Christ Jesus, that in every way you were enriched in him with all speech and all knowledge—even as the testimony to Christ was confirmed among you—so that you are not lacking in any spiritual gift, as you wait for the revealing of our Lord Jesus Christ; who will sustain you to the end, guiltless in the day of our Lord Jesus Christ. God is faithful, by whom you were called into the fellowship of his Son, Jesus Christ our Lord.

The Word of the Lord.

All: Thanks be to God.

Thanksgiving Day Prayer[6]

Lord, we thank you
for the goodness of our people
and for the spirit of justice
that fills this nation.

[6] *Catholic Household Blessings and Prayers*, 177.

We thank you for the beauty and fullness of the land
and the challenge of the cities.

We thank you for our work and our rest,
for one another, and for our homes.
We thank you, Lord:
accept our thanksgiving on this day.
We pray and give thanks through Jesus Christ our Lord.

All: Amen.

SONG SUGGESTION: Now Thank We All Our God

Last Sunday in Ordinary Time: OUR LORD JESUS CHRIST, KING OF THE UNIVERSE (Solemnity)

COLLECT PRAYER

Almighty ever-living God, whose will is to restore all things in your
beloved Son, the King of the universe, grant, we pray, that the whole
creation, set free from slavery, may render your majesty service and
ceaselessly proclaim your praise. Through our Lord Jesus Christ, your
Son, who lives and reigns with you in the unity of the Holy Spirit,
one God, for ever and ever. Amen.

Act of Dedication of the Human Race to Jesus Christ the King[7]

*A partial indulgence is granted to the faithful who piously recite the Act of
Dedication of the Human Race to Jesus Christ the King, a prayer also known
as* Iesu dulcissime, *Redemptor. A plenary indulgence is granted if it is
recited publicly (in a church, family, religious community, or group of friends)
on the feast of Our Lord Jesus Christ, King of the Universe; a partial indulgence is granted for its use in other circumstances.*

---

[7] *Manual of Indulgences*, grant 2. See the introduction of this book for the usual conditions
of indulgences.

Most sweet Jesus, redeemer of the human race, look down upon us humbly prostrate before you. We are yours, and yours we wish to be; but to be more surely united with you, behold, each one of us freely consecrates himself today to your Most Sacred Heart. Many indeed have never known you; many, too, despising your precepts, have rejected you. Have mercy on them all, most merciful Jesus, and draw them to your Sacred Heart. Be King, O Lord, not only of the faithful who have never forsaken you, but also of the prodigal children who have abandoned you; grant that they may quickly return to their Father's house, lest they die of wretchedness and hunger. Be King of those who are deceived by erroneous opinions, or whom discord keeps aloof, and call them back to the harbor of truth and the unity of faith, so that soon there may be but one flock and one Shepherd. Grant, O Lord, to your Church assurance of freedom and immunity from harm; give tranquillity of order to all nations; make the earth resound from pole to pole with one cry: Praise to the divine Heart that wrought our salvation; to it be glory and honor for ever. Amen.

Quas Primas[8]

An excerpt from the encyclical of Pope Pius XI on the institution of the feast of Christ the King in 1925. In case you ever wondered why the Church institutes feast days, this encyclical explains why!

That these blessings may be abundant and lasting in Christian society, it is necessary that the kingship of our Savior should be as widely as possible recognized and understood, and to the end nothing would serve better than the institution of a special feast in honor of the kingship of Christ. For people are instructed in the truths of faith, and brought to appreciate the inner joys of religion, far more effectually by the annual celebration of our sacred mysteries than by any official pronouncement of the teaching of the Church. Such pronouncements usually reach only a few, and the more learned among the faithful; feasts reach them all. The former speak but once; the latter

---

[8] Pius XI, encyclical *Quas Primas* (December 11, 1925), http://www.vatican.va/content /pius-xi/en/encyclicals/documents/hf_p-xi_enc_11121925_quas-primas.html.

speak every year—in fact, forever. The Church's teaching affects the mind primarily; her feasts affect both mind and heart, and have a salutary effect upon the whole of man's nature. Man is composed of body and soul, and he needs these external festivities so that the sacred rites, in all their beauty and variety, may stimulate him to drink more deeply of the fountain of God's teaching, that he may make it a part of himself, and use it with profit for his spiritual life.

History, in fact, tells us that in the course of ages these festivals have been instituted one after another according as the needs or the advantage of the people of Christ seemed to demand: as when they needed strength to face a common danger, when they were attacked by insidious heresies, when they needed to be urged to the pious consideration of some mystery of faith or of some divine blessing. Thus in the earliest days of the Christian era, when the people of Christ were suffering cruel persecution, the cult of the martyrs was begun in order, says Saint Augustine, "that the feasts of the martyrs might incite men to martyrdom". The liturgical honors paid to confessors, virgins, and widows produced wonderful results in an increased zest for virtue, necessary even in times of peace. But more fruitful still were the feasts instituted in honor of the Blessed Virgin. As a result of these, men grew not only in their devotion to the Mother of God as an ever-present advocate, but also in their love of her as a mother bequeathed to them by their Redeemer. Not least among the blessings which have resulted from the public and legitimate honor paid to the Blessed Virgin and the saints is the perfect and perpetual immunity of the Church from error and heresy. We may well admire in this the admirable wisdom of the providence of God, who, ever bringing good out of evil, has from time to time suffered the faith and piety of men to grow weak, and allowed Catholic truth to be attacked by false doctrines, but always with the result that truth has afterward shone out with greater splendor, and that men's faith, aroused from its lethargy, has shown itself more vigorous than before.

November 30: Saint Andrew, Apostle (Feast)

The entry for Saint Andrew's feast day can be found on p. 39.

ACKNOWLEDGMENTS

During the three years in which I actively searched for and compiled the prayers and devotions included in this book, I felt rather like an expert on one of those reality television shows in which antique specialists come and search through people's attics and barns, looking for neglected heirlooms among the sawdust and debris. You find a lot of junk. But you also find priceless treasures of our faith, dusty and forgotten. I'm so grateful to be able to uncover them, clean them up a bit, and bring them to a new generation of Catholics.

I'm indebted to the Holy Spirit, who inspires; to all the original authors of these beautiful prayers; to all the people who have compiled them into other books over the decades; and to people who have put them in the nooks and crannies of libraries and on the Internet, where they were waiting to be found.

I'm grateful to the members of our bishops' conference for the work they've done recently to bring liturgical living and prayerful traditions back to our parishes, homes, and family lives, and to the many ministries (online and in real life), individuals, and families who are working alongside me in this apostolate of liturgical living in the home.

Thank you to my husband, Jim, who is a loving helpmeet and a good father and an honorable man. Jim, your leadership as the head of our domestic church is bearing very good little fruits. I pray we'll have many more liturgical years together.

Thank you to my children: Jack, Betty, Bobby, Gus, Anita, Frankie, Lulu, Midge, George, and Barbara. To my littlest ones: you keep me inspired to add and maintain traditions. To my middle ones: you remind and help and plan, and I couldn't and wouldn't do it without you. To my oldest ones: through your formation and your lives, you give me hope that liturgical living in the home really is a path to faith, understanding, and increased personal holiness.

Thank you to my parents and in-laws, who are an invaluable source of love and support.

Thank you to my pre-readers Grace Brown, Theoni Bell, Kariana Frey, Rosie Hill, and Curt Dosé, who gave helpful insight and commentary and made this book better and more useful.

Thank you to Grace and to Laura Peredo, who helped keep me organized and on the up-and-up in the process of researching and properly citing, sourcing, and licensing hundreds of vintage prayers. And to Mark Brumley, Anthony Ryan, my editors Vivian Dudro and Gail Gavin, and the whole team at Ignatius Press, with whom it is a pleasure to work.

Thank you to Francesca Angeletti and Maria Grazia Traini of the Libreria Editrice Vaticana, Joseph Livingston with the International Commission on English in the Liturgy, Father Andrew Menke and David Ringwald at the Committee on Divine Worship, and Mary Sperry of the USCCB for reviewing the manuscript and allowing me to include blessings and prayers from the rich tradition of the Catholic liturgy.

Thank you to the publishers, organizations, apostolates, and religious communities who have generously shared prayers and devotions to which they own copyrights, including the Friars Minor Conventual at the Basilica of Saint Anthony in Padua, the Marian Fathers of the Immaculate Conception of the B.V.M., Precious Blood International, the Order of the Brothers of the Blessed Virgin Mary of Mount Carmel, Chorbishop John D. Faris of the Maronite Catholic Church, Franciscan Media, Angelico Press, Foundation of Prayer for Priests, Benziger Brothers, Apostleship of Prayer, Ignatius Press, Sophia Institute Press, New Advent, CatholiCity, Pray More Novenas, Father Jordi Rivero, Rhina Espillat, Fundación Studium, and the Oblates of Saint Joseph, Holy Spouses Province, U.S.A.

And thank you to you! Thank you for bringing this book into your home. I hope that you will find it useful and that it will enrich your spiritual life. Please keep my family in your prayer intentions!

APPENDIX A

Daily Prayers and Prayers for Special Occasions

The Most Frequently Used Prayers

Sign of the Cross

Use your right hand to make the sign of the cross.

1. In the name of the Father (*on the word* Father, *touch the center of your forehead*)
2. and of the Son (*on the word* Son, *touch the center of your chest*)
3. and of the Holy (*on the word* Holy, *touch your left shoulder*)
4. Spirit (*on the word* Spirit, *touch your right shoulder*).
5. Amen (*on the word* Amen, *bring your hands together*).

Our Father (Pater Noster)

Our Father, who art in heaven, hallowed be thy name. Thy kingdom come. Thy will be done, on earth as it is in heaven. Give us this day our daily bread, and forgive us our trespasses, as we forgive those who trespass against us. And lead us not into temptation, but deliver us from evil. Amen.

Pater noster, qui es in caelis, sanctificetur nomen tuum. Adveniat regnum tuum. Fiat voluntas tua, sicut in caelo et in terra. Panem nostrum quotidianum da nobis hodie, et dimitte nobis debita nostra, sicut et nos dimittimus debitoribus nostris. Et ne nos inducas in tentationem, sed libera nos a malo. Amen.

Hail Mary (Ave Maria)

Hail Mary, full of grace, the Lord is with thee. Blessed art thou among women, and blessed is the fruit of thy womb, Jesus. Holy Mary, Mother of God, pray for us sinners, now and at the hour of our death. Amen.

Ave Maria, gratia plena, Dominus tecum. Benedicta tu in mulieribus, et benedictus fructus ventris tui, Iesus. Sancta Maria, Mater Dei, ora pro nobis peccatoribus, nunc et in hora mortis nostrae. Amen.

Glory Be (Gloria Patri)

Glory be to the Father, and to the Son, and to the Holy Spirit; as it was in the beginning, is now, and ever shall be, world without end. Amen.

Gloria Patri, et Filio, et Spiritui Sancto; sicut erat in principio, et nunc, et semper, et in sæcula sæculorum. Amen.

Morning Prayers

Morning Offering

This prayer invoking the Sacred and Immaculate Hearts was first composed in 1844 by Father François Xavier Gautrelet, S.J., in Vals, France. There are now many versions. A Morning Offering of any kind is a beautiful way to make all the actions of one's day into a prayer.

O my Jesus, through the Immaculate Heart of Mary, I offer you all my prayers, works, joys, and sufferings of this day, for all the intentions of your Sacred Heart, in union with the Holy Sacrifice of the Mass offered throughout the world, in reparation for my sins, for the intentions of all my relatives and friends, and in particular for the intentions of the Holy Father. Amen.

Domine, Deus omnipotens (for beginning the day)

Lord, God almighty, you have brought us safely to the beginning of this day. Defend us today by your mighty power, that we may not fall into any sin, but that all our words may so proceed and all our thoughts and actions be so directed, as to be always just in your sight. Through Christ our Lord. Amen.

Additional Morning Prayers

Canticle of Zechariah (the Benedictus), *p. 267.*
Saint Patrick's Breastplate, *p. 183.*
Guardian Angel Prayer, *p. 322.*
Act of Spiritual Communion I and II, *p. 255.*

Prayers for Meals

Blessing before Meals

Bless us, O Lord, and these thy gifts, which we are about to receive from thy bounty, through Christ our Lord. Amen.

Grace after Meals

We give thee thanks for all your benefits, O almighty God, who live and reign forever; and may the souls of the faithful departed, through the mercy of God, rest in peace. Amen.

Prayers for Work, Study, and Home

Actiones nostras (for beginning work)

Direct, we beseech you, O Lord, all our actions by your holy inspiration; carry them on by your gracious assistance, that every word and work of ours may always begin from you and by you be happily ended. Amen.

A Student's Prayer (by Saint Thomas Aquinas)

See p. 127.

Agimus tibi gratias (for ending work)

We give you thanks, almighty God, for all your blessings: who live and reign for ever and ever. Amen.

Visita, quaesumus, Domine (for the home)

Visit, we beg you, O Lord, this dwelling, and drive from it all snares of the enemy: let your holy angels dwell herein, to keep us in peace; and let your blessing be always upon us. Through Christ our Lord. Amen.

Prayers for Birthday, Name Day, and Baptismal Anniversary

Blessing on a Child's Birthday[1]

From Jeremiah 1:5.

The Lord said to Jeremiah:
Before I formed you in the womb I knew you,
before you were born I dedicated you.
May God, in whose presence our ancestors walked,
bless you.

All: Amen.

May God, who has been your shepherd from birth
until now, keep you.

All: Amen.

May God, who saves you from all harm, give you peace.

All: Amen.

[1] *Catholic Household Blessings and Prayers*, 242.

Godparent's Blessing of a Child[2]

At baptism, godparents promise to help parents in their duties as Christian mothers and fathers. Throughout the years of childhood it is appropriate for a godparent to bless his godchild, perhaps with a cross traced on the child's forehead.

N., blessed be God who chose you in Christ.

Renewal of Baptismal Promises[3]

Our family renews our baptismal vows a lot. We do it at the Easter Vigil Mass, and at home on the anniversary of each family member's baptism day, for which there are plenary indulgences available.[4] As a bonus, we also do it on the feast of the Baptism of the Lord. The highlight of the devotion is holding our lighted baptismal candles (or another candle if that's not available) and Dad winging everybody in the face with holy water at the end. Also, we think the "I do" part should be enthusiastically shouted.

Leader: Do you renounce Satan?

All: I do.

Leader: And all his works?

All: I do.

Leader: And all his empty show?

All: I do.

Leader: Do you believe in God,
the Father Almighty,
Creator of heaven and earth?

All: I do.

Leader: Do you believe in Jesus Christ, his only Son, our Lord,
who was born of the Virgin Mary,
suffered death and was buried,
rose again from the dead
and is seated at the right hand of the Father?

[2] Ibid., 241.

[3] *Roman Missal*, The Easter Vigil, no. 55.

[4] *Manual of Indulgences*, grant 28.1–2. See the introduction of this book for the usual conditions for indulgences.

All: I do.

Leader: Do you believe in the Holy Spirit,
the holy catholic Church,
the communion of saints,
the forgiveness of sins,
the resurrection of the body,
and life everlasting?

All: I do.

Leader: And may almighty God, the Father of our Lord Jesus Christ,
who has given us new birth by water and the Holy Spirit
and bestowed on us forgiveness of our sins,
keep us by his grace,
in Christ Jesus our Lord,
for eternal life.

All: Amen.

Prayer to One's Patron Saint (for name days)

O Heavenly Patron, in whose name I glory, pray ever to God for me: strengthen me in my faith; establish me in virtue; guard me in the conflict; that I may vanquish the foe malign and attain to glory everlasting. Amen.

Prayers for Others

Thanksgiving Prayer for a Newborn Child[5]

O Saint Joseph, you witnessed the miracle of birth, seeing the infant Jesus born of your most holy spouse, the Virgin Mary. With wonder and awe, you took into your arms the Savior. With gratitude that only a parent can know, you glorified God for the birth of his Son, entrusted to your fatherly care.

---

[5] "Thanksgiving Prayer for a Newborn Child" (2020), a devotion of the Oblates of St. Joseph, Holy Spouses Province, U.S.A., http://osjusa.org/prayers/newborn-child/. Used with permission.

Like you, Saint Joseph, I too give praise and glory to God for the birth of my child. This child's life is such a miraculous testimony of God's loving presence. My heart is filled with grateful joy. Join me, dear Saint Joseph, in offering thanks to God for the gift of my child.

What great trust and confidence God placed in you, Saint Joseph, by entrusting his only Son into your fatherly care. This inspires me to entrust the spiritual care and protection of my newborn child into your competent and loving hands. Teach, guide, and support me to fulfill well my awesome vocation to be a worthy parent to this child. Amen.

Children's Prayer[6]

O Jesus, the friend of little children, bless the little children of the whole world. Amen.

Prayer of Parents for Their Children

O God the Father of mankind, who has given me these my children, and committed them to my charge to bring them up for you, and to prepare them for eternal life: help me with your heavenly grace, that I may be able to fulfill this most sacred duty and stewardship. Teach me both what to give and what to withhold; when to reprove and when to forbear; make me to be gentle yet firm; considerate and watchful; deliver me equally from the weakness of indulgence, and the excess of severity; and grant that, both by word and example, I may be careful to lead them in the ways of wisdom and true piety, so that at last I may, with them, be admitted to the unspeakable joys of our true home in heaven, in the company of the blessed angels and saints. Amen.

O heavenly Father, I commend my children to your care. Be their God and Father, and mercifully supply whatever is lacking in me through frailty or negligence. Strengthen them to overcome the corruptions of the world, whether from within or without; and deliver them from the secret snares of the enemy. Pour your grace into their

[6] *Raccolta*, no. 78.

hearts, and strengthen and multiply in them the gifts of your Holy Spirit, that they may daily grow in grace and in knowledge of our Lord Jesus Christ; and so, faithfully serving you here, may come to rejoice in your presence hereafter. Amen.

See also Prayer for Children, p. 46.

Prayer of Children for Their Parents

O almighty God, you gave us the commandment to honor our father and mother. In your loving kindness hear my prayer for my parents. Give them long lives and keep them well in body and spirit. Bless their labors; keep them always in your care. Bless them generously for their loving care for me. Grant that, through your grace, I may always be their support and comfort, and that, after our life together on earth, we may experience the joy of together praising you forever. Amen.

Prayer of Spouses for Each Other

Lord Jesus, grant that I and my spouse may have a true and understanding love for each other. Grant that we may both be filled with faith and trust. Give us the grace to live with each other in peace and harmony. May we always bear with one another's weaknesses and grow from each other's strengths. Help us to forgive one another's failings, and grant us patience, kindness, cheerfulness, and the spirit of placing the well-being of the other ahead of self. May the love that brought us together grow and mature with each passing year. Bring us both ever closer to you through our love for each other. Let our love grow to perfection. Amen.

Retribuere dignare, Domine (for benefactors)

May it please you, O Lord, to reward with eternal life all those who do good to us for your name's sake. Amen.

Prayer for Vocations

O Father, you desire all of us to be happy. Stir up the grace of a religious vocation in the hearts of many men and women. Grant to them the willingness and generosity to give of themselves, their lives, their time, and their talents to the service of Jesus Christ, your Son, our Lord and Savior, and to his holy Church. May more of your faithful go forth as priests, deacons, brothers, and sisters to bring the truths of our Catholic faith to all others, so that soon they, too, may know you better and love you more, and serving you, be truly happy. Amen.

Prayers Immediately after Death[7]

The following prayers may be recited immediately after someone's death and may be repeated in the hours that follow.

Leader: Saints of God, come to his (her) aid!
Come to meet him (her), angels of the Lord!

All: Receive his (her) soul and present him (her) to God the Most High.

Leader: May Christ, who called you, take you to himself;
may angels lead you to Abraham's side.

All: Receive his (her) soul and present him (her) to God the Most High.

Leader: Give him (her) eternal rest, O Lord,
and may your light shine on him (her) forever.

All: Receive his (her) soul and present him (her) to God the Most High.

Leader: Let us pray.
All-powerful and merciful God,
we commend to you N., your servant.
In your mercy and love,
blot out the sins he (she) has committed
through human weakness.

---

[7] *Catholic Household Blessings and Prayers*, 268.

In this world he (she) has died:
let him (her) live with you forever.
Through Christ our Lord.

All: Amen.

Leader: Eternal rest grant unto him (her), O Lord.

All: And let perpetual light shine upon him (her).

Leader: May he (she) rest in peace.

All: Amen.

Leader: May his (her) soul and the souls of all the faithful departed, through the mercy of God,
rest in peace.

All: Amen.

Additional Prayers for Others

Prayer for Priests, *p. 102*.
Prayer for Holy Bishops by Saint John Fisher, *p. 266*.
Prayer for the Pope, *p. 154*.
Prayer for the Missions, *p. 127*.
Saint Elizabeth Ann Seton Prayer for Students, *p. 114*.
Saint Elizabeth Ann Seton Prayer for Teachers, *p. 115*.
Prayer for Nurses, *p. 148*.
Prayer for Catholic Schools, *p. 116*.
Prayer to Saint Luke for Physicians, *p. 329*.
Prayer to Saint Thomas More for Lawyers and Judges, *p. 256*.

Prayers for Self

Short Invocation against Sudden Death

From a sudden and unprovided death, deliver us, O Lord.

In the Hour of Our Death

Grant unto us, Lord Jesus, ever to follow the example of your Holy Family, that in the hour of our death your glorious Virgin Mother together with blessed Joseph may come to meet us, and we may be worthily received by you into everlasting dwellings: who lives and reigns world without end. Amen.

Prayer for Patience[8]

This prayer was composed by Servant of God Cardinal Merry del Val (+1930).

My dearest Jesus, teach me to be patient, when all the day long my heart is troubled by little but vexatious crosses. Amen.

Prayer to Know One's Vocation

O Lord, help me know your will for me. Let your light shine in the depths of my heart, that I may know what you want me to do with my life. Help me believe that you have a special plan for me. Lord, I know I pass through this life only once; help me decide how you want me to make a difference. Like our Blessed Mother, give me the wisdom to hear your voice and the courage to answer your call. Above all give me peace of mind and heart. I offer this prayer in the name of Jesus Christ our Lord. Amen.

Act of Faith

O my God, I firmly believe that you are one God in three Divine Persons, Father, Son, and Holy Spirit. I believe that your divine Son became man and died for our sins and that he will come to judge the living and the dead. I believe these and all the truths that the Holy Catholic Church teaches because you have revealed them who are eternal truth and wisdom, who can neither deceive nor be deceived. In this faith I intend to live and die. Amen.

---

[8] *Raccolta*, no. 94.

Act of Hope

O Lord God, I hope by your grace for the pardon of all my sins and after life here to gain eternal happiness because you have promised it who are infinitely powerful, faithful, kind, and merciful. In this hope I intend to live and die. Amen.

Act of Love

O Lord God, I love you above all things and I love my neighbor for your sake because you are the highest, infinite, and perfect good, worthy of all my love. In this love I intend to live and die. Amen.

Litany of Humility[9]

Lord Jesus, meek and humble of heart, *hear me.*
From the desire of being esteemed, *deliver me, Jesus.*
From the desire of being loved, *deliver me, Jesus.*
From the desire of being extolled, *deliver me, Jesus.*
From the desire of being honored, *deliver me, Jesus.*
From the desire of being praised, *deliver me, Jesus.*
From the desire of being preferred to others, *deliver me, Jesus.*
From the desire of being consulted, *deliver me, Jesus.*
From the desire of being approved, *deliver me, Jesus.*
From the fear of being humiliated, *deliver me, Jesus.*
From the fear of being despised, *deliver me, Jesus.*
From the fear of suffering rebukes, *deliver me, Jesus.*
From the fear of being calumniated, *deliver me, Jesus.*
From the fear of being forgotten, *deliver me, Jesus.*
From the fear of being ridiculed, *deliver me, Jesus.*
From the fear of being wronged, *deliver me, Jesus.*
From the fear of being suspected, *deliver me, Jesus.*

---

[9] This litany is appropriate for personal use but isn't one of the six litanies approved for public devotion. See p. 31 for an explanation. Once attributed to Servant of God Cardinal Merry del Val, its true authorship is unknown.

That others may be loved more than I, *Jesus, grant me the grace to desire it.*

That others may be esteemed more than I, *Jesus, grant me the grace to desire it.*

That, in the opinion of the world, others may increase and I may decrease, *Jesus, grant me the grace to desire it.*

That others may be chosen and I set aside, *Jesus, grant me the grace to desire it.*

That others may be praised and I unnoticed, *Jesus, grant me the grace to desire it.*

That others may be preferred to me in everything, *Jesus, grant me the grace to desire it.*

That others may become holier than I, provided that I may become as holy as I should, *Jesus, grant me the grace to desire it.*

Additional Prayers for Self

Wedding Ring Prayer, *p. 286.*
Prayer to One's Patron Saint, *p. 354.*

Midday Prayers

Angelus

This devotion, commemorating the Incarnation, developed out of a medieval monastic tradition of ringing bells at various times of day to call the monks to prayer. The current form of the Angelus has been in use since at least the sixteenth century. It is most commonly said daily at noon but is sometimes also said at six in the morning and six in the evening. The usual practice is to cease work and stand to say the prayers.

Leader: The angel of the Lord declared unto Mary,

All: And she conceived of the Holy Spirit.

Leader: Hail Mary, full of grace, the Lord is with thee. Blessed art thou amongst women, and blessed is the fruit of thy womb, Jesus.

All: Holy Mary, Mother of God, pray for us sinners, now and at the hour of our death. Amen.

Leader: Behold the handmaid of the Lord.

All: Be it done unto me according to thy word.

Repeat the Hail Mary.

Leader: And the Word was made flesh,

All: And dwelt among us.

Repeat the Hail Mary.

Leader: Pray for us, O holy Mother of God,

All: That we may be made worthy of the promises of Christ.

Leader: Let us pray. Pour forth, we beseech thee, O Lord, thy grace into our hearts; that we to whom the Incarnation of Christ, thy Son, was made known by the message of an angel, may by his Passion and cross be brought to the glory of his Resurrection. Through the same Christ our Lord.

All: Amen.

Regina Caeli

During the Easter season, the Regina Caeli is usually substituted for the daily Angelus prayer. See it in Latin on p. 223.

Leader: Queen of Heaven, rejoice, alleluia;

All: For he whom you did merit to bear, alleluia;

Leader: Has risen, as he said, alleluia.

All: Pray for us to God, alleluia.

Leader: Rejoice and be glad, O Virgin Mary, alleluia;

All: For the Lord has truly risen, alleluia.

Leader: Let us pray. O God, who gave joy to the world through the Resurrection of your Son, our Lord Jesus Christ, grant, we beseech you, that through the intercession of the Virgin Mary, his Mother, we may obtain the joys of everlasting life. Through the same Christ our Lord. Amen.

Marian Prayers

Maria, Mater gratiae

Mary, Mother of grace and Mother of mercy, shield me from the enemy and receive me at the hour of my death. Amen.

Memorare

Saint Teresa of Calcutta received so many prayer requests that she developed what she called the "flying novena". Instead of spreading her prayers over nine days or nine months, she would pray nine Memorares at once. Then, confident of heaven's help, she would immediately add a tenth Memorare of thanksgiving. Her Missionaries of Charity continue this practice.

Remember, O most gracious Virgin Mary, that never was it known that anyone who fled to thy protection, implored thy help, or sought thy intercession was left unaided. Inspired by this confidence, I fly unto thee, O Virgin of virgins, my Mother; to thee do I come, before thee I stand, sinful and sorrowful. O Mother of the Word incarnate, despise not my petitions, but in thy mercy hear and answer me. Amen.

Sancta Maria, succurre miseris

Holy Mary, succor the miserable, help the fainthearted, comfort the sorrowful, pray for thy people, plead for the clergy, intercede for all women consecrated to God; may all who keep thy holy commemoration feel now thy help and protection. Amen.

Prayers Using Rosary Beads

The Rosary

The Rosary is a beloved Catholic practice that combines meditation and vocal prayers. While holding rosary beads or counting on our fingers, we pray certain prayers while contemplating with Mary the mysteries of the life of Jesus. The mysteries listed here include related Scripture citations with the page numbers where those verses can be found in this book.

It's impossible to overstate the beauty and power of a family Rosary. The Church recommends the practice, offering a daily plenary indulgence (subject to the usual conditions)[10] *when five mysteries of the Rosary (called decades for the ten Hail Marys that are recited) are prayed together with family members. The Rosary has been recommended by countless saints and by Our Lady herself in many apparitions, including at Lourdes and Fatima.*

While a family Rosary is often a challenge, I find solace in this quote: "The devil, of course, hates the Rosary, precisely because it changes hearts, detaches from sin, attaches to the all-pure Mother of God, and leads to conversion. One of the ploys he uses to deter people from praying it is to suggest that unless one can pray it well, in other words, perfectly, one shouldn't pray it at all. I would suggest, rather, that the Rosary, even prayed badly, is better than no Rosary at all."[11]

The Five Joyful Mysteries *(prayed on Mondays and Saturdays)*

1. The Annunciation: The angel Gabriel appears to the Virgin Mary and gains her consent to be the Mother of Jesus. (Lk 1:26–38, p. 71)
2. The Visitation: Mary travels to visit her cousin Elizabeth, who is pregnant with Saint John the Baptist. (Lk 1:39–45, 56, p. 248)
3. The Nativity: Jesus is born in Bethlehem, laid in a humble manger, and exalted by angels, shepherds, and kings. (Lk 2:1–20, p. 95)
4. The Presentation of Jesus in the Temple: Mary and Joseph bring the baby Jesus to the temple, where he is recognized as the Savior by the prophet Simeon. (Lk 2:22–38, p. 144)
5. The Finding of Jesus in the Temple: Mary and Joseph search for the twelve-year-old Jesus, eventually finding him in the temple, where he is instructing the teachers. (Lk 2:39–52, p. 105)

The Five Sorrowful Mysteries *(prayed on Tuesdays and Fridays)*

1. The Agony in the Garden: In anguish, Jesus prays in the Garden of Gethsemane before his arrest. (Mk 14:32–42, p. 204)

2. The Scourging at the Pillar: Jesus is lashed with whips by Roman soldiers. (Mk 15:6–15, p. 204)
3. The Crowning with Thorns: The soldiers mock Jesus by dressing him in a purple cloak and crowning him with a crown of thorns. (Mk 15:16–20, p. 204)
4. The Carrying of the Cross: Jesus carries the cross upon which he will be crucified. (Mk 15:21–24, p. 204)
5. The Crucifixion and Death: Jesus is nailed to the cross and dies upon it three hours later. (Mk 15:33–39, p. 204)

The Five Glorious Mysteries *(prayed on Wednesdays and Sundays)*

1. The Resurrection: Jesus rises from the dead and appears to many of his disciples. (Lk 24:1–5, p. 225)
2. The Ascension: Forty days after the Resurrection, Jesus ascends to heaven. (Acts 1:6–11, p. 228)
3. The Descent of the Holy Spirit: With wind and tongues of fire, the Holy Spirit comes upon Mary and the disciples gathered in prayer. (Acts 2:1–4, p. 249)
4. The Assumption: At the end of her life on earth, Mary is assumed bodily, by God's power, into heaven. (Lk 1:46-49, p. 80)
5. The Coronation of Mary: Mary is crowned Queen of heaven and earth to advocate and intercede for us. (Rev 12:1, p. 297)

The Five Luminous Mysteries *(prayed on Thursdays)*

1. The Baptism of Christ in the Jordan: Jesus is baptized by Saint John the Baptist before beginning his public ministry. (Mt 3:13–17, p. 119)
2. The Wedding Feast at Cana: Jesus performs his first public miracle at the request of his mother Mary. (Jn 2:1–5, p. 124)
3. Jesus' Proclamation of the Kingdom of God: Jesus announces union with God through the Beatitudes. (Mt 5:3–12, p. 335)
4. The Transfiguration: Upon a mountain, Jesus' face, body, and clothing become dazzling white before the eyes of Peter, James, and John. (Mk 9:2–8, p. 291)
5. The Institution of the Eucharist: At the Last Supper on Holy Thursday, Jesus offers his disciples his Body and Blood, the source and summit of the Christian life. (Mt 26:17–29, p. 202)

To pray a customary Rosary, begin by holding the crucifix. Make the sign of the cross, form the intention of gaining an indulgence, and pray the Apostles' Creed.

Sign of the Cross

Devoutly cross oneself, touching first the forehead, followed by the chest, then the left shoulder, then the right shoulder, while saying:

In the name of the Father, and of the Son, and of the Holy Spirit. Amen.

Apostles' Creed

I believe in God, the Father almighty, Creator of heaven and earth, and in Jesus Christ, his only Son, our Lord, who was conceived by the Holy Spirit, born of the Virgin Mary, suffered under Pontius Pilate, was crucified, died and was buried; he descended into hell; on the third day he rose again from the dead; he ascended into heaven, and is seated at the right hand of God the Father almighty; from there he will come to judge the living and the dead.

I believe in the Holy Spirit, the holy catholic Church, the communion of saints, the forgiveness of sins, the resurrection of the body, and life everlasting. Amen.

If you have particular intentions for this Rosary, mention them here. In the interest of time, we limit each family member to three intentions offered aloud.

Then, on the first bead, pray an Our Father for the Holy Father (see prayers below). On the next three beads, pray three Hail Marys (one per bead) for an increase in faith, hope, and charity. Between the fourth and fifth beads, pray one Glory Be and one Fatima Prayer. Announce the first mystery. For the first decade, pray an Our Father on the single bead, followed by ten Hail Marys on the ten beads, while meditating on the mystery.

Our Father

Our Father, who art in heaven, hallowed be thy name. Thy kingdom come. Thy will be done, on earth as it is in heaven. Give us this day our daily bread, and forgive us our trespasses, as we forgive those who trespass against us. And lead us not into temptation, but deliver us from evil. Amen.

Hail Mary

Hail Mary, full of grace, the Lord is with thee. Blessed art thou amongst women, and blessed is the fruit of thy womb, Jesus. Holy Mary, Mother of God, pray for us sinners, now and at the hour of our death. Amen.

After the tenth Hail Mary, pray the Glory Be and the Fatima Prayer.

Glory Be

Glory be to the Father, and to the Son, and to the Holy Spirit; as it was in the beginning, is now, and ever shall be, world without end. Amen.

Fatima Prayer

O my Jesus, forgive us our sins, save us from the fires of hell. Lead all souls to heaven, especially those most in need of thy mercy.

Move on to the next mystery, praying as before: announce the mystery, pray one Our Father, then ten Hail Marys, and end with the Glory Be and the Fatima Prayer.

At the end of the fifth decade, pray the Glory Be and the Fatima Prayer as usual, then finish the Rosary with a Marian prayer. We use the Hail Holy Queen, followed by the Rosary Prayer, and add the Saint Michael Prayer for good measure.

Hail Holy Queen

This translation from the Latin Salve Regina (see p. 250) is by Father Adrian Fortescue, 1913.

Hail, holy Queen, mother of mercy, our life, our sweetness, and our hope. To thee we cry, poor banished children of Eve; to thee we send up our sighs, mourning and weeping in this valley of tears. Turn, then, most gracious advocate, thine eyes of mercy toward us; and after this, our exile, show unto us the blessed fruit of thy womb, Jesus. O clement, O loving, O sweet Virgin Mary.

Leader: Pray for us, O holy Mother of God,

All: That we may be made worthy of the promises of Christ.

Rosary Prayer

Let us pray. O God, whose only-begotten Son, by his life, death, and Resurrection, has purchased for us the rewards of eternal life, grant, we beseech thee, that while meditating on these mysteries of the most holy Rosary of the Blessed Virgin Mary, we may imitate what they contain and obtain what they promise, through the same Christ our Lord. Amen.

Saint Michael Prayer

Saint Michael the archangel, defend us in battle. Be our protection against the wickedness and snares of the devil. May God rebuke him, we humbly pray; and do thou, O prince of the heavenly host, by the power of God, cast into hell Satan and all the evil spirits, who prowl about the world, seeking the ruin of souls. Amen.

Make the sign of the cross, and you're done! Unless you wish to add:

To You, O Blessed Joseph[12]

Written by Pope Leo XIII, a partial indulgence is attached to this prayer at any time. He asked that it would be said after the Rosary, especially in October.

To you, O blessed Joseph,
do we come in our tribulation,
and having implored the help of your most holy Spouse,
we confidently invoke your patronage also.

Through that charity which bound you
to the Immaculate Virgin Mother of God
and through the paternal love
with which you embraced the Child Jesus,
we humbly beg you graciously to regard the inheritance
which Jesus Christ has purchased by his blood,
and with your power and strength to aid us in our necessities.

---

[12] *Manual of Indulgences*, grant 19. See the introduction of this book for the usual conditions for indulgences.

O most watchful guardian of the Holy Family,
defend the chosen children of Jesus Christ;
O most loving father, ward off from us
every contagion of error and corrupting influence;
O our most mighty protector, be kind to us
and from heaven assist us in our struggle
with the power of darkness.

As once you rescued the Child Jesus from deadly peril,
so now protect God's holy Church
from the snares of the enemy and from all adversity;
shield, too, each one of us by your constant protection,
so that, supported by your example and your aid,
we may be able to live piously, to die in holiness,
and to obtain eternal happiness in heaven. Amen.

Divine Mercy Chaplet[13]

Based on the messages of love and mercy for all mankind contained in the apparitions of Jesus to Saint Faustina in Poland in the 1930s, the Divine Mercy Chaplet is said using a traditional five-decade rosary. It is prayed as part of the Divine Mercy Novena (see those prayers on pp. 211–16) or daily at three in the afternoon, known as the hour of Divine Mercy.

Begin with the sign of the cross on the crucifix.

On the bead closest to the crucifix, pray:

You expired, Jesus, but the source of life gushed forth for souls, and the ocean of mercy opened up for the whole world. O Fount of Life, unfathomable Divine Mercy, envelop the whole world and empty yourself out upon us.

---

[13] "How to Recite the Chaplet", The Divine Mercy, Marian Fathers of the Immaculate Conception of the B.V.M., https://www.thedivinemercy.org/message/devotions/pray-the-chaplet. Prayers in the chaplet are from Faustina Kowalska, *Diary of Saint Maria Faustina Kowalska: Divine Mercy in My Soul* (Stockbridge, Mass.: Marian Press, 1987). Used with permission of the Marian Fathers of the Immaculate Conception of the B.V.M.

Repeat three times: O Blood and Water, which gushed forth from the Heart of Jesus as a fountain of Mercy for us, I trust in you!

On the three beads, pray an Our Father, a Hail Mary, and an Apostles' Creed.

For each decade, on each Our Father bead, pray:

Eternal Father, I offer you the Body and Blood, Soul and Divinity of your dearly beloved Son, our Lord Jesus Christ, in atonement for our sins and those of the whole world.

On each Hail Mary bead, pray:

For the sake of his sorrowful Passion, have mercy on us and on the whole world.

After you have finished all five decades, on the medallion pray:

Repeat three times: Holy God, Holy Mighty One, Holy Immortal One, have mercy on us and on the whole world.

Once: Eternal God, in whom mercy is endless and the treasury of compassion inexhaustible, look kindly upon us and increase your mercy in us, that in difficult moments we might not despair nor become despondent, but with great confidence submit ourselves to your holy will, which is love and mercy itself. Amen.

Finish with the sign of the cross.

Chaplet of Reparation[14]

Also known as the Offering of the Precious Blood for Priests, this chaplet of reparation and intercession is recommended in the excellent book In Sinu Jesu.

Make the sign of the cross. On the crucifix:

Incline unto my aid, O God; O Lord, make haste to help me. Glory be to the Father, and to the Son, and to the Holy Spirit; as it was in the beginning, is now, and ever shall be, world without end. Amen.

---

[14] A Benedictine Monk, *In Sinu Jesu: When Heart Speaks to Heart; The Journal of a Priest at Prayer* (Kettering, Ohio: Angelico, 2016), 269. Used with permission.

Alleluia. (DURING LENT: *Instead of "Alleluia"*: Praise be to thee, O Lord, King of eternal glory.)

On the Our Father beads:

Eternal Father, I offer thee the Precious Blood of thy beloved Son, our Lord Jesus Christ, the Lamb without blemish or spot, in reparation for my sins and for the sins of all thy priests.

On the Hail Mary beads:

By thy Precious Blood, O Jesus, purify and sanctify thy priests.

After each decade:

O Father, from whom all fatherhood in heaven and earth is named, have mercy on all thy priests, and wash them in the blood of the Lamb.

After you have prayed all five decades and are on the centerpiece, make the sign of the cross to finish.

Evening and Night Prayers

Penitential Prayer of Saint Ambrose

O Lord, who has mercy upon all, take away from me my sins, and mercifully kindle in me the fire of your Holy Spirit. Take away from me the heart of stone, and give me a heart of flesh, a heart to love and adore you, a heart to delight in you, to follow and enjoy you, for Christ's sake. Amen.

Examination of Conscience[15]

This short examination of conscience from the United States Conference of Catholic Bishops is based on the Ten Commandments.

---

[15] United States Conference of Catholic Bishops, "A Brief Examination of Conscience Based on the Ten Commandments" (2013), https://www.usccb.org/prayer-and-worship /sacraments-and-sacramentals/penance/upload/Examination-of-Conscience.pdf.

1. I am the LORD your God: you shall not have strange Gods before me.

   Have I treated people, events, or things as more important than God?

2. You shall not take the name of the LORD your God in vain.

   Have my words, actively or passively, put down God, the Church, or people?

3. Remember to keep holy the LORD's Day.

   Do I go to Mass every Sunday (or Saturday vigil) and on holy days of obligation (January 1; the Ascension; August 15; November 1; December 8; December 25)? Do I avoid, when possible, work that impedes worship to God, joy for the Lord's Day, and proper relaxation of mind and body? Do I look for ways to spend time with family or in service on Sunday?

4. Honor your father and your mother.

   Do I show my parents due respect? Do I seek to maintain good communication with my parents where possible? Do I criticize them for lacking skills I think they should have?

5. You shall not kill.

   Have I harmed another through physical, verbal, or emotional means, including gossip or manipulation of any kind?

6. You shall not commit adultery.

   Have I respected the physical and sexual dignity of others and of myself?

7. You shall not steal.

   Have I taken or wasted time or resources that belonged to another?

8. You shall not bear false witness against your neighbor.

   Have I gossiped, told lies, or embellished stories at the expense of another?

9. You shall not covet your neighbor's spouse.

   Have I honored my spouse with my full affection and exclusive love?

10. You shall not covet your neighbor's goods.

   Am I content with my own means and needs, or do I compare myself to others unnecessarily?

Act of Contrition

O my God, I am heartily sorry for having offended you, and I detest all my sins, because I fear the loss of heaven and the pains of hell, but most of all because they offend you, my God, who are all good and deserving of all my love. I firmly resolve, with the help of your grace, to confess my sins, to do penance, and to avoid the near occasion of sin. Amen.

Daily Blessing of a Child[16]

This short blessing may be said by parents at various times, such as when a child is going to play or to school, but especially when the child is going to bed each night. The parent makes the sign of the cross on the child's forehead and says the following blessing.

May God bless and protect you.

Rest and Peace

May the all-powerful Lord grant us a restful night and a peaceful death. Amen.

Night Prayer of Saint Augustine

Watch, O Lord, with those who wake, or watch, or weep tonight, and give your angels charge over those who sleep. Tend your sick ones, O Lord Christ. Rest your weary ones. Bless your dying ones. Soothe your suffering ones. Pity your afflicted ones. Shield your joyous ones. And all for your love's sake. Amen.

Pious Invocations

Pious invocations, also called ejaculatory prayers or aspirations, are a long tradition of the Church that was inappropriately secularized. The practice is

[16] *Catholic Household Blessings and Prayers*, 239.

now rather misunderstood but still very much officially recommended—with a partial indulgence even! These are short (sometimes very short) prayers that can be said or thought mindfully before beginning a task, or in a moment of joy or frustration, and are meant to be so second nature that one would say or think them automatically in a moment of fear or panic. Irish-grandma swearing like "Jesus, Mary, and Joseph!" and what might be thoughtless blasphemies like "My God!" and "Jesus!" are actually good prayers if they can be said with good intention. More examples can be found in the first appendix of the Manual of Indulgences.

Some Recommended Pious Invocations

> Praised be Jesus Christ.
> Lord, I adore you.
> Christ conquers! Christ reigns! Christ rules!
> All for love of you.
> Glory be to the Father and to the Son and to the Holy Spirit.
> Heart of Jesus, in you I trust.
> Holy Mary, Mother of God, pray for me.
> Your kingdom come.
> Your will be done.
> Lord, increase our faith.
> Lord, save us or we perish.
> Lord, send laborers into your harvest.
> As God wills.
> Lord, have mercy.
> Mother of Sorrows, pray for us.
> My Lord and my God!
> O God, be merciful to me, a sinner.
> O Queen conceived without original sin, pray for us.
> Pray for us, O holy Mother of God, that we may be made worthy of the promises of Christ.
> Remain with us, O Lord.
> Jesus, save souls.
> You are the Christ, the Son of the living God.
> We adore you, O Christ, and we praise you, because by your holy cross you have redeemed the world.

APPENDIX B

Dates of Movable Feasts and Devotions

First Sundays of Advent

November 28, 2021	November 30, 2025	December 2, 2029
November 27, 2022	November 29, 2026	December 1, 2030
December 3, 2023	November 28, 2027	November 30, 2031
December 1, 2024	December 3, 2028	November 28, 2032

Seven Sundays of Saint Joseph Begin

January 31, 2021	February 2, 2025	February 4, 2029
January 30, 2022	February 1, 2026	February 3, 2030
January 29, 2023	January 31, 2027	February 2, 2031
February 4, 2024	January 30, 2028	February 1, 2032

Ash Wednesday

February 17, 2021	March 5, 2025	February 14, 2029
March 2, 2022	February 18, 2026	March 6, 2030
February 22, 2023	February 10, 2027	February 26, 2031
February 14, 2024	March 1, 2028	February 11, 2032

Easter

April 4, 2021	April 20, 2025	April 1, 2029
April 17, 2022	April 5, 2026	April 21, 2030
April 9, 2023	March 28, 2027	April 13, 2031
March 31, 2024	April 16, 2028	March 28, 2032

Ascension (Thursday or Sunday)

May 13 or 16, 2021	May 29 or June 1, 2025	May 10 or 13, 2029
May 26 or 29, 2022		May 30 or June 2, 2030
May 18 or 21, 2023	May 14 or 17, 2026	
May 9 or 12, 2024	May 6 or 9, 2027	May 22 or 25, 2031
	May 25 or 28, 2028	May 6 or 9, 2032

Pentecost

May 23, 2021	June 8, 2025	May 20, 2029
June 5, 2022	May 24, 2026	June 9, 2030
May 28, 2023	May 16, 2027	June 1, 2031
May 19, 2024	June 4, 2028	May 16, 2032

Trinity Sunday

May 30, 2021	June 15, 2025	May 27, 2029
June 12, 2022	May 31, 2026	June 16, 2030
June 4, 2023	May 23, 2027	June 8, 2031
May 26, 2024	June 11, 2028	May 23, 2032

Corpus Christi

Sunday, June 6, 2021	Sunday, May 30, 2027
Sunday, June 19, 2022	Sunday, June 18, 2028
Sunday, June 11, 2023	Sunday, June 3, 2029
Sunday, June 2, 2024	Sunday, June 23, 2030
Sunday, June 22, 2025	Sunday, June 15, 2031
Sunday, June 7, 2026	Sunday, May 30, 2032

Sacred Heart of Jesus, a Friday
(Immaculate Heart of Mary is the next day)

June 11, 2021	June 27, 2025	June 8, 2029
June 24, 2022	June 12, 2026	June 28, 2030
June 16, 2023	June 4, 2027	June 20, 2031
June 7, 2024	June 23, 2028	June 4, 2032

APPENDIX C

Family Special Days Register

These pages are intended for keeping track of birthdays, baptism days, and name days or patron saint days for members of the family. List the date first, then the type of special day, so that you can easily see which dates require planning each month.

January

_____   _____

_____   _____

_____   _____

_____   _____

_____   _____

_____   _____

February

_____   _____

_____   _____

_____   _____

_____   _____

_____   _____

_____   _____

March

_____   _____
_____   _____
_____   _____
_____   _____
_____   _____
_____   _____

April

_____   _____
_____   _____
_____   _____
_____   _____
_____   _____
_____   _____

May

_____   _____
_____   _____
_____   _____
_____   _____
_____   _____
_____   _____

June

_____   _____
_____   _____
_____   _____
_____   _____
_____   _____
_____   _____

July

_____   _____
_____   _____
_____   _____
_____   _____
_____   _____
_____   _____

August

_____   _____
_____   _____
_____   _____
_____   _____
_____   _____
_____   _____

September

_____   _____
_____   _____
_____   _____
_____   _____
_____   _____
_____   _____

October

_____   _____
_____   _____
_____   _____
_____   _____
_____   _____
_____   _____

November

_____ _____
_____ _____
_____ _____
_____ _____
_____ _____
_____

December

_____ _____
_____ _____
_____ _____
_____ _____
_____ _____

ESSAY ON SOURCES

Unless otherwise indicated, Scripture verses in running text are from Revised Standard Version of the Bible—Second Catholic Edition published by Ignatius Press, copyright 2006 by the National Council of the Churches of Christ in the United States of America. These Bible readings aren't necessarily those of the readings for the day's Mass; I just find them relevant to our discussion of the feast day. Scriptures associated with the official liturgical texts of blessings are from the New American Bible (NAB), published by the United States Conference of Catholic Bishops (USCCB), copyright 2002.

The Collect (pronounced *kol*-ekt) prayers are almost all from the third edition of the *Roman Missal* (Catholic Book Corp, 2011) and are used with permission. For the few included saints whose feast days don't occur on the current universal calendar, historical or other Collects are given. The Collect occurs during the Mass immediately before the Liturgy of the Word. It "collects" all the intentions of the faithful and offers them together to God. Saints' days for which specific Masses are offered have particular Collect prayers. It's best, of course, to hear them at the day's Mass. But we also like to incorporate them into our prayers at home.

Blessings are largely from *Catholic Household Blessings and Prayers*, published by the USCCB in 2007, for the use of laypeople in the home, and the *Book of Blessings*, by the International Commission on English in the Liturgy (ICEL). Both organizations were kind enough to allow me to include them. A few are from various older editions of the *Missale Romanum*. Language and gestures appropriate for priests and deacons and not for laypeople are noted in some cases.

Lyrics for some hymns and songs that we use on particular feast days are included, and many more are suggested. Some of the older songs can be sung to more than one traditional tune. Since we sing some of these songs only once per year, we usually print out the lyrics and pull up a version online and listen to it a couple times through, then practice singing the song together.[1]

Cited papal encyclicals, letters, homilies, prayers, and so on, are used with permission and available in their full-length versions at vatican.va. I highly recommend reading them in their entirety.

Included prayers are from all over the world and throughout time, from various cultures and rites. None are composed by me. A good-faith effort was made to find reliable sources and obtain permission to use everything. If a prayer isn't credited in a footnote, it's because I believe it to be of unknown authorship or in the public domain. There is a preference for "approved versions" of prayers in the Catholic Church, which we can see by the fact that many indulgences are conditional on the use of an approved version of a prayer. This isn't because the Church disapproves of spontaneous or original prayer from individual members of the faithful; rather, it is to avoid the widespread dissemination of prayers that might contain heresies, errors, or misrepresentations.

Stop by any church vestibule and you're likely to find fliers or prayer cards with prayers on them that claim "*never* to have failed" to get you what you ask for. Some claim that particular devotions like wearing a scapular or attending Masses on a particular schedule will "guarantee" your entrance into heaven. The Catholic Church does not support claims like these.

We do not say a prayer as if it's an incantation that will bind God to do our will. We do not see God as a piñata and prayer as the stick with which we poke him until we get what we want. We do not pray because it changes God. We pray because it changes us. The goals of prayer are to honor God as he deserves and to bring our own will into accord with the will of God.

Many of the prayers included in this book are approved versions from the current (2006) *Manual of Indulgences* by the USCCB; from the *Roman Missal* (2011) and *A Tradition of Prayer* (1982), both prepared by ICEL; and from the USCCB and Vatican websites, especially in the case of prayers associated with plenary and partial indulgences. Others

---

[1] The versions to which we sing along can be found collected in a Spotify song playlist and a YouTube video collection, both searchable under my name (Kendra Tierney). Lyrics are available from various online sources and as a printable booklet at CatholicAllYear.com.

are from the *Raccolta*, an out-of-print, seven-hundred-plus-page book of indulgenced prayers authorized by the Holy See between 1807 and 1950. The *Raccolta*'s attached indulgences have been superseded by the most recent version of the *Manual of Indulgences*. However, it's a treasure trove of hundreds of beautifully worded approved prayers and devotions for just about any occasion, from "A prayer for the grace of preaching holily and fruitfully" to "An invocation to be said when people are engaged in making and repairing the ornaments of churches and liturgical vestments" to "Prayer to be said by Christians confined in prison" and "Prayer to be said by motorists".

Other included prayers are from miscellaneous books and online sources. I'm especially indebted to Catholic Culture (catholicculture. org), Pray More Novenas (praymorenovenas.com), Catholic Online (catholic.org), and Sancta Missa (sanctamissa.org) for their amazing online collections of traditional prayers and ways to pray.

In most cases, spelling, capitalization, punctuation, and wording have been adjusted to fit with current publishing norms and ways of speech.

A few prayers and hymns are included in both Latin and English, as we aim to facilitate at least a rudimentary familiarity with Latin in our home. I think it's a good practice for all Catholics.

ADDITIONAL RESOURCES

Many of the prayers, blessings, and devotions included in this book are available as printable resources at CatholicAllYear.com.

The Basics

Catechism of the Catholic Church. 2nd ed. Vatican City: Libreria Editrice Vaticana / Washington, D.C.: United States Catholic Conference), 1997.

Hahn, Scott; Curtis Mitch; and Dennis Walters. *Ignatius Catholic Study Bible: Revised Standard Version.* San Francisco: Ignatius Press, 1999.

The Holy Bible, Revised Standard Version, Second Catholic Edition. San Francisco: Ignatius Press, 2005.

International Commission on English in the Liturgy Corporation. *The Roman Missal.* 3rd ed. Approved by the United States Conference of Catholic Bishops and confirmed by the Apostolic See. New Jersey: Catholic Book Publishing Corp., 2011.

Socías, James. *Daily Roman Missal: Complete with Readings in One Volume, with Sunday and Weekday Masses ... and the Order of Mass in Latin and English on Facing Pages, and Devotions and Prayers for Use throughout the Year.* 7th ed. Woodridge, Ill.: James Socías for Midwest Theological Forum, 2012.

Trese, Leo J. *The Faith Explained.* Princeton, N.J.: Scepter, 1959.

The Saints

Beutner, Dawn Marie. *Saints: Becoming an Image of Christ Every Day of the Year.* San Francisco: Ignatius Press, 2020.

de Voragine, Jacobus. *The Golden Legend: Readings on the Saints.* Translated by William Granger Ryan. Princeton, N.J.: Princeton University Press, 2012.

Wallace, Carey, and Nick Thornborrow. *Stories of the Saints: Bold and Inspiring Tales of Adventure, Grace, and Courage.* New York: Workman, 2020.

The Sacraments

Kelley, Bennet. *The New Saint Joseph First Communion Catechism.* No. 0. New York: Catholic Book Publishing Corp., 2012.
————. *The New Saint Joseph Baltimore Catechism.* No. 1. New York: Catholic Book Publishing Corp., 2012.
————. *The New Saint Joseph Baltimore Catechism.* No. 2. New York: Catholic Book Publishing Corp., 2011.
Tierney, Kendra. *A Little Book about Confession for Children.* New York: Magnificat, 2014.

Prayer

Apostolic Penitentiary. *Manual of Indulgences: Norms and Grants.* Washington, D.C.: United States Conference of Catholic Bishops, 2006.
A Benedictine Monk. *In Sinu Jesu: When Heart Speaks to Heart; The Journal of a Priest at Prayer.* Kettering, Ohio: Angelico, 2016.
Bishops' Committee on the Liturgy. *Catholic Household Blessings and Prayers.* Washington, D.C.: United States Conference of Catholic Bishops, 2007.
Christopher, Joseph Patrick; Charles E. Spence; and John F. Rowan. *The Raccolta; or, A Manual of Indulgences, Prayers, and Devotions Enriched with Indulgences.* New York: Benziger Brothers, 1957.
Fernandez, Francis. *In Conversation with God: Meditations for Each Day of the Year.* London: Scepter, 1993.
Gaitley, Michael E. *33 Days to Morning Glory: A Do-It-Yourself Retreat in Preparation for Marian Consecration.* Stockbridge, Mass.: Marian Press, 2014.
International Commission on English in the Liturgy. *Book of Blessings.* Collegeville, Minn.: Liturgical Press, 1989.
Tierney, Kendra. *My Superhero Prayer Book: Traditional Catholic Prayers for Awesome Catholic Kids.* Scotts Valley, Calif.: Createspace, 2018.

Liturgical Living in the Home

Foley, Michael P. *Drinking with the Saints: The Sinner's Guide to a Holy Happy Hour.* Washington, D.C.: Regnery History, 2015.
Newland, Mary Reed. *The Year and Our Children: Catholic Family Celebrations for Every Season.* Manchester, N.H.: Sophia Institute, 2007.

Tierney, Kendra. *The Catholic All Year Compendium: Liturgical Living for Real Life*. San Francisco: Ignatius Press, 2018.

—————. *O Come, Emmanuel: Advent Reflections on the Jesse Tree for Families*. Steubenville, Ohio: Emmaus Road, 2020.

Trapp, Maria Augusta; Franz Wasner; Rosemary Trapp; and Nikolaus E. Wolff. *Around the Year with the Von Trapp Family*. Manchester, N.H.: Sophia Institute, 2018.

KEY TO CHRISTIAN SYMBOLS
ON THE COVER

Clockwise from the top, the Christian symbols included in the cover art (by the fabulously talented Tricia Hope Dugat of Providential Co.) are as follows:

1. *The Eucharist:* This symbol shows the wheat and the grapes, and the bread and the wine into which they are made. In the Mass, these are transfigured at the consecration and become the actual Body and Blood of our Lord, Jesus Christ—*not* a symbol.

2. *Star of Bethlehem:* This is the star that rose over the humble stable in Bethlehem at the birth of Jesus. It is a symbol of the Incarnation, that God became flesh, assumed a human nature, and became a man in the form of Jesus, the Son of God.

3. *Anchor:* Frequently found in the catacombs of the earliest Christians, the anchor symbolizes our faith in Jesus as our hope for the future. "We have this [hope] as a sure and steadfast anchor of the soul" (Heb 6:19).

4. *Chi-Rho:* If Jesus had fancy guest towels, this is the monogram that would be on them. The Chi-Rho is formed by superimposing the first two letters chi and rho (XP) of the Greek word for Christ: ΧΡΙΣΤΟΣ.

5. *Triquetra:* Also called a Trinity knot, it is a symbol of the three-in-one God—Father, Son, and Holy Spirit. It also indicates unity and eternity. It is often found in Celtic art and architecture.

6. *Pelican in her piety:* In medieval Europe, the pelican was thought to sustain her young with her own blood by wounding her breast when no other food was available. As a result, the pelican became a symbol of Jesus, who sustains us with the Eucharist.

7. *Memento mori skull:* Latin for "Remember your death", a memento mori is a symbolic reminder that each of us will die, and face judgment, and should live our life accordingly. "In all

you do, remember the end of your life, and then you will never sin" (Sir 7:36).

8. *Jerusalem cross:* A symbol in the heraldic tradition of early crusaders to the Holy Land, its five crosses indicate Christ and the four quarters of the world. One tattoo shop in the Holy Land has been marking pilgrims with the Jerusalem cross for seven hundred years!

9. *Alpha and Omega:* The first and last letters of the Greek alphabet superimposed on one another, it is one of the earliest Christian symbols, inspired by Jesus' words "I am the Alpha and the Omega, the first and the last, the beginning and the end" (Rev 22:13).

10. *Manus Dei:* The hand of God is a symbol found in Jewish and Christian art, popular in ancient times through the Middle Ages. It is used to indicate intervention in or approval of affairs on earth by God.

INDEX